MARY MAGDALENE

and the

Mysteries of the Divine Feminine

Elizabeth Clare Prophet

with Annice Booth

SUMMIT UNIVERSITY PRESS®

Gardiner, Montana

Mary Magdalene and the Mysteries of the Divine Feminine
by Elizabeth Clare Prophet with Annice Booth

For information, please contact:
Summit University Press
63 Summit Way
Gardiner, MT 59030 USA
Tel: 1-800-245-5445 or 406-848-9500
TSLinfo@TSL.org
SummitLighthouse.org

Library of Congress Control Number: 2024930916
ISBN: 978-1-60988-465-9 (softbound)
ISBN: 978-1-60988-466-6 (eBook)

SUMMIT UNIVERSITY PRESS®

Cover: Mother of the World, by Nicholas Roerich.

27 26 25 24   3 4 5 6

Contents

Introduction

The almost forgotten story of Mary Magdalene is one that has intrigued many throughout the last two thousand years. Hers is the poignant tale of one who sinned and was redeemed. Somehow, we can all relate to Mary Magdalene—the plight of her soul helps us to have compassion for our own.

Now once more, Mary Magdalene steps into the glare of the spotlight after centuries of neglect. Unexpectedly for some, but in reality long overdue, she emerges from the dusty corners of forgotten churches and even from the hidden recesses of our own memory.

Authors and scholars have explored Mary Magdalene's renewed importance. New evidence has come to light about her role in the early Church, and many have asserted that she had a much more prominent role than we have been led to believe over the centuries.

One key source for this new study is the Gnostic Gospels,[1] some of which speak of Mary Magdalene as the principal disciple of Jesus. Early Gnostic Christian texts describe Mary Magdalene as "the woman who knew the All";[2] she was the one whom Christ loved more than all the disciples.[3] She was the apostle endowed with knowledge, vision and insight far exceeding Peter's.

For some, she is seen as the centerpiece of an underground stream of mystical Christianity, emerging once more on the world scene. This radical reinterpretation of Christianity has been found in several best-selling books.[4] There have also been documentaries that aired on television—*The Two Marys* and *Jesus, Mary and DaVinci.*[5]

According to these hypotheses, Jesus was the rightful heir to the Palestinian throne, married Mary Magdalene, had several children and fled either to Kashmir, India; Alexandria, Egypt; or France following the crucifixion. Meanwhile, Magdalene and the other disciples sought refuge in southern France, where Jesus' bloodline became the foundation of the French Merovingian dynasty of kings of the fifth to the eighth century. The authors of these books propose that the *Sangreal,* the Holy Grail of Arthurian legend, is a code for the *sang real,* the "blood royal," of Jesus and his descendants, and they claim to trace this royal bloodline of the House of David down into modern times.

While we neither affirm nor deny these claims, and while the definitive proof of many of these theories may be lacking, we provide in *Mary Magdalene and the Mysteries of the Divine Feminine* another side of the story of Mary Magdalene, as it has been told by Elizabeth Clare Prophet. Through her personal reading of the akashic records* of the events of history and in the teachings released through her by the great masters of wisdom, Mrs. Prophet has new perspectives and much to offer devotees of Mary Magdalene.

---

* The akashic records are the impressions of all that has ever transpired in the physical universe, recorded in the etheric substance and dimension known by the Sanskrit term *akasha.* These records can be read by those with developed soul faculties.

She opens a door to the soul of Mary Magdalene and her relationship with Jesus—a relationship that transcends the historical details that may be argued by scholars for decades or centuries to come.

Mary Magdalene is one of the most controversial figures of the New Testament. Even in the Bible itself, there is much uncertainty about her. Was she the woman with the alabaster box who anointed Jesus' feet in Luke's gospel? Was she the woman in Matthew, Mark and John who anointed Jesus with the oil of spikenard? Was she the woman taken in adultery whom the scribes and Pharisees wanted to stone and whom Jesus forgave, saying, "Go, and sin no more"?[6]

Jesus has revealed to Mrs. Prophet that all of these are indeed episodes in the life of the Magdalene.[7] While modern scholars may debate, the story written on the ethers—and in the soul memory of those who were there—reveals the true life of a soul redeemed through her love for her Saviour and his love for her. For the love between Jesus and Mary Magdalene was not something that was defined by a flesh-and-blood relationship. Whether they were married or not, the inner record is clear that Mary Magdalene was the twin flame[8] of Jesus, and together they shared a profound and deep love—one that extends beyond that lifetime and into eternity.[9]

Some of the controversy over Mary Magdalene and her role has arisen because of a misunderstanding (and even suppression) of Jesus' true teaching on Woman. Jesus honored Woman. He had women in his closest circles of disciples—a radical liberation of Woman for his day. Yet many in the early Church were not ready to accept this liberation, and therefore Jesus' teachings on Woman did not make it into the Bible. Many were lost and are only now being rediscovered.

Magdalene's role as a disciple has been controversial; the evidence for this survives in the orthodox scriptures—she was, after all, the first to see the risen Christ.[10] Even more controversial is the idea that she and Jesus may have been married. William Phipps addresses this question in his book *Was Jesus Married?* But why should this be so controversial? Is it necessary for Jesus to be so unlike us as to be unapproachably perfect? And in any case, why should perfection necessarily entail not being married?[11]

Elizabeth Clare Prophet asserts that if Jesus were married, it would not in any way detract from his mission or his role as the Piscean conqueror. In her best seller *The Lost Years of Jesus,* she has published the manuscripts that reveal Jesus went to India as a youth, and these manuscripts include some of his lost teachings on Woman. Jesus' teachings on Woman are also found in many of the Gnostic gospels that have recently been rediscovered. It is a tragedy that these teachings were lost and suppressed for two thousand years. Indeed, if the true teachings of Jesus on women's rights had been known and taught in this age, the role of women and the course of civilization would most likely have been vastly different.

Perhaps most importantly, Mrs. Prophet explains that Jesus came to reveal a spiritual path and called us to walk in his footsteps. Whether any of these new theories about his life that are circulating are true or not, it would make no difference to the true spiritual understanding of the path that Jesus and his disciples taught and lived—including the crucifixion, resurrection and ascension that he demonstrated. These are spiritual initiations.

She cautions us not to indulge in a flesh-and-blood religion. Your spiritual body is more real, more solid, more vibrant than the physical body you wear, which is simply a vehicle for the spirit. One day you will lay down your physical body. If you are a true disciple of Christ and have walked in his ways and fulfilled the requirements of the Law, you also can be resurrected—your soul in its spiritual body, wed to

Christ, will be infilled with the upward spiraling resurrection flame. The flame of life can fill your being, and you will find that your sense of immortality and everlasting life is not wed to the flesh—nor is the process of the ascension. Rather, you can live forevermore apart from the clay vessel, just as Jesus demonstrated—"Jesus Christ the same yesterday, and to day, and for ever."[12] And the proof of this path is also seen in the souls of Mary Magdalene, Mary of Bethany,[13] Mary, the mother of Jesus, John the Beloved and others of the apostles who have followed in the footsteps of their Lord and demonstrated this same ascension process.

Jesus' life and mission did not end on the cross. He was indeed resurrected, and he made his exit from a very controversial situation. The second-century Church Father Irenaeus wrote that Jesus taught until he was forty or fifty years old.[14] The third-century Gnostic text Pistis Sophia records that after the resurrection, Jesus "passed eleven years discoursing with his disciples."[15] And the Bible itself records that Paul received his teaching directly from Jesus.[16] In fact, for two thousand years, the Master has not ceased to walk and talk with his disciples.

But what of Mary Magdalene? Perhaps the mystery of Mary Magdalene is like the black keys on the piano. It is possible to make music without them—but a tune played only on the white keys may be a very different melody. The adoration of Mary Magdalene has long been in secret and deeply devotional. Some claim that the mysterious Black Madonna, found in so many of the great cathedrals in Europe, is really Mary Magdalene. There has long been a hidden stream of devotion to her, but now the underground stream is returning to the surface.

Much of what is now coming to light about Mary Magdalene is well out of the realm of the traditional Catholic and Protestant faith. When seen from a different perspective, the history of persecution within Christianity is more readily explained—the churches have often felt threatened by the power of the divine feminine in both man and woman. And sometimes in trying to stamp out the vestiges of Babylon, the Great Whore, and the misuses of the light of the Mother in ancient pagan cults, they also suppressed the emergent light of the Woman Clothed with the Sun.[17]

Yet given all this, while scholars debate and students research, some things remain.

Mary Magdalene lived and still lives, and it is time for the secrets of her life to be revealed.

Who, then, was Mary Magdalene? What was her role in the early Church and in the last two thousand years? Who is she now and what can she teach us today? And what relevance does the message of her life have for our own soul?

Mary Magdalene and the Mysteries of the Divine Feminine reveals this enigmatic and yet strangely familiar character. Now at last, the long-lost Magdalene, the Black Madonna if you will, can emerge from the shadows to unveil herself as someone we have all known intimately after all. Perhaps now that she is "redeemed" once more, our own souls can find the answers and the acceptance we seek. For when one soul is restored to her rightful place, the feminine aspect in all of us can be raised up once again.

Annice Booth

Managing Editor, Summit University Press
Paradise Valley
Montana

Foreword

As a well-known female religious leader of the latter twentieth century, the subject of Woman's role in the Church was something that was very important to Elizabeth Clare Prophet—not only on a personal level, but also as she defined her role and calling in her own organization and on the world scene. She spoke on this subject many times during her nearly forty years of active ministry. The material in this book is compiled from many sources in her lectures and published and unpublished works, particularly a series of lectures she delivered on "The Lost Teachings of Jesus on Women's Rights."

Since those lectures were delivered, the subjects of Mary Magdalene and Jesus' teachings on Woman have come to the forefront of popular and scholarly debate.

Central to the whole question about the role of Woman in Christianity is Mary Magdalene. Was she a leader in the early Church? What was her role in relation to the twelve apostles? Was she, as some have claimed, the wife of Jesus? What is the role of Woman in the Church? And what is the spiritual understanding of male and female?

With all that has been written in recent years on Mary Magdalene and the divine feminine, the question arises as to whether there is anything new that can be said. Mrs. Prophet brings a unique perspective to the subject. In her lectures, writings and reconstructions of Jesus' lost teachings on Woman, Mrs. Prophet draws on historical sources, including the Gnostic texts. But most importantly, she brings an understanding of the Gnostics and their teachings that comes not only from a study of their texts but that is also deeply rooted in her own spiritual experience.

Like the Gnostics, she believes in the present possibility of contacting Jesus, even after his ascension (in her terms, as an ascended master). She therefore approaches the Gnostic texts not just through an analysis of their teachings but as someone who has sought and personally experienced the path of which they spoke. Gnosticism for her is not simply an ancient spiritual tradition but a path that she can understand and know more deeply because it parallels her own life and path. Her lectures include the results of her research, but her understanding of the Gnostic teachings is also drawn from her own inspiration and revelations from Jesus.

This, of course, may make her conclusions controversial for some. Not everything will be open to historical verification and analysis. Some things must remain matters of faith and belief and of what rings true in one's heart and in one's personal experience. Some scholars are not comfortable entering this realm. Yet it really is the essence of what the Gnostics taught: their path could not really be understood from an intellectual level but only by entering deeply and *experiencing* it from within. Mary Magdalene did not become "the one who knew the All" by study and analysis but by the closeness of her heart to the Saviour.

We invite you similarly to seek to enter in, to join with Mrs. Prophet in her journey to find the essence of Mary

Magdalene and Jesus' teachings on the divine feminine. And above all, we invite you to weigh these things in your heart as well as your mind.

The Editors
Summit University Press

CHAPTER 1

Jesus Prepares for His Mission

Previous page: *Jesus Approaching Ladakh as a Youth,*
by J. Michael Spooner

CHAPTER 1

Jesus Prepares for His Mission

The Lost Years of Jesus

This book, *Mary Magdalene and the Mysteries of the Divine Feminine,* is not only about women or for women. It is a book about your right to become who you really are, whether you are in a male or a female body. The leaders of the early Church did not accept this message. And so for more than two thousand years, Jesus' teaching on Woman has been lost. His message on reverence for Woman and on the feminine potential of both man and woman was almost unknown until recently, when newly discovered texts have brought to light some of Jesus' lost teachings.

One source of these teachings is found in manuscripts that speak of Jesus' "lost years" in the East. His profound reverence for Woman has been captured in an ancient Eastern text written down by Buddhist historians. These historians chronicled Jesus' words and deeds during what are called his "lost years." I have published this text in my book *The Lost Years of Jesus,*[1] which tells the story of these documents, how they were found and what Jesus did during the years that are not mentioned in the recorded scriptures that the Church councils put together.

We have absolute silence in the gospels as to where Jesus was from age thirteen to twenty-nine. It is pure speculation that he was a carpenter in Nazareth all of that time. But it is no longer speculation what he did elsewhere, because these documents, discovered in Ladakh in a monastery, tell the whole story. The people who went there and saw them and wrote down what they saw are all profiled in my book. This is not a book on religion; it's a book on history, the most important history of our time.

As you know, there is no record in our Bible of Jesus' whereabouts between the age of twelve (when he was found at the Temple discoursing with the doctors[2]) and about age thirty (when he was baptized by John the Baptist in the Jordan River[3]). Ancient Buddhist manuscripts say Jesus spent these "lost years" in the East, where he was known as Saint Issa.

Saint Issa

In my book, I have published three independent translations of the manuscript about the life of Saint Issa. The first was made by Nicolas Notovitch, a Russian journalist who, in 1887, found the manuscripts in a Buddhist monastery near Leh, Ladakh (a region in northern India bordering Tibet). He published his text in 1894 as *The Life of Saint Issa: Best of the Sons of Men.*

Swami Abhedananda, a scholar and a disciple of Ramakrishna, saw the document at Himis in 1922. Abhedananda journeyed to the Himalayas, determined to find a copy of the Himis manuscript or to expose the "fraud." His book of travels, entitled *Kashmir O Tibbate,* tells of a visit to the Himis *gompa* and includes a Bengali translation of portions of a manuscript that he saw there that closely paralleled the Notovitch text. I had Abhedananda's version of the manuscript translated from Bengali into English for the first time

Nicolas Notovitch

Swami Abhedananda

Nicholas Roerich

Elisabeth Caspari

Four eyewitnesses to the Buddhist manuscripts
that describe Jesus' "lost years" in the East

specifically for my book.

The same, or a similar, text was seen by the Russian artist, archaeologist and author Nicholas Roerich in 1925. Roerich, who spent more than five years traveling through central Asia, also found accounts of Jesus' journey to the East recorded in the oral tradition of the region.

The Lost Years of Jesus also includes the eyewitness account of Dr. Elisabeth Caspari.[4] In 1939, she was at Himis and the librarian presented a set of parchments to her with these words: "These books say your Jesus was here!"

"These books say your Jesus was here!"

In 1951, we find Supreme Court Justice William O. Douglas traveling to Himis. He later wrote in his book *Beyond the High Himalayas*:

> There are those who to this day believe that Jesus visited the place, that he came here when he was fourteen and left when he was twenty-eight, heading west, to be heard of no more. The legend fills in the details, saying that Jesus traveled to Hemis* under the name of Issa.[5]

For more than a century, these documents have been known to be there and have been seen. The manuscript and oral tradition about Saint Issa reveal that the seventeen years Jesus spent in the East were a dress rehearsal for his Palestinian mission.

---

* Some authors prefer this alternate spelling.

Monks at Himis Monastery

Jesus' Preparation for His Mission

According to Notovitch's translation of the Buddhist texts, Jesus left home with the goal of "perfecting himself in the Divine Word and of studying the laws of the great Buddhas."[6] Think of this! He had the goal of perfecting himself in the Word! It is a liberating statement! It tells us that Jesus walked a path of discipleship under the great lights of the East—Lord Maitreya, Gautama Buddha and Sanat Kumara, who is known as the Buddha Dipamkara.

Maitreya

Jesus is our role model. The Jesus of the New Age movement, the Jesus who is the universal avatar of all ages is far grander, far more profound than the Jesus of orthodox Christianity. That Jesus sought the perfecting of his heart and mind, his soul and spirit tells me that although he was born an avatar—truly the incarnation of God—he still had to take the necessary human footsteps. And if he had to do it, we also have to do it. He had to do this to accomplish his soul's integration with the Word in preparation for his baptism, his transfiguration, crucifixion, resurrection and ascension.

The Gospel of Luke testifies to this growth process. I emphasize it because orthodox Christianity tells us today that Jesus was born a god, far removed from all of us. And yet we see that he unfolded that God flame throughout his life. He reached the culmination of its manifestation when he began his Palestinian mission.

To know that he was not simply that God, with nothing to do about realizing or integrating with God, we simply need to read Luke: "And the child grew, and waxed strong in spirit, filled with wisdom: and the grace of God was upon him."[7]

Waxing strong in spirit means that from the time of your conception, through all of the stages of growth, your spirit and your soul are integrating with your mind, your heart, your physical body, your chakras. A little baby cannot contain the fullness of God that is there at age thirty-three. And so we see that Jesus is the role model from birth for us to externalize our personal Christhood, our personal God-manifestation.

Writing of him at age twelve, Luke again observes the increase of his soul's integration with the Word: "And Jesus increased in wisdom and stature, and in favor with God and man."[8]

Jesus journeyed to the East to study and to prepare for his mission. This is a Jesus much closer to our hearts. We understand how arduous the journey, how difficult the soul testing, that he had to face the forces of hell and of darkness as well as the greatest light and keep his balance between both. If he could do it, we can do it also, because he said, "He that believeth on me, the works that I do shall he do also; and greater works than these shall he do; because I go unto my Father."[9] Jesus is a how-to teacher. He teaches us by example, and he expects us to follow.

Jesus prepared for his mission with all due diligence. It is not blasphemy to affirm that Jesus had to work to internalize and bring forth the fullness of his Christhood. He said it himself: I must work the works of him that sent me. My Father worketh hitherto, and I work.[10]

What Jesus learned in the East he has brought back today. I have published his teachings in *The Lost Teachings of Jesus*.[11] You can learn how to do the things Jesus did, and that is the reason for being. That's why you came into embodiment at the conclusion of the twentieth century, because God needs you to manifest your own Christ perfection.

The Son of God, the Christ Incarnate, knew all these things, the things that he went to the East to perfect. But Jesus, the evolving Son of man, must learn through the mastery of the lower bodies what his soul had known from the beginning. So it is with you. The God Presence is with you and in you. The Christ light is the flame in your heart. Your soul has existed for aeons, but when you come into a new body, you must integrate with the physical body and brain and mind. You must integrate with the desires that you bring back with your karma. You must bring down from your Higher Self momentums of the past of mastery, of creativity. And all of this you put together.

So we have to go to school and study and learn all over again what is in the memory bank of our beings. That doesn't mean to say that God is not perfect in us already. It means we, this outer mind and soul, have to once more mesh with the Reality of being.

Jesus moved among Hindus, Buddhists, Zoroastrians and pagans while he was in the East. He championed the poor, taught the people to stop worshiping idols and challenged the false priests who subjugated the people. He told the lower castes: "God the Father makes no difference between his children; all to him are equally dear."[12] The text also says: "He denied with his full force the right of man to take upon himself the power to deny his fellows of human dignity."[13]

Now that wasn't exactly a message that the priest class wanted to hear. During his sojourn in the East, Jesus' life was threatened more than once for his outspoken challenges of the priesthood. But each time, he escaped.

A Chronology of Jesus' Life as We Know It

It is your divine right to know where Jesus was between the ages of thirteen and twenty-nine. Scripture makes no mention of these years, and yet those who have come back from the East with the message of his journey, reporting this to Rome, were told a century ago that there are at least sixty-three documents in the Vatican brought back by various travelers speaking of Jesus' journey.[14] We have a right to know why Rome did not impart this information to us and to think for a moment why the most powerful Church in the world would not want its members to know what Jesus did during those "lost years."

Before we continue with Jesus' pilgrimage in the East, let us review his early years and the chronology of his life as we know it. He was born sometime between 8 and 4 B.C.[15] He spent his early life in Palestine. He may have moved to Memphis, Egypt, shortly after his birth and lived there until the death of Herod. You remember it is written: Out of Egypt have I called my son.[16] So the scripture was fulfilled; he was called out of Egypt upon the death of Herod.

Legends from the British Isles say that his great-uncle Joseph of Arimathea, who took care of him after the death of his father, Joseph, was a tin merchant who, with a fleet of ships, regularly sailed to the Isles.[17] It is said that he took Jesus to Glastonbury as a youth to be educated before we read about him in the temple at the age of twelve. At that time, the most famous universities in Europe were in Britain. They were the Druid universities.

Sometimes we overlook the normal questions we should be asking. Where did Jesus learn and study to be so wise at the age of twelve? If you are of the view that, contrary to all of the laws of our own lifetimes, he automatically had the knowledge of his time, had mastered other languages, memorized the Old

Testament and even Apocryphal books that are not in the Old Testament that he quotes—the knowledge that Jesus had is a knowledge that is gained through education. Wisdom is gained from God, but knowledge comes through education.

I believe that Jesus had a very rich childhood, was watched over carefully by his mother, by his father, Joseph, and then by his great-uncle Joseph of Arimathea and that he was fully prepared with all of the knowledge that our teenagers must wait till they are eighteen to receive and much, much more by the time he was age twelve.

We look, then, elsewhere for proof, for some clue to the mystery of our Lord's doings. And we find our answers in the ancient Buddhist manuscripts that say that Jesus spent his "lost years" in the East. These texts were originally recorded by Buddhist historians in Pali, the sacred language of the Theraveda Buddhist canon. Later they were translated into Tibetan.

Jesus' Travels in the East

From the texts themselves, we have pieced together a chronology of Jesus' travels. It begins at age thirteen: he set out towards the Sind (a region in present-day southeast Pakistan in the lower Indus River valley).

The Life of Saint Issa records:

> When Issa had attained the age of thirteen years, the epoch when an Israelite should take a wife, the house where his parents earned their living by carrying on a modest trade began to be a place of meeting for rich and noble people, desirous of having for a son-in-law the young Issa,

> already famous for his edifying discourses in the name of the Almighty. Then it was that Issa left the parental house in secret, departed from Jerusalem, and with the merchants set out towards Sind, with the object of perfecting himself in the Divine Word and of studying the laws of the great Buddhas.[18]

Who are the great Buddhas? They are simple people and lifestreams like you and me who sought to embody that Universal Christ. And the term *Buddha* means one enlightened by that Universal One, one whose consciousness has budded and opened, whose seven chakras (see page 83) have become orifices for the receiving and the distributing of that light.

At the age of fourteen, Jesus crossed the Sind. His fame spread far and wide. The Jains asked him to stay, but he went instead to Juggernaut "where the white priests of Brahma made him a joyous welcome." The priests "taught him to read and understand the Vedas," the ancient scriptures of the East. They taught him "to cure by aid of prayer, to teach, to explain the holy scriptures to the people, and to drive out evil spirits from the bodies of men, restoring unto them their sanity."[19]

Most of us have believed that Jesus did not need to be taught anything. And yet his entire childhood is a record of learning and receiving the Word of God and of mastering the Old Testament scriptures and the prophets and texts that were a part of the Essene community at Qumran.

Jesus was familiar with all of the background and history of his people. Somehow we are led to believe in a magical Jesus, someone entirely different from the laws of life on earth.

What Jesus did and what he said between these ages, these "lost years," is priceless, essential and fundamental to our own evolution and our psychological development. We do not understand our psychology if we assess it only as ourselves being humans, subject only to the conditions of this life.

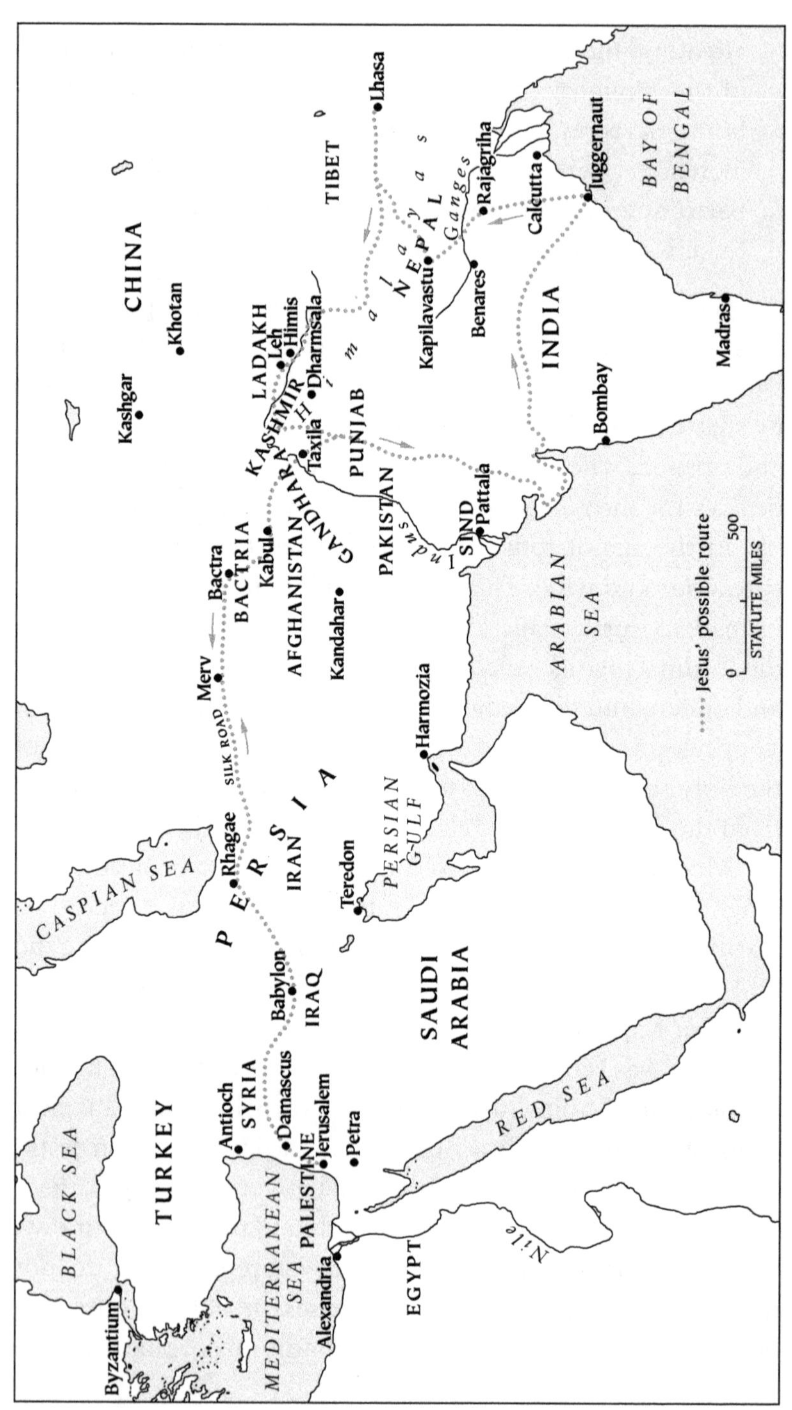
BLACK SEA
TURKEY
Byzantium
MEDITERRANEAN SEA
Alexandria
EGYPT
Nile
PALESTINE
Antioch
SYRIA
Damascus
Jerusalem
Petra
RED SEA
SAUDI ARABIA
IRAQ
Babylon
CASPIAN SEA
PERSIA
IRAN
Rhagae
Teredon
PERSIAN GULF
SILK ROAD
Merv
Harmozia
BACTRIA
Bactra
AFGHANISTAN
Kandahar
Kabul
GANDHARA
KASHMIR
Taxila
PAKISTAN
Indus
SIND
Pattala
PUNJAB
ARABIAN SEA
Kashgar
Khotan
CHINA
LADAKH
Leh
Himis
Dharmsala
Himalayas
TIBET
Lhasa
NEPAL
Kapilavastu
Benares
Ganges
Rajagriha
Calcutta
Juggernaut
INDIA
Bombay
Madras
BAY OF BENGAL
Jesus' possible route
0 500
STATUTE MILES

Psyche is from the Greek, meaning "soul." Psychology is the study of the soul, not in one life but in many lifetimes, which culminate at the conclusion of the final incarnation in reunion with God. Jesus, the Son of God in the Son of man, did determine to demonstrate for us all this union with the light, producing works out of it, establishing the Word that is the divine direction for us.

The Buddhist texts say Jesus spent six years at Juggernaut, Rajagriha, Benares and other holy cities. He eventually became embroiled in a conflict with the Brahmins and Kshatriyas (the priestly and warrior castes) for teaching the holy scriptures to the lower castes. His enemies plotted to kill him. He left Juggernaut by night and went to the foothills of the Himalayas in southern Nepal, the birthplace of Gautama.

Five hundred years before, Gautama Buddha had taught, had achieved enlightenment, had internalized the Word. Does that detract from the Son of God? No, it enhances the Son of God, because it tells us that what man has done, man can do—that along the lines of history for millions of years throughout a Matter cosmos, the soul that descends has found a way to internalize a higher light and to ascend. There is hope for all of us, not merely because we believe in Jesus Christ, but because we believe in the Christ of him[20] and in his promise that we must do the greater works, for he has ascended to the Father.[21]

Gautama had lived and preached a way of peace, an Eightfold Path. He had the same desiring that Jesus did. He saw human suffering. He wanted to find its cause and its cure. He said that the cause of human suffering is wrong desire, inordinate desire. Don't we all suffer when we can't have our desires fulfilled until we recognize that that it is not possible in life? We begin to sublimate desires and to have wisdom and maturity in determining goals that we can make happen.

Inordinate desire, then, must be conquered. But right desire, the desiring to embody the light, is the reason for being. And therefore, Gautama defended his right to be doing what he was doing, and he ascended that golden crystal coil of light. He went into samadhi. He brought back the understanding of the cause of suffering and his Eightfold Path, which is a path of exercises for the balancing of the seven chakras and the eighth chakra—the eight-petaled chakra, the secret chamber of the heart.

What did Jesus do next? He spent six years in Nepal. He mastered the Pali language and became "a perfect expositor of the sacred writings" of Buddhism.

According to tradition, sometime during his sojourn in the East, Jesus also traveled to Lhasa, Rajputana and Ladakh. Between the ages of twenty-seven and twenty-nine, he left the Himalayas and journeyed west, preaching along the way. He passed through Kabul in Afghanistan and through Persia, where he rebuked the false priesthood of Zoroastrianism even as he had rebuked the false priesthood of Hinduism. They cast him out of their town, leaving him prey to the wild beasts.

Was Jesus' Revolution for Woman Founded in the Concepts He Learned in the East?

If Jesus indeed journeyed to the East, he would have come into contact with several different cultures and peoples, including Hindus, Buddhists, Zoroastrians, Greeks and possibly even Egyptians. These cultures had a radically different view of women and of God—one that honored the feminine. Was the revolution for Woman that Jesus began in Palestine founded on these concepts?

At some time during his journey, Jesus may have traveled through Alexandria, a Greek city in Egypt. Alexandria was a main port of travel to and from the East. It was a meeting place not only of travelers and traders from East and West, but of their philosophical ideas as well.

God as Mother—Isis: The Universal Mother

One idea that was prominent in Alexandria and in the East was the concept that God had a feminine side—a stark contrast to the Jewish depiction of an exclusively patriarchal God.[22] Alexandria was the center of devotion to the goddess Isis, the best-loved representative of the Divine Mother in the ancient civilizations of the Mediterranean. Isis was a healer, a champion of justice and the embodiment of Divine Wisdom and philosophy. Isis was known as the "Universal Mother." She was able to perform miracles by using "words of power." Through her words of power, she restored her husband (and by extension all men) to life.

In the ancient world, women were more highly respected in Egypt than in the Middle East or in the Greek or Roman cultures. An Egyptian woman's legal rights were equal to those of a man of the same social class. Unlike Greek or Jewish women, Egyptian women were permitted to appear in public with their husbands.

Women in Rome also held greater freedom than in Greece or Israel. John Temple Bristow, author of *What Paul Really Said about Women*, writes,

> A woman living in Rome . . . often accompanied her husband on outings and to social affairs. Roman women of the upper class were allowed to organize meetings and pursue academic studies.
>
> The spread of the Isis cult from Egypt affirmed these freedoms for women as they gathered together (without

> men) and learned to offer thanks to this goddess, who—they were taught to say—"gavest to women the same power as to men."[23]

Jesus Returns to Palestine

And we pick up with his life story as we find him being baptized by John in Jordan, the Holy Spirit descending upon him and the approbation given, "This is my beloved Son, in whom I am well pleased."[24]

The Baptism of Jesus, by Gustave Doré

When he arrived in Palestine, at the age of twenty-nine, Jesus found the people of his native land in despair. He adjured them not to give up their faith in God, not to resort to debauchery or the worship of idols, "but be imbued with hope and with patience."[25]

Now, Pilate didn't like Jesus any better than the priests of India did. The Buddhist historians, who chronicled all of this, recorded that "Pilate, ruler of Jerusalem, gave orders to lay hands upon the preacher Issa and to deliver him to the judges without, however, arousing the displeasure of the people."[26] In short, Jesus ruffled the feathers of both Church and State.

> But Issa taught: "Do you not see that the rich and the powerful ones are sowing the spirit of revolt against the eternal consciousness of heaven? Lo, I tried to revive the laws of Moses in the hearts of the people. And I say that you do not understand their true meaning because

they do not teach revenge but forgiveness. But the meaning of these laws is distorted."

But the ruler, waxing wroth, sent to Issa his disguised servants that they should watch his actions and report to him about his words to the people. "Thou just man," said the disguised servant of the ruler of Jerusalem approaching Issa, "teach us, should we fulfill the will of Caesar or await the approaching deliverance?"

But Issa, recognizing the disguised servants, said, "I have not said unto you that you would be delivered from Caesar; but I said that the soul which was immersed in sin would be delivered from sin."

At this time, an old woman approached the crowd, but was pushed back by one of the disguised ones.[27]

"Reverence Woman, Mother of the Universe"

The text that follows is the most important document in existence that establishes Jesus' revolution and reverence for Woman:

> Then Issa said, "Reverence woman, mother of the universe. In her lies the truth of creation. She is the foundation of all that is good and beautiful. She is the source of life and death. Upon her lies the life of man, because she is the succor of his labors. She gives birth to you in travail, she watches over your growth. Until her very death you bring anguish to her. Bless her. Honor her. She is your only friend and sustenance upon earth. Reverence her. Defend her. Love your wives and honor them, because tomorrow they shall be mothers, and later—the mothers of the human race. Their love ennobles man, soothes the embittered heart and tames the beast. Wife and mother—invaluable treasure. They

> are the adornments of the universe. From them issues all which peoples the universe.
>
> "As light divides itself from darkness, so does womankind possess the gift to divide in man good intent from the thought of evil. Your noblest thoughts shall belong to woman. Gather from them thy moral strength, which you must possess to sustain your near ones. Do not humiliate her, for therein you will humiliate yourselves. And through this shall you lose the feeling of love without which naught exists upon earth. Bring reverence to thy wife and she shall defend you. And all which you will do to mother, to wife, to widow or to another woman in sorrow—that shall you also do for the Spirit."[28]

That was Jesus Christ. That is his liberating revolution. That flame he ignited has never truly gone out except through ignorant pronouncements of ignorant men. I want to remind you that those statements were not made by Gloria Steinem or Betty Friedan.[29] They were made by Jesus Christ for you and for me.

The Meaning of "Mother of the Universe"

The true meaning of the title *Mother of the Universe* is that it belongs to every woman. Every incarnation of the feminine ray is the keeper of the *Mater* (which is Latin for "mother"), or the Matter, universe. And she is sent into life to keep the flame of the Divine Mother as well as of the Trinity on behalf of her children, her father, her husband, her brothers, her friends. This is the role and office of Woman and it is the role and office of Woman in the Church.

Therefore, the primary destiny of everyone who incarnates as a woman (and we all do at one time or another though we may be wearing a masculine body at this time[30]) is to keep the flame of the Mother and to raise up that Mother flame.

It is the Divine Mother, Omega, whom we ought to worship just as we worship our Divine Father, Alpha. The worship of the Divine Mother and our absolute oneness with her enable the raising of her sacred fire in our temple whereby we achieve a state of being androgynous.

Mother of the World, by Nicholas Roerich

We can affirm in our heart that every woman, no matter what her station, is yet the Mother of the Universe in the sense of bringing forth life and in the sense of keeping the flame of life. Only one who possessed the highest love and the highest respect for Woman could speak such words of transcendent tenderness in her defense. Let us be comforted by them.

Jesus Walked a Path That We Can Follow

We find these footsteps of Jesus in the East ones in which we can comfortably place our own feet because we can understand that there is a salvation to be won before we have the full realization of the Christ within this body, within this mind, within this temple. Jesus walked a path that we can follow.

We can know him as a teenager, and he is a role model for our teenage years and for our years when we prepare for our profession and study—the years of his twenties. This account shows that he was not just born a god but that he descended into human form and had to prepare for that mission and that he did so diligently.

I believe that orthodoxy has removed this path from us because they wanted to make Jesus into a flesh-and-blood god to be worshiped instead of seeing him as a brother and a friend and someone who is approachable and reachable. This does not detract from the divinity of Jesus, but it restores the divinity of yourself. It doesn't make you equal to Jesus, for he is the avatar, but he gives us the example that we can follow.

It is no blasphemy to affirm that Jesus was God incarnate and yet that he came toward that route and toward that goal in the same manner as we have, even by reincarnation. We see signs of him in the Old Testament[31] and even all the way back to Atlantis,[32] always the one who comes as the great Saviour and the great converter of our souls back to God.

That Jesus was a diligent student means that we must also be diligent students and not dilettantes, not going here and there but recognizing that the kingdom of God is within us. The light is there, and those who have gone before us, our elder brothers and sisters—the ascended masters—are guiding us every step of the way. This is my mission, to bring to you the understanding of the ascended masters' teachings. This message on Woman is central, but only one chapter in those teachings.

Jesus gives us the same message today as he did in the East and in Palestine. He is our Lord and Saviour, and no one can take his place. Yet all can follow him to arrive at that kingdom of God and to be part of the company of saints robed in white who come from every religion and every creed who gather around the throne of God.[33] And they are known as the Great White Brotherhood.*

---

* A spiritual fraternity of ascended masters, archangels and other advanced spiritual beings. The term "white" refers not to race but to the aura of white light that surrounds these immortals. The Great White Brotherhood works with earnest seekers of every race, religion and walk of life to assist humanity.

The Beginning of Our Own Quest

We have a trek to make, not necessarily physically to the Himalayas, but we must climb the highest mountain of being;[34] we must accelerate and go beyond the consciousness and worldliness. We must find the inner teachers, and this through the Holy Spirit. We must drink of their cups, walk in their footsteps, be willing to understand that there is a price to be paid to carry the light, and pay it.

Someone has paid the price that you could be reading this book. We must be ready to pay the price for our children and our youth. Therefore, because Jesus submitted to John the Baptist,[35] that tells me he also submitted to the great lights of the East, because he is the greatest light, the *summum bonum* of all the world's religions. He rises to the highest awareness of all peoples' sense of the divine man incarnate. Notovitch referred to him as "the best of the sons of men."

Sometime, somewhere every one of you must come to that moment and that lifetime when you are called to embody that light. This could be that lifetime. This could be why you are reading this book, because this is the end of the Piscean age and the beginning of the age of Aquarius. It is a time of the harvest of souls and a great awakening.

Some of you are old souls. You have been on this planet a long time. You want to get on with your reason for being. You sense the call of higher octaves. You know you must access the light of that great causal body (shown as the spheres of light surrounding the upper figure in the Chart of Your Divine Self, page 80).

Then begins the quest. How? Why? How to call forth that light? How to feel more of that light and Reality here below? All of this is a part of the lost teachings of Jesus. The ascended masters[36] who have followed in his footsteps have also given that teaching to us by the Holy Spirit. And it is all the same teaching of the path of the soul. It is rich and full of treasure, and it covers whatever you might face on your path of overcoming.

You might experience exactly what happened to Jesus between the age of fourteen and twenty when he traveled to Juggernaut, Rajagriha, Benares and other holy cities and came into conflict with the Brahmins and Kshatriyas. This might happen to you when in the firmness and in the fire of youth, you take a stand against entrenched materialism or a dead-lettered orthodoxy or any other limitation that may be imposed upon the people. Youth have a great sense of justice and, correspondingly, a sense of injustice. It is the fire in us that impels us to change and uplift life, to make things better.

Jesus took their holy scriptures and gave them to the lower castes. It was unthinkable and unheard of—that they should be given the means to implement the Word and one day to fully embody that light. The priests said, "They are not worthy." Therefore his enemies plotted to kill him. He was warned by the people and escaped by night.

The encounter with Darkness or Evil that denies the Light within us all is something that we all come to when we are the servants of truth, when we know the truth and have that truth and see it. We want to champion the cause of those who are oppressed, whether by big government or big business, whether by World Communism or any of the other forces that deprive the individual of his right to be the fullness of that light.

This is a part of the experience of overcoming as you move through the institutions of higher learning and the professions and see the limitations imposed in every field—if you don't think a certain way and write a thesis a certain way, you're not accepted in that field or institution. When you see the limitations of science, if you have a new idea, you may be outside of its community.

There is a fire that burns in us, and we say we must take our stand for Truth. Because somehow we know that Truth translates as the person of Christ and that the person of Christ emerging in every single man, woman and child upon earth will be crushed, will be denied, will be set aside if we don't say, "Here I stand. And I will stand for this light, so help me, God." And by that individual stand, the world moves up in the spiral.

We need to know that all the revolutionaries of the Spirit who have ever gone before us have come to that crossroad: whether to go the way of mediocrity, to not make waves, to just do everything the way everybody else is doing it and has ever done it—or to say, "There is a better way. And I will fight for the right of people to know that better way."

That's what the life of Jesus is telling us. That is what we have to know. We have to know how he dealt with all these specific situations that we are facing. That's why we need his lost years and his lost teachings.

Jesus, being the world teacher and the Saviour in Pisces, came to show the people the way of the internalization of this light from their own scriptures. Jesus, achieving the highest manifestation and goal of all religions, our reunion with God, must speak to the people in their own language, in their own traditions, must live with them, love them, be trusted by them and trust them, heal them and give to them the lost Word, awaken their memory to their origin in the heart of the Great Central Sun and tell them that all that he was, they, too, can become.

CHAPTER 2

Jesus' Revolution for Woman—The Women of the Church, Then and Now

Previous page: *Madonna and Child between St. Catherine and Mary Magdalen* (detail), by Giovanni Bellini

CHAPTER 2

Jesus' Revolution for Woman—The Women of the Church, Then and Now

Jesus' Message for Woman

Jesus came with a revolutionary message for Woman. But the leaders of the early Church didn't pass the torch! They dropped it! And for two thousand years, Jesus' message on Woman has been lost. His message on the feminine potential of both man and woman has also been lost.

To understand the revolutionary nature of Jesus' teachings, let us look at women's position when Jesus entered the scene in Palestine. At that time, social convention in the Greco-Roman world did not allow women to play a leadership role in the public domain. That was the man's field of influence. Women did, however, take leadership roles in the private domain where they were respected managers of their household estates.

Karen Jo Torjesen explains in her book *When Women Were Priests* that ancient households presented complex duties for their managers. There were many slaves to raise, educate and oversee. Great estates produced, harvested and stored their own food. Clothing was made on the premises, and the manager saw to it that all supplies were inventoried and distributed where needed.

"The role of household manager would be closer to the job of manager of a small factory than to the role of the contemporary housewife,"[1] Torjesen concludes. Thus woman's position and practical experience in the ancient world shows that she was certainly capable of leadership though she wasn't allowed to exercise it in the public arena.

Jewish women's role in the synagogue was more complicated, depending on whether the synagogue was considered to be a private or a public one. Torjesen shows that Jewish communities in the cities of the Roman Empire were considered to be separate nations, or *politeumas*. Synagogues in these communities were regarded by the Roman government as private associations. Therefore, Torjesen writes, Jewish women were allowed to "lead synagogue worship," which could have included reading aloud the Torah (the Pentateuch).

In a public synagogue, however, women were not allowed to read the Torah. A section from the Talmud (Jewish law) reads: "All are qualified ... [to read the Torah,] even a minor and a woman, but a woman should not be allowed to come forward and read the law in public."[2]

The proscription against women's having public training in the Torah was reflected in the Jewish prayer of the early centuries A.D.: "Praised be God that he has not created me a gentile; praised be God that he has not created me a woman; praised be God that he has not created me an ignorant man."[3]

Jewish women were relegated to the same category as Gentiles and ignorant men because they were not permitted to study the law.

Jesus Broke with Tradition

It was not socially acceptable for Jewish women of the first century to enter into close association with men apart from their families, and therefore women were not allowed to study under a rabbi. In such a setting, it was not only unheard of for a woman to leave home and accompany a rabbi on his itinerant ministry—it was scandalous. But that is just what the women who worked and served with Jesus did.

Jesus broke with the traditions of his day. He spoke openly to women. He taught women. Some of his close companions were women, including Mary Magdalene, Martha and Mary of Bethany, Salome, Joanna and Susanna.

Tuning in to the akashic records, we read what the scriptures also record: These women and many others were also his disciples.

What better example is there of Jesus' high regard for Woman than this familiar scene at the home of Mary, Martha and Lazarus in Bethany? Martha complains to Jesus that her sister, Mary, is sitting at the Master's feet listening to his teachings rather than helping with household duties (the expected role of a woman at that time). Jesus replies to Martha, "Mary hath chosen that good part, which shall not be taken away from her."[4]

Jesus defends Woman's right to be the disciple of the Christ and to be the repository of the sacred mysteries and to keep the flame of the Divine Mother on behalf of all life. He shows both men and women, rich and poor alike, that the soul must defend her* right to be—and first and foremost to be a living disciple of the living Word.

---

* The soul of man and woman is feminine is relation to the masculine, or spirit, portion of being. The soul is therefore often referred to as "she."

The Female Apostles

The Gospel of John also records what I consider one of the most important statements about Jesus in the Gospels. Martha confesses that Jesus is "the Christ." This means that she recognizes his spiritual attainment.

Martha makes her confession as Jesus arrives at her home following the death of her brother Lazarus. Jesus promises Martha that her brother "shall rise again."[5]

Although the orthodox hierarchy of the Church has never proclaimed Mary Magdalene to be an apostle, some early Christian Gnostics considered her an apostle of equal standing to the twelve, or even of higher standing. Some saw her as the apostle who was closest to Jesus and the true spiritual leader of the early Christian community.

The Gnostics were followers of Jesus in the second and third centuries who claimed to possess the secret teachings he had handed down through his closest disciples. Unlike orthodox Christians, the Gnostics championed women's right to be leaders. As we will see in the next chapter, the Gnostics were truly the stewards of Jesus' original message on Woman and the feminine potential of every soul. Their teachings and their texts were suppressed by early Church Fathers and were believed lost until recent discoveries at Nag Hammadi.

Apostolic Succession: Can Women Convey the Holy Spirit?

We look, then, to the roots of the early Church. The criteria for papal authority and apostolic succession of bishops were established around the apostle Peter to whom Jesus said: "Thou art Peter, and upon this rock I will build my church."[6] The antecedent of this quote, of course, is Jesus' asking Peter who he is. And Peter says, "Thou art the Christ, the Son of the living God."[7] And Jesus answers, "And I say thou art Peter

Saint Peter, by Ribera

and upon this rock [of my Christhood, which you also can become], I will build my church."

It is the confession of the Christ in Jesus upon which the Church is built and not upon any human being whatsoever—especially Peter.

The authority of Peter was also legitimized by those who claimed he was the first witness of the resurrection. Now, we know that Mary Magdalene was the first witness of the resurrection, so named in the Gospels of Mark and John.[8] But Peter is traditionally considered the "first witness of the resurrection" in Catholic and some Protestant churches.[9] This is because Woman was of no account in those days.

Mary Magdalene Was First at the Tomb

Now, to me that tells the whole tale of orthodoxy and apostolic succession. Only the ones who were at the tomb, and first at the tomb, and those who were the descendants from them spiritually have the right to tell us exactly what was Jesus' teaching. Well, they have forgotten that Mary Magdalene was the first at the tomb and that she was a woman.

First of all, it should be understood that Jesus chose Mary Magdalene and not the apostles as the first one to see him after his resurrection. The claim of orthodoxy today rests upon the testimony of the supposed eyewitnesses, the apostles—all of whom were men. But as a matter of fact, Jesus gave to Mary Magdalene the revelation of his resurrection.

This particular moment, captured in the painting *Rabboni*, captures the fire of the resurrection initiation, not merely the ascension. The ascension comes later, so we are not seeing

Jesus in the ascension pose. Mary reaches out her hand, and you remember the words Jesus spoke, "Touch me not; for I am not yet ascended to my Father: but go to my brethren, and say unto them, I ascend unto my Father, and your Father; and to my God, and your God."[10]

Rabboni

In those very simple words, we realize that Jesus has a God Presence and Mary Magdalene has a God Presence. And that God Presence is the presence of the Father, the I AM Presence, which is shown in the Chart (see page 80), above Jesus and above Mary Magdalene. How else can you explain his very statement? He is acknowledging the individualization of the God Presence for each one. And he is saying, "I have not yet accelerated into that sacred fire. I am in the midst of that initiation. Touch me not."

Here, then, you see the soul of Mary Magdalene. She has fallen from heaven into the planes of Matter, into density. She has lost the way. She has received the call of her Lord. Jesus has cast out of her seven devils.[11] He has raised her up. She has been a part of the inner circle. And within the Gnostic text of the Gospel of Mary, she begins to give the inner mysteries of the initiations of the seven chakras.

This, then, is a picture of self-knowledge. And what is being imparted by Jesus in the great tradition of the raising up of the light of God is the initiation of the crucifixion and the resurrection. "As I have done it, so shall you."

Gender Has No Bearing on Spiritual Attainment

The truth is that during his ministry, Jesus was the emissary of the Universal Christ, the second person of the Trinity. He was an extension of God's light into material form.

Gender has no bearing on individual spiritual attainment. That Jesus was male does not determine his spirituality. Men and women have equal access to the light of God, and that light can be transmitted through all. Anyone who becomes one with the Spirit as Jesus did is worthy of being called the Christ.

The Church hierarchy prohibits women from entering the priesthood because they question a woman's ability to be a link in the chain of apostolic succession. Can Christ's light and authority be transmitted to and through women?

The pope says no.

But I ask, is there really any intrinsic difference between man and woman that renders woman incapable of participating in and transmitting Christ's mystery?

Paul did not think so. I have taken to heart his profound message to the Galatians in which he says that all men and women who have "put on Christ," being of Abraham's seed, are "heirs according to the promise."[12] Now, if men *and* women are heirs, what are they heirs *of* if not Christ's light essence and the authority to convey it?

The Descent of the Spirit, by Gustave Doré

When the Holy Spirit descended on those who were gathered together at Pentecost, its cloven tongues of fire "sat upon each of them."[13] It blessed both men and women alike. If the women lacked the capacity to assimilate the Holy Spirit, why would God have anointed them? Having been anointed, why would they not be able to transmit that spirit of the living God to others?

Today some scholars argue that the early prominence of women in the Jesus movement was at first clearly written into the New Testament but that bishops and Church Fathers later had second thoughts about the spiritual and leadership ability of women. Changes were made and passages were inserted into the Gospels that reflected a return to a more male-oriented point of view. Scholars say this continued until the canon was finalized in the fourth century.*

Jesus came not only to raise up Woman but to raise up the feminine potential of both man and woman. But early on, Church Fathers amended and added to his teachings things that Jesus never taught. Thus, Jesus' liberal vision of Woman's role and rights was suppressed.

Paul Reinforces Jesus' Teaching on Woman

The early Christians followed Jesus' example in their treatment of women. Paul also spoke of women as leaders, teachers and fellow missionaries.

Paul expressed the newfound freedom for women in Christ when he wrote in Galatians 3:

> *For ye are all the children of God by faith in Christ Jesus. For as many of you as have been baptized into Christ have put on Christ.*
>
> *There is neither Jew nor Greek, there is neither bond nor free, there is neither male nor female: for ye are all one in Christ Jesus.*†

---

* See chapter 6 for a discussion of the suppression of Jesus' true teachings.

† Editor's note: We will be using this scripture throughout the book as a running theme.

In Romans 16:7, Paul refers to Junia as one of his "kinsmen" or "compatriots." He calls her "an outstanding apostle" (Jerusalem Bible). Apostle? Would any church today allow a woman to be called an apostle? Yet Paul called women by that title.

Paul gives Phoebe the title *diakonos* (meaning minister, deaconess, missionary or servant).

In Romans 16:6 and 12, Paul also commends other women disciples who "work hard for the Lord" (JB).

In Philippians 4:3, Paul speaks of two women who worked with him when he was "fighting to defend the Gospel."

Women were also given the status of prophet in the Christian community. Acts 21:9, for instance, records that Philip had four daughters, all of whom prophesied.

Paul and Jesus, then, do not distinguish between men and women.

Misinterpretation of Paul's Statements

Before I go any further, I would like to address one point that inevitably comes up in Christian circles when discussing the status of women. And usually this point carries the day against women. In contrast to the teachings of Paul and Jesus that I have just recounted, there are statements in I Timothy and in I Corinthians that seem to support a subordinate role for women.

This is the crux of the matter. And on this passage turns Woman's place in society as well as in the Church for two thousand years. The fate of women in and out of the Church has rested upon these verses. And the irony is that *Paul didn't write them.*

I Timothy 2:8–15 reads:

> *I will therefore that men pray every where, lifting up holy hands, without wrath and doubting.*

In like manner also, that women adorn themselves in modest apparel, with shamefacedness and sobriety; not with braided hair, or gold, or pearls, or costly array;

But (which becometh women professing godliness) with good works.

Let the woman learn in silence with all subjection.

But I suffer not a woman to teach, nor to usurp authority over the man, but to be in silence.

For Adam was first formed, then Eve.

And Adam was not deceived, but the woman being deceived was in the transgression.

Notwithstanding she shall be saved in childbearing, if they continue in faith and charity and holiness with sobriety.

This teaching is markedly different from other New Testament writings that tell us that the women who served with Jesus and Paul were esteemed and held positions of importance. Why the discrepancy? Simply because Paul was not the author of I Timothy!

Today most scholars doubt that the Pastoral Epistles—which are I and II Timothy and Titus—were written by the apostle Paul. I Timothy does contain Pauline ideas, but it is less mystical in its approach than are Paul's writings.

Scholars say the author is addressing matters that were of importance at the end of the first century—thirty-five years after Paul's time. The author of I Timothy is most concerned about rules and regulations in the Church.

As Howard Clark Kee and Franklin W. Young explain: "The author, clearly a great admirer of the apostle Paul, wrote in Paul's name not only because he believed what he said fully accorded with Paul's thought, but also because he wanted the apostle's authority for his message."[14]

This may sound farfetched today, but it was not out of the ordinary for the first century A.D. As a matter of fact, the authorship of many New Testament writings is questionable. And several are considered to have been written under pseudonyms—assumed names.

Pseudonymous biblical works were written in the tradition of a genre of a religious literature known as *pseudepigrapha.*[15] These were composed between 200 B.C. and A.D. 400. Pseudepigrapha are not among the approved canonical books of the Bible, but they are often associated with the Bible. Some are ascribed to biblical figures, such as Moses, Abraham, Enoch and the apostles. The authors of these documents assumed the name of a patriarch or apostle in order to lend authority to their teachings or for symbolic significance. They did not consider this practice deceitful but believed they were carrying on the tradition of a certain teacher or author.

St. Paul Preaching to the Thessalonians, by Gustave Doré

In other words, two thousand years of submission to a male hierarchy in Church and State because somebody decided to put words in Paul's mouth so they could quote his authority ever thereafter!

Professor Ralph P. Martin states that one theory about the authorship of the Pastorals is that a follower of Paul took fragments of Paul's writing and wove these letters around them "to relate Paul's teaching, as he understood it, to a fresh set of circumstances that arose after Paul's martyrdom in A.D. 65."[16]

Scholars say the author may well have taken something Paul said in response to a specific problem at a specific church and carried it much farther than Paul ever intended. In so doing, he crystallized a particular instruction intended for one situation into a doctrinal position.

One of Paul's statements to the Christians at Corinth may have been the basis for the statement in I Timothy. In I Corinthians 14:34, Paul writes:

> *Let your women keep silence in the churches: for it is not permitted unto them to speak; but they are commanded to be under obedience.*

Because this verse is at odds with other passages in Paul's writing that champion women's full participation in church worship and leadership, some scholars believe that a later author inserted it into a genuine letter of Paul.

However, working from the assumption that Paul is the author of this verse, scholar Norman Hillyer says:

> Paul's famous instruction that *women should keep silence in the churches* and *not ... speak* is still much misunderstood by being divorced from its local and contemporary context.... He is keenly aware of the need for emancipated Christian women to avoid unnecessary scandal through flouting the social conventions of the day. Women had to be wise in using their newly-given liberty in Christ. Paul is here protesting against the disturbance of services by feminine chatter—the meaning of *speak* in vv. 34, 35. Some women (they sat apart from men) were perhaps calling out questions, and commenting knowingly on things said in the service. Paul did not condemn women to complete silence in church for he mentions some able to prophesy,... and this was a gift exercised in public.[17]

Scholars and theologians say it is unlikely that Paul meant his words in I Corinthians 14:34 to be taken as a blanket statement since he rarely made blanket statements. Furthermore, Paul makes a comment elsewhere in the same epistle that assumes women do have the right to speak in church but says that they should follow the social custom of covering their heads when they prophesy.

Paul writes in I Corinthians 11:5:

> *Every woman that prayeth or prophesieth with her head uncovered dishonoureth her head.*

In I Corinthians 11:3, Paul gives further instruction on the role of women that again has been misinterpreted. It needs to be understood in the context of the first century. The apostle writes:

> *But I would have you know, that the head of every man is Christ; and the head of the woman* is *the man; and the head of Christ* is *God.*

Norman Hillyer writes in his commentary on this passage:

> Although the *woman* is subject to *her husband* (and decidedly so in ancient days), his authority is significantly modified because of his own subjection to *Christ.*[18]

I believe Paul is saying woman is subject to her husband only insofar as he subjects himself to Christ and, through him, to God. Hillyer continues,

> The principle does not interfere with the personal relationships of men and women to Christ. It must be applied today against the background of the different sociological situation. (Otherwise we must revert to the clothes—and slavery—of those times.)[19]

In addition, Paul closes his teaching on this subject in I Corinthians 11:11–12 by acknowledging that men and women are mutually dependent upon one another (Jerusalem Bible):

> *Though woman cannot do without man, neither can man do without woman, in the Lord; woman may come from man, but man is born of woman—both come from God.*

In sum, Paul's statements in Corinthians and those made by the author of I Timothy need to be placed against the backdrop of the strict social customs of the first century. In reality, Paul's teaching in regard to women was radical for his day. He forged the way for a new equality in Christ when he wrote in Galatians: "There is neither male nor female: for ye are all one in Christ Jesus."

Even if the first Christian women did not officially share the mantle of "apostle" with the original twelve for practical reasons, they were full-fledged disciples, leaders, missionaries and prophets. Apart from this evidence that we have gleaned from the Bible, there are also traditions that say a band of Jesus' disciples, including women, traveled with Joseph of Arimathea to France as missionaries. Martha is said to have ministered in the town of Tarascon and Mary Magdalene in Aix. The gender of the body one wears does not determine the fitness of the soul to be a servant at the altar of God, but the quality of your spirit and your heart and your mind does.

Omission from the Bible: When Women Were Priests

Following Jesus' example, early Christians were very open toward women. But the orthodox clergy decided that the teachings on the Divine Mother and the feminine principle were not the true teachings of Jesus Christ and therefore should not be included in the Bible. As Elaine Pagels, professor of Religion at Princeton University, points out,

> From the year 200, we have no evidence for women taking prophetic, priestly, and episcopal roles among orthodox churches.
>
> This is an extraordinary development, considering that in its earliest years the Christian movement showed a remarkable openness toward women. Jesus himself violated Jewish convention by talking openly with women, and he included them among his companions.[20]

Orthodox clergy, pretenders to the throne of Saint Peter and the like, dropped the torch of the revolution Jesus started for Woman! And it's up to us to pick it up and to run with it—to pick it up and run with it until the full rights of woman and man under Jesus Christ and God alone are guaranteed on earth as in heaven!

The fourth-century Synod of Laodicea proclaimed that "women are not allowed to approach the altar."[21]

The Apostolic Constitutions, a fourth-century collection of Church law, banned women from holding any positions in the Church.

In 829, the Reform Synod of Paris called it "shameful" that in some provinces the women came close around the altar, touched the holy vessels, handed clerics their priestly vestments and dispensed the Body and Blood of the Lord.[22]

The twelfth-century Decree of Gratian, a compilation of centuries of canon law, declared,

> We do not permit women to exercise the office of teaching in the Church; rather they are simply to pray and listen to the teachers.

Why? The Decree of Gratian explains,

> Our Teacher and Lord Jesus himself sent only the Twelve to us, to teach the people and the gentiles. But he never sent women, although there was no lack of them. . . . If it had been seemly for women, he would have called them himself.[23]

You can see how far removed from the Gnostic texts, which are sitting in the Vatican Library and which have been denounced by Church Fathers—how far removed from those true teachings the hierarchy of the Church had become by the twelfth century.

In 1917, the Roman Catholic Church's revised code of canon law stated,

> A female person may not minister. An exception is allowed only if no male person can be had and there is a good reason. But female persons may in no case come up to the altar, and may only give responses from afar.[24]

Ruth Tucker and Walter Liefeld explain in their book *Daughters of the Church* why Jesus may have declined to include women among the twelve apostles. They point out,

> First of all, from a practical standpoint, it would have been logistically difficult for a woman to travel alone as an itinerant missionary in the first-century world. Second, from a social viewpoint, a woman would not have been accepted as a religious teacher in most areas. . . . Third, women were not accepted as witnesses. The basic function of the apostle was to witness to the words, deeds, resurrection, and person of the Lord Jesus Christ. . . . Fourth, the apostles symbolically represented the twelve tribes of Israel. . . . If this symbolic group was to gain acceptance among Jews, it was unthinkable that one of them be a woman.[25]

In 1977, Pope Paul VI stated that women could not become priests "because our Lord was a man."[26] In 1988, Pope John Paul II condemned sexual discrimination in the Church but stated that "women cannot become priests because Jesus Christ chose only men as his apostles."[27]

As in Gratian's decree, this has long been the line of an all-male Church hierarchy. It is nothing short of blasphemy against the Blessed Mother of our Lord and all of her daughters on earth! It denies the entire legacy of women's rights championed by Jesus Christ and the apostle Paul that is as plain as day in the New Testament, in the Gnostic scriptures and in the records carefully penned and preserved by Buddhist historians who chronicled the life of Saint Issa.

Two thousand years after Jesus started his revolution for Woman, the Roman Catholic Church is finally allowing women to serve at the altar to assist the priest during mass.

But women still do not have the right to be priests.

The Gnostics' Views on Apostolic Succession

The Gnostics, on the other hand, did not agree that religious authority was restricted to the first apostolic generation or to the bishops.

Pagels outlines the three ways in which Gnostics received their understanding of spiritual matters: first, through secret teachings handed down by the apostles to an elect group of Gnostic initiates; second, through inspired teachers who were revered as visionaries because one could testify to the presence of the Holy Spirit with them; and third, from within—through direct spiritual experience and inspiration.

They did not believe that when the forty days between Jesus' resurrection and ascension were up, the door of access to the Master was forever shut. The Gnostics maintained that they themselves could experience Jesus' continuing presence through intimate communion with the Master or visions in which he would impart new revelations and insights. They considered that those who received these revelations thereby shared in, or even surpassed, the authority vested in the apostles and their representatives—the bishops.

In fact, writes Pagels,

> The bishops' promise to "remain bound by original apostolic witness"... means something else to Gnostic Christians: they take it as proof of the severe limitation of the bishops' authority.... Belonging to the original circle of "apostles"... matters less than receiving new and continuing visions.[28]

For instance, some Gnostic texts depict Mary Magdalene as a higher initiate than Peter because she received direct communications from the risen Christ and exceeded Peter in gaining gnosis.

Although some clergymen favored the active participation of women in church affairs, the majority supported the view of second-century Church theologian Tertullian, who wrote: "It is not permitted for a woman to speak in the church, nor is it permitted for her to teach, nor to baptize, nor to offer [the eucharist], nor to claim for herself a share in any masculine function—least of all, in priestly office."[29]

Current Views on Women Priests

This view has essentially remained unchanged. As we said previously, as recently as 1977, Pope Paul VI said that a woman cannot be a priest "because our Lord was a man"! That is the reason he gave! Evidently he had forgotten Paul's message to the Galatians.

One of the reasons why it is thought that Jesus appointed Peter as "prince of the apostles" and head of the Church is the episode recorded in the Book of Matthew where Jesus asks the disciples: "Whom say ye that I am?"

We need to look deeply into this scene. It is my conviction that here Jesus, in his use of words, is already rebuking the idolatrous nature of Peter. When Jesus asks, "Whom say ye that I am?" Peter answers, "Thou art the Christ, the Son of the living God."

Jesus says in return, "Blessed art thou Simon Barjona: for flesh and blood hath not revealed it unto thee, but my Father which is in heaven. And I say also unto thee, That thou art Peter, and upon this rock I will build my church; and the gates of hell shall not prevail against it."[30]

As you know, this is a play on words, for the name Peter means "rock." So he is saying to Peter, "On the witness that you have made of my Sonship, which is not of flesh and blood, I am founding this church." If the witness is not of flesh and blood, it is of the Christ truth. And he is saying to Peter, "Upon this rock I am building my church. So don't ever think that I will build it on the rock of Peter, Cephas—upon flesh and blood. Because I am rejecting the flesh-and-blood testimony of the human. And I am praising you at this moment for being the instrument of Christ's recognition that I am the Son of the living God."

Regarding the interpretation of this passage, Dr. G. Campbell Morgan has noted, "If we trace the figurative use of the word *rock* through the Hebrew Scriptures, we find that it is never used symbolically of man, but always of God."[31] Upon the rock of God, I build my church, to which, Peter, you have given witness. Peter the little rock, Christ the big Rock.

Mother Mary has told us:

> It is upon the Rock of the individual Christ Self [of every member of the mystical body of God] and not upon the flesh-and-blood consciousness of Peter or of

> his successor that the rising or the falling of the Church must rest. Would we, then, place something so divine as the institution in heaven and on earth of the mystical body of God in the fragile chalice of the human will or the human frailty? I tell you nay! The Rock of the Church lives today in the hearts of those who are its true saints both within and without its ranks East and West and even those who may be devotees of Zarathustra or of the Lord Confucius....
>
> 
>
> 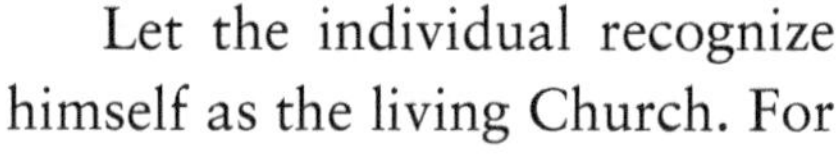
>
> Let the individual recognize himself as the living Church. For not a cathedral nor an institution but a heart that beats one with the heart of God, *this* is my definition of Church.[32]

I believe with all my heart—I know it, I remember it, because I was Jesus' disciple Martha—that our Lord respected women and gave female disciples equal opportunity and gave them status equal to that of male disciples. And I believe, as every good Christian should, in the imitation of Christ.

I believe that if it is your calling from God to serve in any office of the Church, you should be allowed to do so if you study to show yourself approved unto God—rightly dividing the word of truth—regardless of your sex.

There is nothing wrong with a woman's being a priest. The right women would make fine priests. And for that matter there is nothing wrong with a woman's becoming the pope of the Roman Catholic Church. The right woman would make a fine pope.

When I am at the altar, I don't identify myself as male or female. I remember the words of Saint Paul,

There is neither Jew nor Greek, there is neither bond nor free, there is neither male nor female: for ye are all one in Christ Jesus.

This is a revolution for Woman started by Jesus Christ. And this revolution, by God's grace, we will finish!

The Suppression of Jesus' True Teachings on Woman and the Soul

Jesus' teaching on the nature and destiny of the soul was suppressed. He taught that our souls had their origin in God and have the potential to return to God through a disciplined path of soul evolution.

From the time of the Council of Nicaea in A.D. 325, when it was written into Church dogma that Jesus was the only Son of God, it became heresy to think that we too could become sons and daughters of God.

Yet the attack on Jesus' teaching on the soul as the potential to become godlike had begun before Nicaea. Certain Church Fathers started the process when they suppressed the Gnostic belief in the spiritual capacity of Woman and the divine origin of the soul.

In the early centuries of Christian thought, Church Fathers took exception to Jesus' teaching. They decided that the soul did not come from God. Instead they linked the soul to the body, saying that both were formed "out of nothing," meaning that God created life not from his own being but from the "nothing" that was outside himself. Only Jesus' soul, they claimed, was made from God's essence.[33]

This new doctrine devalued the soul and thus compromised our ability to follow Jesus' example and return to God as his son or daughter. Not only did the Church lose the spirit of what Jesus was all about, but it effectively ruled out the possibility that we could become like him and have our own one-on-one relationship with God. The Church concluded that the only way we could attain salvation was through the formal steps of instruction offered by Church rules and rituals.

As we will see in chapter 3, the thread of Paul and Jesus' original message on Woman has been found in the writings of the Christian Gnostics. However, orthodoxy has turned Jesus into a flesh-and-blood god, someone we cannot relate to and who doesn't always seem to relate to us because he never had to experience the problems we have had to experience. That is not the real Jesus.

CHAPTER 3

The Gnostics—Inheritors of Jesus' True Teachings

Previous page: *Christ and the Rich Young Ruler* (detail),
by Heinrich Hofman

CHAPTER 3

The Gnostics— Inheritors of Jesus' True Teachings

A Treasure Chest in an Earthen Jar

Apart from the Bible itself and the Buddhist text on the life of Saint Issa, we have yet another record of Jesus' outspoken defense of Woman and of each soul's potential to become one with God. Enter the Christian Gnostics.

Up until the middle of the twentieth century, most of what we knew about the early Christian Gnostics came from what their enemies among the Church Fathers had written about them.

The first two original Gnostic manuscripts (Codex Askewianus and Codex Brucianus) were actually acquired by two British collectors in the eighteenth century. But these rare and precious documents remained untranslated—the first for about eighty years and the second for a hundred and twenty years.

But in 1945, an Arab peasant accidentally discovered fifty-two Gnostic texts near Nag Hammadi, Egypt—a village located about sixty miles north of Luxor, along the Nile River. The texts were hidden in a large earthen jar that had been buried at the foot of a high cliff. They were Coptic translations made in about A.D. 350 from original Greek texts that may date as far back as the first or early second century. (Coptic is a vernacular form of the Egyptian language used by the earliest Egyptian Christians.) Some scholars have speculated that a monk from a nearby monastery hid the banned Gnostic manuscripts in the jar around A.D. 400 to prevent them from being destroyed.

Nag Hammadi, Egypt

These manuscripts, dubbed the Nag Hammadi library, were published for the first time in English in 1977. They have provided valuable information on some of the early controversies in the Church as well as what might have been some of the secret teachings of Jesus.

What Were the Gnostics' Beliefs?

Gnosticism is a term applied to a diverse group of religious sects, some Christian and some not, that existed before and after the birth of Christianity. They believed that the most important element in the soul's spiritual quest was *gnosis,* a Greek word meaning "knowledge."

Although the Gnostics' origins are debated today, many scholars now believe that a Jewish Gnosticism existed before Christianity and probably continued to develop alongside it.[1]

The Christian Gnostics claimed that they were the recipients of Jesus' secret teaching handed down to them by the apostles and the inner circle of disciples. These Gnostics understood that Jesus had come to demonstrate a mystical path to which all could attain.

They honored disciples such as Mary Magdalene, Salome, Thomas and James as the foremost spiritual leaders of the Church, whereas the orthodox factions preferred Peter and Andrew.

Christian Gnostic sects were especially active in the second century A.D. Prior to that time, Christianity was characterized more by its diversity than by a unified body of beliefs. In fact, the orthodox Christians developed their doctrines, creeds and canon in response to what they considered the heresies of their Gnostic rivals.

While Gnostic groups differed in many ways, they shared a common belief that the means to salvation was not primarily through faith or through the Church but through gnosis. But for the Gnostics, gnosis was not worldly or intellectual, rational knowledge. Gnosis was knowledge of God, knowledge of the True Self as God—knowledge of the universe in which they lived and an understanding of their relationship to each other. The term gnosis as it was used by the Gnostics has also been translated as "understanding," "insight" or "acquaintance." Gnosis is true self-knowledge, based on a real acquaintance of God.

However, gnosis itself was not the Gnostics' ultimate goal. We gain a higher understanding of where their sights were set from one of the first Gnostic translators and authorities. G. R. S. Mead explains that

> one of [the Gnostics'] earliest existing documents expressly declares that Gnosis is not the end—it is the beginning of the path, the end is God—and hence the Gnostics would be those who used the Gnosis as the means to set their feet upon the Way to God....
>
> They strove for the knowledge of God, the science of realities, the gnosis of the things-that-are; wisdom was their goal; the holy things of life their study.[2]

Scholar Hans Jonas writes that for the Gnostics

> "knowledge" has an eminently practical aspect. The ultimate "object" of gnosis is God: its event in the soul transforms the knower himself by making him a partaker in the divine existence.[3]

This inner self-knowledge is what the New Age is really all about. Everyone is seeking, in one way or another, inner self-knowledge:

What is consciousness?

What is the divine spark within me?

What is the Inner Christ?

Who is the Inner Buddha?

In fact, who or what or where is God?

The Gnostics considered themselves the keepers of Christ's inner teachings, passed down to them by his disciples. They also believed that after Jesus' resurrection, he continued to reveal higher spiritual mysteries—not only to chosen apostles and disciples, but to all who would become quickened to his message and mission.

They claimed that this progressive revelation was imparted through visions, dreams or direct communication with the person of Christ.

The Gnostics wrote down these teachings as collections of sayings, parables and proverbs; exhortations or sermons; interpretations of scripture; stories; or dialogues between Jesus and one of the disciples. The dialogues—often written in the name of a disciple or a biblical figure—did not necessarily include the words of the disciple himself but were written, for example, in the spirit of Philip, John or Mary Magdalene as a continuation of their original experience of communion with the Master.

One of the central themes among Gnostics was Jesus' high esteem for his female disciples. Their texts tell us that Mary

Magdalene, Martha and Salome were among those Jesus chose to receive his secret teachings and revelations.

The Gnostic work entitled the Gospel of Philip says, "There were three who always walked with the lord: Mary his mother and her sister[4] and the Magdalene, the one who was called his companion. His sister and his Mother and his companion were each a Mary."[5] (The Greek word translated here as "companion" can also mean partner, spouse or wife.)

In another Gnostic text, the Dialogue of the Saviour, Mary Magdalene is called the "woman who knew the All."[6] She knew the allness of God by her devotion to Jesus, in whom she saw God fully incarnate as the Word. Jesus came to teach Mary Magdalene—and you and me—the meaning of the All and how to attain oneness with the All. He came to restore the soul to her divine estate. And through his adoration of Magdalene's soul, he drew her back into her divine image.

As Gnostic beliefs grew more popular, they presented a challenge to the unity of the Church. The Gnostics refused to recite new creeds written by men or to conform to the emerging doctrines of the Church. They had the teachings of Jesus' inner circle, of his disciples and the holy women. They didn't need dogma and doctrine. They were carrying on the traditions of the mystic John the Beloved, of Mary Magdalene, of Martha and of the Mother of Jesus.

Eventually the Gnostics were expelled from the Church—they complicated matters—and the orthodox clergy attempted to destroy all traces of them and their teaching. They were so successful that few Gnostic works have survived to the present.

The Gnostics' Quest for an Individual Experience of God

At first, Gnostic groups were part of early Christianity, and their leaders held prominent positions in Christian communities. The Gnostic teacher Valentinus began his career as a Christian teacher. In about A.D. 140, Valentinus left his native Egypt to go to Rome, where he expected to be elected bishop. When he failed to receive that position, he left the Church there and continued to teach on his own. The philosophical school he founded produced an extensive body of writings.

Valentinus wrote visionary poetry and claimed that his teaching was based on divine revelations. His and other Gnostic spiritual practices centered around the individual quest for an experience of God. The Gnostics' mystical experiences were meant to culminate in the state of divine union—a state in which the soul would be permanently reunited with God.

Gnostics tended to gather in small circles around a charismatic teacher, such as Valentinus, from whom they were seeking instruction. They valued this form of group interaction more than membership in a Church that stressed ritual and a formal creed.

Although Christian Gnostic groups differed in many ways, they shared the common belief that our soul's origin is divine and her goal is to return to God. They believed that God had given them a seed of light, a divine spark, that represented their divine potential.

They saw Jesus as their Redeemer—but a very different sort of Redeemer than the one the orthodox Christians claimed to know. To the Gnostics, Jesus had come to breathe life into that spark and awaken them to their own divinity. For them, Jesus was a wayshower who had attained gnosis, experienced union with the Father and had come to show them how they could do the same.

Today, the belief in an indwelling God is common to many spiritual seekers who are searching for their own "inner man" of the heart. They look for their true identity by asking the important questions:

What is my destiny?

Where did my soul come from and where is she going?

How can I unlock my divine potential and become my Real Self?

The early Christian Gnostics also asked these questions and proposed answers for them, sometimes in the form of complicated theories. Gnostics were some of the first Christian theologians, weaving together Greek philosophy, Jewish mysticism and allegorical interpretations of Jesus' sayings and deeds.

These are Jesus' lost teachings that are returning to our awareness today.

The Gnostic Paul

Let us repeat: Gnosticism has been used to describe a group of diverse religious movements that existed first within Christianity and then as a rival of it—especially during the second century A.D. when standards for Christian belief and practices had not yet been clearly defined.

The Gnostics sought self-knowledge of the inner Christ, revealed to the disciples by Jesus himself. Even the apostle Paul was a Gnostic.[7] He makes very clear that he learned all things from Jesus himself who personally taught him. And even the scriptures themselves note that Paul was initiated on the road to Damascus.[8] He was blinded by Jesus' light and then healed, raised up to be an apostle, and through him the power of the Holy Spirit flowed.

We find, then, that the apostle Paul was taught by Jesus over many years. And our inner reading of the records of akasha shows that he was taken up, when he spent that period of his life on the Arabian desert, into the etheric or heaven-world retreat of Jesus that is to this day over the Holy Land.[9] And there, in that inner tutoring of his soul, Paul received the

Paul at Mars' Hill, Athens

fullness of the mysteries of Christ. He was empowered as the greatest of the apostles to spread Christianity to the Gentiles.

You can read about the apostle Paul in our book *The Masters and Their Retreats,* which also tells you how you can journey to these etheric or heaven-world retreats of the masters as your soul journeys out of the body during sleep at night.[10]

So then, the apostle Paul, being a Gnostic, did teach a way of self-knowledge. And we find in many of his epistles glimpses of the truth that remain.

Self-knowledge was the gift to the inner circle, and Paul speaks of veiled truths reserved for those who are "perfect" or "mature," that is among those who are initiated into the deeper mysteries Jesus taught:

> *Howbeit we speak wisdom among them that are perfect: yet not the wisdom of this world, nor of the princes of this world, that come to nought: but we speak the wisdom of God in a mystery, even the hidden wisdom, which God ordained before the world unto our glory.*[11]

The idea that there could be an inner circle of initiates who might be more advanced, more in touch with the Lord than those who determined to establish the Christian Church and orthodoxy was simply unacceptable. Therefore, for purposes of power and for holding the power in this world of the authority of Christ, these teachings have not come down as a tradition.

The Gnostics emphasized knowledge as the means to salvation. Jesus has taught us that salvation means *self-*

elevation, not the lower self elevated but Christ in you elevated. Thus, the elevation of Christ in you is the means to salvation. Jesus said, "And I, if I be lifted up from the earth, will draw all men unto me."[12] The "I" he spoke of is the "I AM," the I AM THAT I AM, or the living Presence of God. It is the light—so he taught the inner circle.

The early Church Fathers put the entire emphasis of salvation on faith—believe in the Lord Jesus Christ and thou shalt be saved. This is the common parlance of Christianity today. Conversion begins with believing in Jesus Christ or believing that Christ was embodied in Jesus, for that is the open door for the same experience for each one of us. It begins here but it is fulfilled in recognizing that Christ is within oneself. There is nothing to be denied of what outer Christianity has to say. There is only to be added the inner mysteries whereby every man sits under his own vine and fig tree, his own I AM Presence and Holy Christ Self.[13]

Your Divine Self

Let us now discuss the Chart of Your Divine Self (pictured on page 80) so that I can more clearly explain the sharing of the Christ between ourselves and Jesus Christ and all avatars. First of all, the word *Christ* comes from the Greek word *Christos*, meaning "anointed." A Christed one is one who is "anointed" with the light of the I AM THAT I AM.

This is a Chart of you, your divine Reality, your Divine Self. You are the lower figure in the Chart. The center is the Universal Christ individualized. And the upper figure is the I AM Presence, or the I AM THAT I AM, who appeared to Moses.[14]

Jesus the Son of man, the human being who wore a body like our bodies, who could suffer pain, who could fall under the weight of the cross, who could be weary, who could cry—

The Chart of Your Divine Self

that Jesus, that human person is the lower figure. It's also you. Visualize yourself as that person and see that flame around you as the flame of the Holy Spirit, because Paul has told us that we are intended to be the temple of the living God, the temple of the Holy Spirit.

Above you is that Universal Christ individualized for you. This is the Christ, this is the teacher, this is your Real Self. This is the Christ that comes forth from God, and there is one Christ and one Lord. But that one Presence is individually personified for you and for me. The Christ of Jesus, the Christ of you and me is still one Lord and one Christ. One times one times one still equals one. It does not detract from Jesus Christ that you also have a Holy Christ Self.

He is the great example, but in Jesus, the Christ is not above him. This is the difference between the avatar, the God incarnation, and ourselves. Jesus Christ and Jesus the Son of man are fully integrated as one. And by that oneness, he is showing us the goal of our life. The goal for your soul is to fully merge and integrate, to be bonded with that Christ. And when you are one with Christ, you are one with the Christ of Jesus, because they are one and the same. That is what Gnosticism is teaching.

The I AM THAT I AM is the Presence of Almighty God that is always above you. "Draw nigh to God and he will draw nigh to you."[15] That I AM Presence comes very close to you in meditation, enters your temple, directs the light and increases it through your spiritual chakras. When you are depressed or angry or out of alignment with the will of God, that I AM Presence may be fifty feet or a thousand feet above you. The closer you are to God's consciousness, the closer God is to you.

The difference between you and Jesus is that I AM THAT I AM is the Word that he incarnated. We acknowledge Jesus as the Word incarnate. The Word is the name of God, I AM THAT I AM. Jesus embodied that full Godhead, that fullness of Christ and that fullness of the Holy Spirit. And he also embodied the light of the Divine Mother.

He was the integrated personality in God. We are disintegrated personalities. We have gotten away from our integration with our divine Reality. The lost teachings of Jesus Christ bring back to you and people of all the world's religions the Path of how to reintegrate with that only begotten Son of God and with that I AM Presence.

This is the mystery that was recorded by the Gnostics, by the early Christians and handed down. This is the teaching that was taken out of the Church. Why was it taken out?

Because with this teaching, you can attain union with God through your Lord and Saviour Jesus Christ, who uses his supreme power to reconnect you to the living fire and the living Presence. You don't have to go through a series of doctrines and dogmas. You don't have to have eternal condemnation that you are a sinner from the beginning, since the sin of Adam and Eve. You don't have to go around thinking you're going to go to hell if you don't obey this and that rule.

However, this teaching does not liberate us from responsibility. You have to understand that you are absolutely responsible for your actions. When, by our actions, we misuse God's energy, we create negative karma. When we create negative karma, we pay the price; and it is the price of having karma, and we must balance that karma.

This teaching gives back to you your accountability for your thoughts and feelings, your words and deeds and says, "What you do wrong, you must make right." This teaching enables you to discover that you have a path to fulfill, that you can do it, that there is a law and a science that Jesus demonstrated, not as an exception to the rule but in fulfillment of the will of God.

This is the teaching of Jesus that is lost. It is the teaching given to us again as the Everlasting Gospel.[16] And as you listen to the teachings that are recorded in the Gnostic texts, you will begin to see just how relevant is this Chart.

Spiritual Centers in the Body

From this picture, you can see how the chakras, or spiritual centers, are placed in your body and can be thinking about these in terms of Jesus' initiation. The lower figure in the Chart is depicted here as the runner.

There is an angel in Revelation who has a foot upon the land and a foot upon the sea.[17] This individual (in our picture) was not intended to be that angel but may be an angel in any case. As Jesus and Paul said to us, "Be not forgetful to entertain strangers: for thereby some have entertained angels unawares."[18] This is a reference to the teaching that angels have taken embodiment and that angels have come to earth and are wearing forms like ours to be our teachers. So we find that among spiritual movements there are any number of people who are embodied angels, good angels who are actually understanding their mission to be teacher rather than fallen angels.

This is the runner in the race that Paul speaks of, running for the prize of the high calling in Christ Jesus[19] and taking dominion over the sea and over the earth, the lower elements of this octave. The seven chakras represent seven planes of being, seven planes of heaven, seven major initiations.

Jesus spoke of all these things to the inner circle. He sealed these mysteries in their hearts for the hour when two thousand years later they would be published abroad and made available.

It's a very interesting thing about the publishing of the mysteries and the teachings. We have seen that those who are quickened by God fully comprehend and understand the mysteries that are written. Those who are not quickened by the Lord may read these books and not understand a word of them and not have any understanding of why anyone would read these books or get anything out of them. It is amazing to see that though they are published abroad, they are given individually when the pupil is ready.

We are endowed by God with the gift of free will and a divine spark. This is what makes us different from all other species. Yes, you have a tiny flame in your heart, a spiritual flame. It is sealed there. It is a threefold flame of power, wisdom and love. It focuses the consciousness of the Trinity—

The Threefold Flame

of Father, Son and Holy Spirit.

The Divine Mother resides in your temple in the sacred fire that rises on the spinal altar from the base-of-the-spine chakra to the crown chakra.

We are the temple of the living God, and the scriptures say so: "What? Know ye not that your body is the temple of God and that the Spirit of God dwelleth in you?... And ye are not your own, for ye are bought with a price.... As God hath said: 'I will dwell in them and walk in them; and I will be their God, and they shall be my people.'"[20]

If we are the children of God, then we must be born of the essence of God, and that essence is the spiritual fire. The spiritual fire gives us the freedom to obey the voice of God, who speaks to us from the precincts of the heart. This is the voice of conscience. And that conscience we acknowledge and adore as our Holy Christ Self.

Gold in the Mud

In the Gospel of Thomas, we read:

> Jesus said, "Blessed are those who are alone and chosen: you will find the kingdom. For you have come from it, and you will return there again.... If some say to you, 'Where have you come from?' say to them, 'We have come from the light, where the light came into being by itself, established itself, and appeared in an image of light.'"[21]

The juxtaposition of the elements of light and darkness is captured in a fundamental Gnostic image—the image of "gold in the mud." The Greek Church Father Irenaeus left us a record of what the Gnostics meant by the symbol of "gold in the mud." This was in his five-volume refutation against the heresies of the Gnostics written in A.D. 180.

We find that the enemies preserved Gnosticism and we get to read about what they said. Irenaeus says: "Gold, when submersed in filth, loses not on that account its beauty, but retains its own native qualities, the filth having no power to injure the gold."[22]

Professor Werner Foerster explains in his book *Gnosis* that "the image of the 'gold' implies that the 'self' in man [the Real Self] to which it alludes belongs to the sphere of God."[23]

This Real Self is the Christ of you, the divine image in which you are made.

> The image is chosen because it allows the gold to be gold, even in the mud of the world: the divine element in man is not damaged, even if it stays there. The divine element in man cannot be altered in its quality, it is "good."... Perhaps the "gold" must yet be purified, ...[24]

And this element of purification, the purification of the gold until it is refined pure, refers, then, to the soul that is putting on the gold of her Christhood—so the purging and the refining process.

There is in the Old Testament the prophecy of the coming of the messenger of God to purify the sons of Levi.[25] This is a Gnostic teaching. It speaks of the refiner's fire and how this refining process takes place, and is such an intense action of the sacred fire that it says, "But who may abide the day of his coming? and who shall stand when he appeareth?"[26]—the coming of the Divine Mediator, the coming of the Saviour when we must be purged so that we can become a part fully and one of this gold.

Foerster continues:

> … the divine element has still to be trained, but the end is certain: the sphere of the divine….
>
> The mud is that of the world: it is first of all the body, which with its sensual desires drags man down and holds the "I" in thrall…. Thus we frequently hear in Gnosis the admonition to free oneself from the "passions."[27]

In the Gnostic work entitled the First Apocalypse of James, James the Just says to Jesus:

> You descended into a great ignorance, but you have not been defiled by anything in it. For you descended into a great mindlessness, and your recollection remained. You walked in mud, and your garments were not soiled, and you have not been buried in their filth, and you have not been caught.[28]

Thus, we would desire to have this spoken of us as it was said to Jesus.

What we have to understand is that while the soul wears the garments, the fleshly garments that are corruptible, she is yet subject to the corruption of this world because she has the gift of free will. Souls that descend, therefore, as taught by the Gnostics, are in danger—in danger of identifying with the illusion and forgetting their higher Home.

If incarnation is a must, then, one cannot regret, one cannot look back, one can understand that what one is seeing is the acceleration of a life. And if one life can so accelerate in the light, then another can. And this is the proof that we must offer, because when you see this in a loved one, when there is an example where the light becomes so great, then the promise is forever, and by that experience we can impart it to others. If you dedicate your life to have that experience so that others will be sure that death is not real, I can assure you that your reward will be great here and now as well as in heaven.

These words of James the Just are words of promise and of comfort and of the sacred mysteries. And when they appear before our eyes, we know truly that the grace of God is available to all today.

In the Gospel of Thomas, Jesus assures the disciples that they are indeed children of the light:

> The disciples said to Jesus, "Tell us about the end."
>
> Jesus said, "Have you already discovered the beginning, that now you can seek after the end? For where the beginning is, the end will be. Blessed is the one who stands at the beginning: that one will know the end, and will not taste death."[29]

And what does Jesus say in the Revelation of John, the most powerful mantra that you can recite—"I AM Alpha and Omega, the beginning and the ending."[30] Jesus said that in a powerful opening of the first chapter of Revelation. He is affirming Alpha and Omega, the plus and the minus polarity of the light itself. He is saying, "I AM the embodiment of Alpha and Omega. I AM the beginning and I AM the ending of all things. I AM the ascended master Jesus Christ." By his affirmation of it, we can affirm it; we can follow in his footsteps. This is the meaning of the I AM affirmations of Jesus.[31]

This is a Gnostic teaching. It teaches that the light of the Father as the I AM Presence descends unto you; the light of the Divine Mother from the base-of-the-spine chakra, the seat of the sacred fire in our being, ascends within us. When these energies merge, there is a divine caduceus, there is a fusion of this energy in the heart, the threefold flame expands, and the Christ consciousness is born in you because Alpha and Omega, the Father-Mother God, have united in your temple to give birth in you to that Christ-awareness.

The affirmation of that simple mantra—I AM Alpha and Omega, the beginning and the ending—is based on a profound science, a gnosis, a self-knowledge. And then we practice the science of mantra and the mantras that increase this fire in our temple. So, a simple saying of Jesus, when we understand the lost teaching, is the key whereby this mortal shall put on immortality.[32]

The Gospel of Thomas says,

> "If they say to you, 'Is it you?', say, 'We are its children, and we are the elect of the living father.' If they ask you, 'What is the sign of your father in you?', say to them, 'It is movement and repose.'"[33]

The active and the passive, the Alpha, the Omega, the ancient symbol out of China of the T'ai Chi. The movement and the repose, the release of the light and the going within, the great sine wave of being—this is the sign whereby we know we are of the original light and the elect of the living Father.

The Gnostic Gospel of Truth speaks of the children whom the Father loves and "in whose midst there is no lack of him":

> Such are those who possess something of this immeasurable majesty from above.... They do not go down to the underworld, nor do they have envy or groaning, nor is death with them. They rest in one who rests....
>
> They are truth. The father is in them and they are in the father, perfect, inseparable from him who is truly good. They lack nothing at all but are at rest, fresh in spirit.[34]

This rest can refer to the inner experience of samadhi and ultimately of nirvana. It can refer to yourself in inner meditation or even when the physical body is at rest and you are studying in the inner temples.[35] What's more, the quality of these is "they will hearken to their root." The root of the seed of light is Christ. "For the father is good, and his children are perfect and worthy of his name."[36]

The Name of God: I AM THAT I AM

I believe that the Gnostics knew the sacred name given to Moses for all generations as the I AM THAT I AM.[37] This name given to Moses is not spoken or written in the Old Testament again, considered too holy for the common people. It is the Hebrew letters YOD HE VAU HE, I AM WHO I AM. This is what God declares where you are. When you declare it, you confirm it in your soul, and your soul, then, receives the light and has impressed upon her the light of the I AM Presence. And that soul becomes more and more permanent or incorruptible day by day until she literally sheds this garment and becomes permanent in the Being of God through the garment Jesus referred to in scripture as the wedding garment.[38] It is called the Deathless Solar Body. And we are weaving that body daily as we conserve the light of God that is the sacred fire.

The name I AM THAT I AM, then, was taken from the people, but God said to Moses, This is my name for ever, and a memorial to all generations.[39]

The prayers and dynamic decrees that you will find in our teachings are all predicated upon the release of the light through this name. "I AM the resurrection and the life,"[40] said Jesus.

When you are saying that, you are saying, "God in me is the resurrection and the life. God in me is the I AM THAT I AM, and I affirm that I am here below that which I am Above." And when you affirm below what is Above, the two become one because they are the same, but they are in polarity. Above is a positive polarity of Spirit, below is the negative polarity of Matter—Alpha and Omega.

The hermetic axiom of Hermes Trismegistus is simply the same statement—as Above, so below. That is the goal of the disciple or the alchemist, the spiritual alchemist—to reproduce here below in the mirror of self that which is Above. When the image matches, time and space collapse and the soul ascends to God. Each day more of this is taking place as you give your prayers, your decrees, Archangel Michael's Rosary, the violet flame, and pursue this self-knowledge in the teachings of the ascended masters.[41]

A corollary to the Gnostic admonition to "Know thyself," to know (thy divine origin) is the warning: "Know thy enemy"—the enemy who is both within and without. The enemy is the part of the self that has been corrupted, has misqualified the light of God for many incarnations, and therefore poses as a part of oneself, but is anti the light. It is over this self that we must get dominion and self-mastery.[42]

The Call

The Gnostics believed that it is the nature of the soul "stuck in the mud" of this world to forget her divine origin. They described this state as sleepfulness, drunkenness or ignorance. What, then, will awaken the soul? It is "*the call.*"

Foerster explains that the Gnostics taught that

> the "call" reaches man neither in rational thought nor in an experience which eliminates thought.... [Man] *feels* that he is encountered by something which already lies within him, although admittedly entombed. It is nothing new, but rather the old which only needs to be called to mind. It is like a note sounded at a distance, which strikes an echoing chord in his heart.[43]

In Gnostic theology, the instrument of the call usually comes in the figure of a Redeemer. Your Redeemer would be your Holy Christ Self, the presence of Christ with you, or as in Christian Gnosticism, it is Jesus who sounds the call and brings the liberating power of gnosis. This concept is also found in the New Testament, which records Jesus as saying: "the Son of man is come to seek and to save that which was lost."[44] "My sheep hear my voice, and I know them, and they follow me."[45]

The Gospel of Truth describes the impelling power of the call as well as the power of gnosis to break the pall of ignorance that holds the soul in its grips.

> Whoever has knowledge is from above. If called, that person hears, replies, turns to the one who is calling, and goes up to him. He knows how he is called. That person has knowledge and does the will of him who called. That person wishes to please him, finds rest.... Those who have knowledge in this way know where they come from and where they are going....
>
> From the moment that the father is known, deficiency will cease to be. As one's ignorance about another vanishes when one gains knowledge, and as darkness departs when light comes, so also deficiency disappears in completeness....
>
> In Unity all individually will come to themselves. By means of knowledge they will purify themselves from multiplicity into unity, devouring matter within themselves like fire, darkness by light, death by life.[46]

The End of Opportunity

God has given your soul many rounds of opportunity incarnation after incarnation to find your way back to his heart. And some day he expects you to do it, to find your way.

Yes, this incarnation, this life today is your opportunity to reunite with the Spirit of God through the ritual of the ascension.

But there is also an end to opportunity for this soul potential that we have. This is something that it is not taught widely today. But you will find it in both the Old and New Testaments. It is the fact that the soul can be lost. The LORD said through the prophet Ezekiel: "The soul that sinneth, it shall die."[47] What this means is that the soul that sins without repentance and without going through the Saviour to be bonded back to God will not become immortal.

Jesus said to his disciples: "What shall it profit a man, if he shall gain the whole world, and lose his own soul?"[48] Jesus was clearly underscoring here that the soul is the non-permanent point of being. And until she becomes permanent through her fusion with the living Christ and with the I AM Presence, she does not have eternal life.

This is why Mother Mary has told us in her Fátima and Medjugorje messages that we must pray for souls that they be not lost.

CHAPTER 4

The Divine Feminine—East and West

Previous page: *Mother of the World,* by Nicholas Roerich

CHAPTER 4

The Divine Feminine—East and West

At the Dawn of History

The cult of the Mother, destined to come into prominence in the twentieth century, was the foundation of the civilization of Lemuria—that lost continent that sank beneath the Pacific Ocean many thousands of years ago.[1] The evolution of life in the Motherland and her colonies represented the initial thrust of Spirit into Matter on this planet. Here, where the early root races[2] completed the cycles of their divine plan during not one but several golden ages that reached their apex prior to the Fall of man, the masculine ray (the descending spirals of Spirit) was realized through the feminine ray (the ascending spirals of Matter) in the world of form.

In the main temple of Mu, the flame of the Divine Mother was enshrined as the coordinate of the flame of the Divine Father focused in the Golden City of the Sun. Perpetuating the ancient rituals of invocation to the Logos[3] and intonation of sacred sounds and mantras of the Word, priests and priestesses of the sacred fire held the balance of cosmic forces on behalf of the lifewaves of the planet. Throughout the far-flung colonies of Mu, replicas of the temple and its flame-focus were established as shrines of the virgin consciousness, thereby creating between the earth and the sun an arc of light, anchored in the flame below and the flame above, which conveyed the energies of the Logos necessary for the precipitation of form and substance in the planes of Matter.

Far beyond our own meager accomplishments, the great advances in technology made during centuries of continuous culture on Mu were brought forth through a universal *at-one-ment* with the Divine Mother, whose consciousness embraces the laws governing all manifestation in the earth plane. The accomplishments in every field of endeavor of a people dedicated to the plan of God show to what heights a civilization can rise when the Mother flame is honored and adored in every heart and guarded and expanded in shrines dedicated to her name. And it becomes clear that man's fall from grace was, in actuality, the result of his falling away from the cult of the Mother and his misuse of the energies of the seed atom focused in the base-of-the-spine chakra (see page 83), which establishes the light of the Mother flame in the physical body.

The fall of Mu, then, was the direct result of the Fall of man, which reached its lowest point in the desecration of the shrines to the Cosmic Virgin. This came about gradually through compromise with principle, separation from the Holy Ghost and the loss of vision that inevitably results therefrom. Blinded by ambition and self-love, priests and priestesses no longer tended the flames; forsaking their vows, they abandoned the practice of those sacred rituals that had remained unbroken for thousands of years—even as the holy angels keep perpetual watch over the unfed flame that burns upon the altar of the Most High God.

The worship of the Moon Mother, the Great Whore mentioned in the Book of Revelation,[4] replaced the worship of the Sun Mother, the Woman whom John saw "clothed with the sun, and the moon under her feet, and upon her head a crown of twelve stars."[5] A black crystal set in lead and stone became the focus for the perversion of the Mother ray and the symbol of the new religion. One by one, the inner circles of the temple orders were violated through the diabolical practice of black magic and phallic worship taught by the Luciferians,[6] until a completely false theology wiped out the pristine patterns of the Mother Cult.

By and by, the early rumblings of cataclysm were heard by the inhabitants of Mu. The altars of the most remote colonies were the first to topple. When the last strongholds—the twelve temples surrounding the main temple—were taken over by the Satanists, the momentum of light invoked by the remnant of the faithful was not great enough to hold the balance for the continent. Thus Mu finally sank by the sheer weight of darkness that her children had invoked—and which, because their deeds were evil, they had come to love more than the light. She went down in a horrendous mass of volcanic fire and exploding lava, and the flame-focuses that had sustained a mighty people and a mighty civilization were no more. What had taken hundreds of thousands of years to build up was torn down in a cosmic interval—the achievements of an entire civilization lost in oblivion, the spiritual-material evolution of man stripped from his outer memory!

Devastating though that cataclysm was for millions of souls, of far greater consequence was the destruction of the focus of the Mother flame that had blazed on the altar of the main temple—a life-giving fire, the insignia of each man's divinity made manifest as Above, so below. Alas, the torch that had been passed was let fall to the ground. The strategies of the fallen ones, who had worked night and day with a fanatical zeal, were successful in accomplishing their end: the Mother flame was extinguished on the physical plane.

For a time it looked as though the darkness had completely

enveloped the light. Beholding the defection of the race, cosmic councils voted to dissolve the planet whose people had forsaken their God; and this would have been its fate had Sanat Kumara[7] not interceded, offering to exile himself from Hesperus in order to keep the flame on behalf of mankind and to hold the balance of the light for Terra until such time as mankind should return to the pure and undefiled religion of their ancient forebears.

The souls who perished with the Motherland reembodied upon a naked earth. Their paradise lost, they roamed the sands whose atoms were etched with the edict of the LORD God, "Cursed is the ground for thy sake...." Having no recall of their former estate and no tie thereto—for they lacked the flame—they reverted to a primitive existence. Through disobedience to the laws of God, they forfeited their self-mastery, their right to dominion, and their knowledge of the I AM Presence. Their threefold flame was reduced to a mere flicker and the lights in their body temples went out. Man, no longer found in the image of the Christ, became one of the species *(Homo sapiens)*, an animal among other animals, his God-potential sealed for a thousand days of cosmic history. Thus began the tortuous trek of evolution that has brought civilization to its present level and that is intended to culminate in a golden age of Christ-mastery and full God-realization.[8]

What happened to the ancient memory of the Mother flame on Lemuria? We see the threads of it picked up by the avatars of all the world religions. One of these threads leads us back to Gnosticism.

Gnostic Views

A significant feature in some Gnostic writings is the portrayal of the Supreme Being not as a monistic, masculine God, but as God that has both male and female elements.

Elaine Pagels, in her best-selling book *The Gnostic Gospels,* explains that Gnostic texts depict God as Mother in three distinct ways: as part of an original couple; as the Holy Spirit or the Third Person of the Trinity; and as Wisdom.

Some Gnostic texts point out that in the Book of Genesis, God refers to himself as a plurality—"Let us make man in *our* image, after *our* likeness."[9] The Hebrew word for "God" used in this verse of Genesis is the plural noun "Elohim"—a duality in a unity. It is used elsewhere throughout the Old Testament about twenty-five hundred times.

The Gnostics note that if God created man in his own image, and "male and female created he them,"[10] as Genesis goes on to say, then God must also be "male and female"!

The influential Gnostic teacher Valentinus taught that the Divine consisted of two elements: the Primal Father (whom he described as the Ineffable or the Depth) and the Mother of the All (whom he called Grace, Silence, the Womb).[11]

A Gnostic work known as the Great Announcement says that there is

> from above ... a great power, (the creative) Mind of the universe, which manages all things, (and is) a male. The other ... is from below, (and constitutes) a great Intelligence, and is a female which produces all things.... They are ranged in pairs, one opposite the other; for power is in no wise different from intelligence, inasmuch as they are one. For from those things that are above is discovered power; and from those below, intelligence.[12]

Pagels says that in many Gnostic works "the divine is to be understood in terms of a harmonious, dynamic relationship of opposites—a concept that may be akin to the Eastern view of *yin* and *yang,* but remains alien to orthodox Judaism and Christianity."[13]

The Gnostic understanding of the yang-yin of the Father-

Mother God goes back to the Hindu teaching on the interplay of cosmic forces represented by a god and his *shakti* ("wife" or "consort").

In fact, the avatars of all world religions taught the same truths. It is the generations that came after them that embroidered upon and distorted these truths. The religious hierarchies of East and West who did not have the spirit of the original founders created doctrines and dogmas that have separated Christian from Jew from Moslem from Hindu from Buddhist.

But what is God? God is not a belief system. God is not a set of doctrines and dogmas. God is love. And that love is the union of the Father-Mother God in each of us, who give birth to the Christ in us right within our hearts.

And when we can see that, we will break the shackles of a man-made doctrine, because we don't get to heaven by our doctrine! We get to heaven in spite of our doctrine, not because of it! Now I give you the teachings of God, not the doctrines of men.

Who Is the Divine Mother?

Who is the Divine Mother? She is the great Shakti. She is Isis. She is the Woman clothed with the Sun.[14] Our Divine Mother is with us and in us and universally manifest in the Matter cosmos.

In the ancient city of Saïs on the Nile delta stood the temple of Isis on which was written the following inscription: "I, Isis, am all that has been, that is or shall be; no mortal Man hath ever me unveiled."[15] Known by a thousand names, Isis pervades the cultures of the world. Known by any name, she is the Divine Mother who ensouls all life. It is she who gave birth to all things, including the only begotten Son of

God. She remains the Cosmic Virgin; for the Divine Mother preserves the Whole-I-Vision of the Godhead, and through the perception of the Eye of God within her forehead, the Christ victorious appears.

Whereas God the Father is depicted as the Omnipotent One, the impersonal Law and the personal Principle that undergirds the creation, the Mother is personified in and as the creation and is identifiable to man not only through the forces of nature but also through every aspect of the physical universe, including his own four lower bodies. Thus the Divine Mother shows forth the eternal glories of the Father and the Son in the four planes of Matter and balances in man the cosmic energies that ordain his destiny.

Omnipotent is the flame of the Mother, omniscient her wisdom, omnipresent her love.

In Adolph Erman's *Handbook of Egyptian Religion,* we find certain statements attributed to Isis, the personification of the feminine aspect, which recall the identity and purpose of the Divine Mother. They are noteworthy in that they evince the continuity of the teaching of the Great White Brotherhood on the Mother flame from ancient times to the present:

I am Isis, mistress of the whole land:

> *The Earth Mother takes dominion over the entire physical universe.*

I was instructed by Hermes,

> *The God of Science ordains the Mother to teach mankind the laws governing the plane of material manifestation.*

and with Hermes I invented the writings of the nations, in order that not all should write with the same letters.

> *The communication of God-ideas and identifications through the written and spoken Word is the process whereby the Mother makes intelligible to her children the consciousness of the Father.*

I gave mankind their laws, and ordained what no one can alter.

The commandments of the Lord and the laws governing the release of energy from Spirit to Matter, indispensable to the well-being of man, are the unalterable expression of Spirit in Matter.

I am the eldest daughter of Kronos.*

While the Mother embodies the consciousness of the Father in the plane of Matter-earth, her energies issue forth from the plane of Spirit-earth.

I am the wife and sister of the king Osiris.

In referring to feminine goddesses as the wife, sister or daughter of the gods, the ancients indicated the polarity that exists between the yang and yin aspects of the creation. Isis is the twin flame of Osiris; together in their appointed sphere, they coordinate the functions of Alpha and Omega.

I am she who rises in the dog star.

The Image of the Divine Mother is seen in the God Star, Sirius, focus of the Great Central Sun in this sector of our galaxy.

I am she who is called the goddess of women....

The World Mother represents God in the Womb-man.

I am she who separated the heaven from the earth.

With the creation of Matter, the divine Whole became twain.

I have pointed out their paths to the stars.

The Mother delineates the destiny of her sons and daughters and imparts to them the wisdom and the love necessary to fulfill the divine blueprint.

I have invented seamanship....

---

* Cronus, the earth god.

The Mother, often called the Star of the Sea, is the mistress of the seas—water being the most feminine, or yin, aspect of the material creation.

I have brought together men and women....

The love aspect of the Divine Mother is the cohesive force of atoms, universes and twin flames.

I have ordained that the elders shall be beloved by the children.

Through the Mother, the continuity of the Flame—of life, culture and the blissful awareness of the Father—is preserved from one generation to the next.

With my brother Osiris I made an end of cannibalism.

Through the Mother, man comes to understand reverence for life, for the God who inhabits his creation.

I have instructed mankind in the mysteries.

Wisdom teaches her children the geometrization of the Spirit of the LORD.

I have taught reverence of the divine statues.

As the statue is the symbol of the identity of God individualized in his manifestation, so every manifestation is the embodiment of Universal Christ Principle. It is to this rather than to the statue or to the person that we bend the knee and direct our devotion.

I have established the temple precincts.

Mater is the temple of Spirit and forms the boundaries thereof, enshrining the sacred law, the sacred science and the sacred flame of life.

I have overthrown the dominion of the tyrants.

The perversions of the God consciousness and of the Father Image are exposed by the Divine Mother.

I have caused men to love women.

The Mother is the counterpart of the Divine Magnet as she attracts the flow of Spirit into the womb of Matter.

I have made justice more powerful than silver and gold.

Through the discovery of the Mother Image mirrored in nature, man is no longer wedded to materiality as an end in itself but perceives in the virtues of the Spirit rising out of the crucible of time and space that the material universe is but the means to an end; moreover, he recognizes those virtues as having the power to take dominion over the human spirit, making it to transcend itself and the clay vessel that houses the Spirit.

I have caused truth to be considered beautiful.

Truth, as the arrow of the Father's consciousness, becomes beauty in manifestation through the Image of the Mother.[16]

We also find many images of the Divine Mother in the East.

A stone statue, carved over a thousand years ago in a cave temple in India, is a striking testimony to the Father-Mother God. It portrays the Great God Shiva as an androgynous being—half man, half woman. Known as Ardhanarishvara ("the Lord who is both male and female"), this sculpture of Shiva on Elephanta Island shows him with his left side having all the attributes of a woman and his right side those of a man.

Ardhanarishvara

This image of Shiva is linked in design to the yin-yang symbol of the T'ai Chi, whose light and dark halves—divided by a flowing line in the form of an *S*—form the circle of the Divine Whole. Both works of art are telling us that God is a union of two opposing but complementary forces.

We can see these two images as representations of the Father-Mother God, for God is androgynous, a plus and minus Whole. All heavenly beings are also androgynous, although they can appear to us in either a masculine or a feminine form.

Furthermore, these dual images of God also remind us that long ago, before we lost our immortality and were born on earth, we too were androgynous beings. And our goal is to return to that original state of wholeness.

Hinduism, the oldest religion on this planet, has retained the memory of God as androgynous, a concept that Jesus learned in his travels in the East. Perhaps the Gnostic understanding of the Father-Mother God came down through the centuries from Hinduism or from another ancient source that taught this concept.

The Divine Couple: God as Father-Mother in the Vedas

Western scholars believe that the Vedas, the earliest scriptures of Hinduism, were probably composed between 1500 and 1000 B.C. Hindu scholars push the dates back another two thousand years.[17]

The Rig Veda, the oldest of the Vedas, refers to the Divine Father and Mother as Heaven and Earth. In an early verse of the scripture, the author speaks to "Heaven and Earth," saying:

> I meditate with invocations upon the Father's harmless, undeceiving Mind and the Mother's mighty Self-power, prolific parents who made the world for their children.[18]

David Frawley, an interpreter of the Hindu scriptures and the translator of this verse, comments on its meaning:

> Heaven and Earth as the Divine Father and Mother are the basis of ancient cosmology, Father Heaven and Mother Earth. In this sense they are not simply the worlds, but the transcendent Divine principles which manifest through them. The Father and his harmless, undeceiving Mind is Shiva, the supreme Being. The Mother, who has the mighty Self-power, is Shakti, the supreme Consciousness-force. The beneficence of Heaven and Earth rests upon them. The world of nature is their gift of vision to us to lead us up into the immortalities of their higher nature.[19]

The term *Shakti* that Frawley uses here to define the Mother means "energy," "power" or "force." He is saying that the Hindus see the Divine Mother as the dynamic expression of God's energy. The Shakti is also the creative force of the universe, the manifest power of her masculine counterpart. She is not inferior to her partner, for she has a different but complementary role: she releases the potential of God from Spirit into Matter. The entire universe would collapse if there were not this co-equality of divine energy.

Shiva

The Hindu Mother of the Universe—Vac

The Gnostic teaching on the "Mother of the All" is much like the Hindu teaching on Vac, the Mother of the Universe.

In the Vedas, the Mother is associated with the cosmic Principle and Person of Vac, a Sanskrit word meaning "speech," "word," "voice," or "language." The Mother of the Universe is considered to be the active Creator, creating by the Word. She is the Word with Brahman in the Beginning by which all things are made.

If a Hindu were to hear of Jesus being the incarnate Word, he would understand this in terms of Jesus being the incarnation of the Divine Mother. You might question that teaching, but when you think about Jesus and you think of the tremendous flame of the Divine Mother of love, the tremendous peace and the caring for life, you can see that Jesus is equally balanced as masculine and feminine.

Hindu texts say that Vac contains within herself all worlds of time—past, present and future. She is sometimes identified with Sarasvati, the goddess of learning, eloquence and the arts.

Sarasvati

The Vedic concept of Vac parallels the concept of the Logos, or Word, reflected in the opening verse of the Gospel of John: "In the beginning was the Word, and the Word was with God, and the Word was God.... And without him was not any thing made that was made."[20] You can translate that to say, "In the beginning was the Divine Mother, and the Divine Mother was with God, and the Divine Mother was God. And without the Divine Mother was not anything made that was made."

John Woodroffe, who wrote under the pen name Arthur Avalon, writes in *The Garland of Letters,* "These are the very words of the Veda, *Prajapatir vai idam asit:* In the beginning was Brahman. *Tasya vag dvitiya asit;* with whom was Vak* or the Word ... *Vag vai paramam Brahma;* and the Word is Brahman."[21] Brahman is the Hindu name for the Supreme Being, who represents ultimate Reality, the Absolute.

Hindu texts refer to Vac as the Shakti of the Creator. In Hinduism the Divine Mother is worshiped in the form of many Shaktis. Shaktis are the consorts of the various gods, who actually represent the many virtues and principles of the one God. True Hinduism is not polytheism. Hinduism vividly portrays the many facets of God's personality, masculine and feminine, but acknowledges one God, one supreme Godhead —Brahman.

Woodroffe comments that Vac is spoken of as second to Brahman "because She is first potentially in [Him], and then as Shakti issues from Him."[22] So the Mother is both outside of the creation and in the creation, but Brahman is forever outside of it. And the portion of Brahman that is in the creation is Vac. And that is the role of the feminine ray in each one of us, giving shape to form. Bringing forth the formed from the unformed is the work of the Mother.

Shakti is that point of the feminine principle who releases the potential of God from Spirit to Matter. She is the energy of God. She is the Word of God. When you are in a female body, that is your role. A woman's function is to bring out in her husband, in her children and in society the Spirit of the living God that is in them, to breathe upon it, to give it life, to help them to know who they are from the Beginning. By this continual nurturing, the Mother gives identity and vision to all with whom she serves. She helps them see and develop who and what they are.

I teach that the masculine presence of God can be identified as the Father, the Son and the Holy Spirit—who

---

* Woodroffe uses this alternate spelling of Vac.

ensoul the entire Spirit cosmos. And I teach that the feminine presence of God can be identified with the Divine Mother who embodies the Matter cosmos.

We live in the Matter cosmos. Perfected Being is in the Spirit cosmos. So the Divine Mother is actually much more close to us in the earth body. In fact, our bodies, our vehicles of consciousness, are hers on loan. She has given these to our souls for their evolution. We, as man, as woman, revere these bodies we wear that she has provided for our souls to dwell in.

And in the very center of this temple, she has provided the heart and the secret chamber of the heart. And here the Father, the Son and the Holy Spirit take up their abode in us as Jesus promised: Who will love my Father, who will obey his commandments, the Father and the Son will take up their abode in him.[23]

Secret Chamber of the Heart

So the Trinity does not enter the Matter universe except through the threefold flame in the heart and the body of the Mother. God descends to us through that sacred fire; but the sacred fire must have a temple. And the temple is the Mother's. So in reality, we have a Trinity of God in our hearts, sealed there; and that is the great key of Jesus' lost teachings.

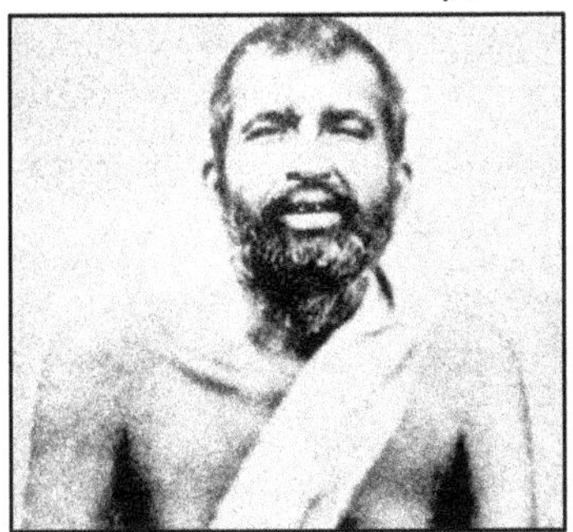

Ramakrishna

In modern India, veneration of the Mother exists far and wide, celebrating her terrible as well as her beautiful aspects. Ramakrishna, the nineteenth-century saint and mystic, served the fearsome Goddess Kali as his preferred representative of the Divine Mother, but he saw her as one with Brahman.

Ramakrishna gave great devotion to his wife, Sarada Devi, and saw her also as the incarnation of the Divine Mother. He liked to quote the mystic Kabir, who used to say, "The formless Absolute is my Father: and God with form is my Mother."[24]

Aurobindo, a twentieth-century devotee of the Mother, born in India but educated in the West, experienced her presence in every center of his consciousness and in every cell of his body. He believed that to experience the transforming power of the Mother we must give ourselves in "unreserved surrender" and "let her do unhindered her work within" us.[25]

Of her sacrificial work in this universe, Aurobindo writes:

> The Mother not only governs all from above but she descends into this lesser triple universe.... In her deep and great love for her children she has ... taken upon herself the pangs and sorrows and sufferings of the creation, since it seemed that thus alone could it be lifted to the Light and Joy and Truth and eternal Life. This is the great sacrifice called sometimes the sacrifice of the Purusha [Spirit], but much more deeply ... the sacrifice of the Divine Mother.[26]

To those like Aurobindo, who prize her transforming power, the Mother becomes their ever-present guide and comfort. This is the path towards the union of soul and Spirit, female and male, earth and heaven aspired to by the mystics, East and West.

Our understanding is that the Mother enters the Matter cosmos. All that is Matter and physical, worlds without end, the Mother embodies and is a part of. Our bodies are the Mother's body. And this is why we should revere our bodies as man and woman as the Mother's temple that she has provided for Father, Son and Holy Spirit to become indwelling in that temple.

We find that God as the masculine presence does not enter the physicality of the Matter cosmos. But by the power of the Word as mantra, as decree, as prayer, as affirmation, by the power of that Word who is Mother, we magnetize and draw down into the physical Matter universe that which is the masculine Godhead—the Father, Son and Holy Spirit.

Because they do not enter this universe except through the Mother, we give mantras and Hail Marys[27] and devotions to that white light, to that personal presence of the Mother. When we do so, her magnet in our being draws down the Father, because the Father-Mother God are the eternal lovers, and they desire to be one. We have two choices: to ascend to the Father, which we may do at the conclusion of this life, having fulfilled all things in this octave;[28] or to draw the Father, Son and Holy Spirit down to us.

We see a Spirit-Matter Cosmos symbolized in the figure eight, and a figure eight establishes a flow. The light of the masculine Trinity is always descending into the physical universe through us as we understand ourselves to be the manifestation of the Shakti. The Shakti is the energy of God. It is the Word of God. It is the Creator of the physical creation.

The masculine descends into form through the feminine, and the feminine ascends into Spirit through the masculine. And they are one. And who can say where the masculine begins and the feminine ends?

Why am I bringing up the Hindu teaching on Shakti in a book on the lost teachings of Jesus?

Simple. It's because the Eastern concept of God the Father and God the Mother as a complementary pair appears in some Gnostic works with stark Reality. You can attribute this to the fact that Jesus went to the East and that he brought back with him the riches of that ancient lore coming down from the ancient texts of the manus, the ancient texts of the Vedas.

We know Jesus studied the words of the sages and Buddhas during his sojourn in the East, and we know that he brought back his conception of the Divine Mother as well as many other teachings.

How else would John be writing in his opening verses of his Gospel a direct quote from the ancient Vedas? (See page 109.)

God as Mother in the Role of Holy Spirit

We have seen how the Christian Gnostics portrayed God as Mother as part of an original divine couple, and how this parallels the Eastern concept of Shakti.

The second way in which the Gnostics depicted God as Mother was in the role of Holy Spirit. While we usually think of the Holy Spirit as a masculine manifestation of God, James M. Robinson, professor of religion at Claremont Graduate University and editor (with others) of *The Facsimile Edition of the Nag Hammadi Codices,* points out that even some early Christian texts present the Holy Spirit as feminine:

> The Hebrew word for "spirit," *ruach,* is usually feminine. In the Semitic branch of early Christianity the femininity of the Spirit and her role as Jesus' mother are made explicit. This is reflected in the apocryphal *Gospel of the Hebrews*.... Here the feminine Spirit as Jesus' mother becomes explicit in a fragment quoted both by Origen and by Jerome: "Even so did my mother, the Holy Spirit, take me by one of my hairs and carry me away to the great mountain Tabor."[29]

The apocryphal Odes of Solomon, written around A.D. 100 to 200, also uses female imagery for the "dove" of the Holy Spirit and the "Spirit of the Lord."

The dove flew upon the head
 of our Lord Christ,
Because he was her head.
And she sang over him,
And her voice was heard....
I rested on the Spirit of the Lord,
And she raised me on high;
And she made me stand on my feet
 on the Lord's heights,
Before his perfection and his glory,
While I was praising *him* in the
 composition of his psalms.[30]

(The Spirit) brought me forth
 before the Lord's face,
And because I was the Son of Man,
I was named the Light, the Son of God.[31]

The Gnostic Gospel of Philip, speaking of the Holy Spirit, says, "Her children are many."[32] The Gospel of Philip also refers to the Holy Spirit as feminine in an argument against the virgin birth* (the doctrine that Jesus was born of a virgin mother). The Gospel says:

> Some said, "Mary conceived by the holy spirit." They are in error. They do not know what they are saying. When did a woman ever conceive by a woman? ... The lord [would]† not have said "My [father who is in] heaven" unless [he] had had another father, but he would have said simply ["My father]."[33]

---

* See pages 257–66 for a further discussion of the virgin birth.

† Brackets in quotations from Gnostic texts indicate that a part of the text is missing because of physical damage to the manuscript. The words supplied inside the brackets are conjectural restorations by the translator.

So it appears that this particular branch of Gnosticism acknowledges Saint Joseph as Jesus' father on earth.

The emphasis on feminine imagery was dropped from later Christian theology as "Father, Son and Holy Spirit" became the all-male Trinity. I myself have always meditated on the Holy Spirit as "cloven tongues of fire."[34]

To me these twin flames of fire (described in the Book of Acts as having descended upon the apostles on the day of Pentecost) are the manifestation of the individed wholeness of our Father-Mother God. I therefore disagree with this Gnostic notion of the Holy Spirit being entirely feminine, but see the Holy Spirit as overshadowing and endowing Mary *and* Joseph as Jesus' earthly parents.

The Divine Mother as Shekhinah

The Holy Spirit also takes on a feminine character in the Jewish mystical teaching on the Shekhinah. *Shekhinah* means "indwelling" or "presence." It refers to the glorious manifestation of the Presence of God that dwells among or in you as his sons and daughters. The Shekhinah glory is the light-emanation of that Presence with us whose name is I AM THAT I AM, the Presence of "God with us," Immanuel.

This I AM Presence, depicted on the Chart of Your Divine Self (see p. 80) is the individualization of our Father-Mother God. And the glory of this LORD—the light that shines forth from it encompassing the whole world—is the Shekhinah, the Mother—the activating principle and energy of the cosmos.

The Talmud speaks of the Shekhinah as the cloud that descended into the tabernacle prepared by Moses in the wilderness, as the cloud of glory that rested on the mercy seat in the Holy of holies, and as the Presence of God that resided in the sanctuary of Solomon's Temple until its destruction.[35]

According to rabbinical tradition, the Shekhinah accompanied the Israelites throughout their wanderings. In contrast to the impersonal, awesome aspect of the Hebrew God, the Shekhinah represented the nearness and ever-presentness of the Divine.

The Shekhinah took on a distinctly feminine quality with the development of the Kabbalah, an esoteric system of interpreting the Old Testament that reached its height in the late Middle Ages. Gershom G. Scholem writes that with the writing of the *Zohar,* the principal book on Jewish Kabbalism, the Shekhinah

> was now identified with the "Community of Israel," a sort of Invisible Church, representing the mystical idea of Israel in its bond with God and in its bliss, but also in its suffering and its exile. She is not only Queen, daughter and bride of God, but also the mother of every individual in Israel.[36]

This is the same as the Christian concept of the Church being the mystical body of God and the Bride of Christ.

Some Rabbis believed that the Shekhinah departed from Israel whenever sins or injustices were committed. In *The Legends of the Jews* (compiled by Louis Ginzberg), we read:

> Originally the real residence of the Shekinah was among men, but when Adam committed his sin, she withdrew to heaven, at first to the lowest of the seven heavens. Thence she was banished by Cain's crime, and she retired to the second heaven.[37]

In fact, throughout the ages the representative of the Divine Mother embodied upon earth has been murdered, has been removed, has been denied, has been desecrated. Woman has been mistreated because she is the power of God that descends into the Matter cosmos for the judgment of the Evil One. It is the Mother who goes forth to defend all of the children of God against the forces of evil.

The Legends of the Jews continues:

> [When] the sins of the generation of Enoch removed her still farther off from men, she took up her abode in the third heaven; then, successively, in the fourth, on account of the malefactors in the generation of the deluge; in the fifth, during the building of the tower of Babel and the confusion of tongues; in the sixth, by reason of the wicked Egyptians at the time of Abraham; and, finally, in the seventh, in consequence of the abominations of the inhabitants of Sodom.[38]

God sent the Divine Mother into the Matter cosmos. And the violations of her light, her sacred fire, have driven her to go into higher and higher octaves because she is God in manifestation, and God cannot be violated in manifestation. God will then withdraw. This author continues:

> Six righteous men, Abraham, Isaac, Jacob, Levi, Kohath, and Amram, drew the Shekinah back, one by one, from the seventh to the first heaven, and through the seventh righteous man, Moses, she was made to descend to the earth and abide among men as aforetime.[39]

Other Jewish commentators characterize the Shekhinah as a source of inspiration and a sort of divine intermediary between God and the world. The *Tikkune Zohar* says: "The creation is the work of the *shekhinah* who takes care of it as a mother cares for her children."[40]

Summarizing the evolution of the concept of the Shekhinah, author Charles Poncé[41] explains that in Talmudic literature:

> The *Shekhinah* is understood as nothing more than the active presence of God in the daily affairs of a nation, specifically Israel.[42]

This concept of the Shekhinah as the active principle directly parallels the Eastern concepts of Vac and Shakti. Poncé continues:

> In the Kabbalah, things change. The *Shekhinah* becomes his feminine counterpart, an intrinsic component of God rather than a mere aspect. On the one hand she is identified with the exiled Israel, and on the other with the soul with which man, along with God, yearns for union.[43]

The medieval Hasidim, members of a Jewish religious movement in the twelfth and thirteenth centuries that stressed austerity combined with mysticism, also associated the Shekhinah with the Holy Spirit. Scholem explains that the Hasidim taught that the glory of God, or Shekhinah, is "the 'holy spirit,' out of whom there speaks the voice and word of God."[44]

Jewish mystics also speak of the Shekhinah as a source of divine inspiration and prophecy. Professor Moshe Idel says that the mystics believed that

> the prophet not only delivers the prophecy by means of his voice, but also receives it "into his throat." There was a wide-spread belief among the Sages that the Shekhinah spoke through the instrument of Moses' voice.[45]

The Hasidim also understood that the Shekhinah dwells not only among men but in them. Summarizing the Kabbalistic view of the Shekhinah as feminine, Ya'qub ibn Yusuf writes:

> With the Jewish notion of the Shekhinah, we go beyond an external consideration of women and men,

> to a sense of the divine feminine within....
>
> In the Jewish tradition, the Shekhinah is approached as within creation, while the God "beyond" is characterized as masculine....
>
> While the Shekhinah is considered feminine and receptive in its relationship with the Divine, it is not a femininity which is restricted to a passive role. According to the *Zohar,* initiative is not only in the hands of God, but in the hands of the Tzaddiqim, the upright of Israel.[46]

The implication here is that Israel is the embodiment of the Mother, and therefore as Mother, they must take an active role in the affairs of state, politics, the economy, and so forth. And this is the real mystery of the traditions that come down to us, the Judeo-Christian tradition in the United States of America, where we are actively engaged as the hands and feet of God.

We are, in fact all of us—men and women and children—the Divine Mother in action. And since the Mother has charge of the Matter universe, we must take charge of our lives and determine that righteousness prevail on earth, that we fulfill our roles and not neglect to do so.

Ya'qub ibn Yusuf continues:

> [The upright of Israel] act on behalf of the Shekhinah, to stimulate the flow of divine mercy upon this world, according to the function of "arousal from below."[47]

By our mantras, our decrees, our prayers we arouse the sacred fire within us. We arouse the presence of the Divine Mother who magnetizes down to us the Divine Father.

> The central problem of the world is that the Shekhinah is in exile. The task of the religious human

> being is to aid in reuniting her with her Beloved, the radiant source of creation.[48]

You could say that the Divine Mother is in exile in you in the base-of-the-spine chakra, the spiritual center where the energy of Mother is anchored in man and woman. That sacred fire of the base chakra is imprisoned in many misuses of energy that we see in society today. When you misuse the light of God, you make the Divine Mother a prisoner within you.

> We are talking about uniting the divine which is immanent in creation, and the divine transcendence—with the human being as the bridge between them.[49]

What is immanent in creation is the Mother and what is the divine transcendence is the Father.

> From this point of view, the human task would be not to leave the material for the spiritual, but to live in such a way as to make it possible for God to come to earth.[50]

Even though the Jews were deprived of the essence and vision of Jesus' lost teachings on women's rights for centuries, their meditation upon God revealed to them that the light-emanation of the I AM THAT I AM is feminine. They discovered the Divine Mother!

Truly the natural inclination of the soul of the mystic is to receive the unveiling of the divine feminine. And mystical Judaism today is the highest branch of Judaism—even as the mystics form the most spiritually evolved "white-fire core" of all the world's religions.

The Divine Mother as Wisdom

We have reviewed God as Mother in the complementary pair and in the Holy Spirit, the Shekhinah. The third way the

Christian Gnostics portrayed the Divine Mother was as Wisdom—and this was not a new concept. Several world religions have honored a female figure who is endowed with the attribute of wisdom, such as the Egyptian goddesses Isis and Maat. But closer perhaps to the Christian Gnostics was the personification of Wisdom as a female in the Apocrypha and in the Old Testament.

In this literature, Wisdom is spoken of in terms that suggest she is an independent heavenly being. Western scholars warn that just because the authors of these writings personified God's quality of Wisdom, we should not assume that they intended to portray Wisdom as a being separate from God. They do, however, acknowledge that Wisdom takes on the character of a "power," "a divine attribute" or a "personification of the functions" of God.[51]

Wisdom is dynamic and intensely involved in what is happening on earth. And that is exactly what the feminine aspect of God is and does.

The Wisdom literature of the Bible includes Proverbs, Job, the Book of Wisdom (also called the Wisdom of Solomon) and Ecclesiasticus (also called Sirach). In these writings, Wisdom plays the role of preacher and prophet, bride and teacher. She is depicted as God's friend, an active participant in the creation and an intermediary between God and man. She communicates to human beings God's teaching, chastisements and prophecy.

The Book of Proverbs has the greatest teaching on the Divine Mother in the Bible. Proverbs chapter 8 tells us that Wisdom was the first creation of God and was with him at the creation of worlds. Proverbs says: "[The LORD] created me when his purpose first unfolded, before the oldest of his works."[52] And this is precisely the concept of Vac.

The apocryphal Book of Wisdom identifies Wisdom as a female consort of God. This book is in the Catholic Bible but not the Jewish or Protestant canon. It was very popular in the early Church. A prayer in the Book of Wisdom reads:

> God of our ancestors, Lord of mercy,... grant me Wisdom, consort of your throne.... With you is Wisdom, she who knows your works, she who was present when you made the world.[53]

Wisdom is also identified as "a spirit, a friend to man."[54] The Book of Wisdom says that wisdom "is a reflection of the eternal light, untarnished mirror of God's active power, image of his goodness.... In each generation she passes into holy souls."[55]

Orthodox Christianity transferred the role of Wisdom in the Old Testament to Christ and called it male. The reality is that the Son is the incarnation of the Word who was in the beginning with God—and that Word is the feminine principle of the creation. Therefore, Jesus Christ was the incarnation of the Divine Mother and his wisdom is hers. He is herself in action in the form and the formless, shepherding her sons and daughters until they too become the incarnation of the Mother—by the flame of the Trinity in their hearts. The Mother through her Son—in and as the "Christ," the light of the World—is the Divine Mediator in this world between God and his children.

All Buddhas and bodhisattvas, all disciples of Jesus Christ, Jesus Christ himself, all who hold the light of nations, though they may be in male bodies, perpetually meditate upon the Divine Mother.

The apostle Paul refers to Christ as "the Wisdom of God,"[56] and so he is. Paul says the Son takes part in the creation and the preservation of the world, and so he does, as the transparent presence of the Mother—with the Father—in our midst.

When we say Jesus Christ is the incarnation of the Word,

we are saying that he is the incarnation of the Divine Mother—as well as of the Divine Father. Masculine in form, feminine in essence, our Lord is androgynous being personified. We love him because we see in him what no male hierarchy has given us—the image of our Father-Mother God.

In the Gnostic tractate Trimorphic Protennoia (literally "The Three-Formed First Thought"), the Divine Mother is portrayed as having the qualities of Thought, Speech and Intelligence. She says:

> [I] am [Protennoia, the] Thought that [dwells] in [the Light.]... I exist before the [All, and] I am the All, since I [exist in] everyone.[57]

Wisdom as Sophia

The Teachings of Sylvanus, another text found at Nag Hammadi, speaks of Wisdom as the Mother of the disciple. In Gnosticism, Wisdom is fully embodied in the divine being called Sophia. She is sometimes called Pistis Sophia (meaning literally Faith-Wisdom). Sophia takes on various roles as Mother and consort of divine beings. In one text, she is the consort of the Son of Man and is named "First Begettress Sophia, Mother of the Universe."[58] Through her disobedience, Sophia is cast out of the heavenly realms into what is called "The Chaos."

Jesus often figures as the redeemer of Sophia. In the Gnostic work Pistis Sophia, Jesus explains to his disciples,

> I came to help her, and led her up out of the chaos, because she had repented, and also because she had had faith in the Light and had endured these great pains and these great perils.[59]

Sophia is the archetype of the fallen souls of humanity, man and woman, who are rescued by Jesus Christ.

The Word of Wisdom

from the book of Proverbs

Happy is the man that findeth wisdom,
And the man that getteth understanding.
For the merchandise of it is better than
the merchandise of silver,
And the gain thereof than fine gold.

She is more precious than rubies:
And all the things thou canst desire
are not to be compared unto her.
Length of days is in her right hand;
And in her left hand riches and honour.

Her ways are ways of pleasantness,
And all her paths are peace.
She is a tree of life to them that lay hold upon her:
And happy is every one that retaineth her.

The LORD by wisdom hath founded the earth;
By understanding hath he established the heavens.
By his knowledge the depths are broken up,
And the clouds drop down the dew....

Get wisdom, get understanding:
Forget it not; neither decline from the words of my
mouth.
Forsake her not, and she shall preserve thee:
Love her, and she shall keep thee.
Wisdom is the principal thing; therefore get wisdom:
And with all thy getting get understanding.

Exalt her, and she shall promote thee:
She shall bring thee to honour,
    when thou dost embrace her.
She shall give to thine head an ornament of grace:
A crown of glory shall she deliver to thee....

I, wisdom, dwell with prudence,
And find out knowledge of witty inventions.

The fear of the LORD is to hate evil:
Pride, and arrogancy, and the evil way,
    and the froward mouth, do I hate.
Counsel is mine, and sound wisdom:
I AM understanding; I have strength.

By me kings reign, and princes decree justice.
By me princes rule, and nobles,
    even all the judges of the earth.
I love them that love me;
And those that seek me early shall find me.[60]

CHAPTER 5

Gnostic Teachings on Male and Female

CHAPTER 5

Gnostic Teachings on Male and Female

Is God Male?

An important chapter in the lost teachings of Jesus on Woman has to do with the question of God's gender: Is God male? Throughout the centuries, orthodox Christianity has affirmed that the Supreme Being is a masculine figure.

But if you could travel back in time to the second century and ask some of the Christian Gnostics, "Is God only male?" they would answer you with a resounding "no." For to them, God was both male and female.

If you look objectively for a moment at the panorama of the world's religions, you will realize that the paternal God of Judaism and Christianity is unusual. In many civilizations—including those of Egypt, Babylonia, Greece, Rome and India—the Divine Mother figures alongside her masculine counterpart.

And if Gnostic ideas had survived those of their orthodox Christian rivals, Christians today could very well be praying to their "Father-Mother" God. I myself have always done so and taught the followers of Jesus Christ in my church to do the same. Didn't Jesus say in Revelation: "I AM Alpha and Omega, the Beginning and the Ending."[1] Alpha and Omega are names for the masculine and feminine God—Alpha masculine, Omega feminine. Jesus was the incarnation of God. He defined his Godhood as the Father-Mother, the plus-minus polarity of being.

There Is neither Male nor Female

Some Gnostic texts use *male* to connote something that is immortal and of the Spirit. The Nag Hammadi text called the First Apocalypse of James says:

> The perishable has [gone up] to the imperishable and the female element has attained to this male element.[2]

Here the female is associated with that which is perishable and the male with that which is imperishable.

Scholar Kurt Rudolph says that, like the Gnostic Gospel of Thomas, other texts speak of the female's being transformed into the male. He writes:

> The same view is also held by the [Gnostic sects] the Naassenes and Valentinians; the former maintain that all who reach "the house of the (good) God" "become bridegrooms, being rendered wholly male through the virgin spirit." The Valentinian Theodotus believed that the "seed of light", so long as it was still unformed (i.e. uneducated, untrained), is a "child of the female", but when it is formed (i.e. trained), it is changed into a man and becomes a son of the (heavenly) bridegroom; no longer is it weak and subjected to the cosmic powers, but having become a man, it becomes a male fruit. As such it can enter into the Pleroma [spiritual universe]

> and unite with the angels.... In Greek, "angel" (i.e. messenger) has the masculine gender.[3]

I believe that God speaks to us not because we're in a male or female body but because we are a soul of God.

The Gnostics devoted themselves to the quest for the God within. Like the sages and mystics, they pursued an inner wisdom that led them to an understanding of the deep and secret things of God.

The Gnostics' Understanding of the Soul

As a corollary to their understanding of God as both Father and Mother, the Gnostics held that the male and female principles could be used to explain the nature of the universe as well as the nature of humanity. That which belonged to the realm of transcendent heavenly Reality was male in nature. That which belonged to the plane of creation was female in nature.

The soul of both man and woman—which had fallen from higher realms into the Matter spheres—was considered to be feminine. The Exegesis on the Soul, a Gnostic text, explains that "wise men of old gave the soul a feminine name. Indeed she is female in her nature as well."[4]

The Gnostics believed that when she fell from grace and higher realms and entered the lowly estate of the flesh, the soul needed to be saved by Christ the Redeemer—the incarnation of the Father-Mother God—who descended through their Son to raise up the fallen potential. The soul is considered our potential to realize God.

This understanding of the masculine and feminine components of being explains some very puzzling passages in Gnostic scriptures. For instance, in the Gospel of Mary, Jesus delivers his parting words to the disciples and then leaves them. The gospel records that after he is gone,

> the disciples were in sorrow, shedding many tears, and saying: "How are we to go among the unbelievers and announce the gospel of the Kingdom of the Son of Man? They did not spare his life, so why should they spare ours?" Then Mary [Magdalene] arose, embraced them all, and began to speak to her brothers: "Do not remain in sorrow and doubt, for his Grace will guide you and comfort you. But rather let us praise his greatness, for he has prepared us and made us into men."[5]

The Conflict between Peter and Mary Magdalene

Some Gnostic works vividly portray conflicts between Mary Magdalene and Peter as to whether women should be considered as legitimate receivers and interpreters of the true teachings of Jesus.

The Gospel of Thomas is of special interest because many of the sayings of this Gospel parallel statements attributed to Jesus in the four New Testament Gospels.

Scholars believe that the Gospel of Thomas could date as far back as the second half of the first century (earlier than, or at the same time as, the Gospel of Mark, which was written in about A.D. 70). And Mark is the earliest of the Gospels.

In Saying 114 of the Gospel of Thomas, we find this disagreement among the apostles. It is one of the most interesting and controversial sayings:

> Simon Peter said to them, "Let Mary leave us, for females are not worthy of life."
>
> Jesus said, "Behold, I shall guide her so as to make her male, so that she too may become a living spirit resembling you males. For every female who makes herself male will enter the kingdom of heaven."[6]

Are both Peter and Jesus exhibiting here a bit of male chauvinism?

In the opinion of the scholar Stephen Patterson,

> this saying does not really free itself from the mistaken notions of its day about the relative worth of men and women. Nonetheless, what it says, in its own "back-handed" way, is very important for the history of early Christianity. First, it probably indicates that not all were in agreement on whether women should be allowed to participate fully in the Jesus movement. The opposition to women voiced by Peter in this saying is not isolated, but reminds one of later evidence of a similar dispute in the Gospel of Mary and Pistis Sophia.[7]

Patterson says the dispute over the participation of females

> was likely one which would be carried on within early Christianity for many years to come. The Gospel of Thomas, of course, comes down [in Saying 114] in favor of women's participation, provided they engage in the same sort of regimen required of the men in the group. What is more, Mary ... is taken as the predecessor of all women who would become disciples. This stands in contrast to the more traditional feminine roles assigned to Mary in the [New Testament gospels] (whether one speaks of Mary the mother of Jesus or of Mary Magdalene).[8]

However, Patterson's assessment that Saying 114 reflects a debate about the role of women is not a complete picture. His perspective does not take into account the context of the times or what other Gnostic works have to say on this issue.

Patterson is taking the words *male* and *female* literally. Yet the author of the Gospel of Thomas tells us that the sayings are enigmatic. In the opening words of the Gospel, he writes, "Whoever finds the interpretation of these sayings will not taste death."[9] Thus we cannot take for granted that the meaning of these sayings is going to be readily apparent.

As I interpret these passages, this is what I understand: The word *male* here does not mean *man* but the I AM THAT I AM, that upper figure in the Chart of your Divine Self, which shows your I AM Presence (see page 80).

There is much evidence that the words *male* and *female* are to be taken symbolically and not literally. But even if these words were to be taken literally, would Jesus have agreed with Peter's statement that "females are not worthy of life"? And would he have said that Mary had to have a male body in order to enter the kingdom of heaven, or a male body to become a teacher, a preacher or a priest? From everything we know about Jesus, it is highly unlikely.

The Spirit of the living God is the plus, or masculine, polarity of being. But within that plus polarity is contained the plus/minus of androgynous being, which we have already called the Father-Mother God. Out of that divine sphere of being, that divine wholeness of the Father-Mother God, the soul has descended into form. Descending into the Matter cosmos, that soul has a minus coefficient, a feminine polarity.

What I believe Jesus means in the Gospel of Thomas when he says that every woman "must make herself male" is that the soul cannot gain her immortality without uniting with the Spirit of God, with the I AM THAT I AM. And when she does, she now has that masculine, plus polarity. This is what Jesus meant by saying, "I will make her male." The Spirit of God manifests the masculine polarity of being as a magnet to draw back to itself the female part of itself, which is the soul.

Without uniting with the Spirit of God, with the I AM THAT I AM, none of us will achieve immortality. We are nonpermanent beings in this octave. To become permanent, we unite with the Universal Christ and the Universal I AM Presence.

Another time, Peter asks Mary to tell the disciples the words that Jesus told her privately and never taught them. Mary Magdalene relates to the disciples a teaching that Jesus gave her in a vision about the ascent of the soul. After she has done so, Andrew challenges her. He says he doesn't believe Jesus taught her these things:

> Andrew answered and said to the brothers, "Say what you think about what she said, but I do not believe the savior said this. These teachings are certainly strange ideas."
>
> Peter voiced similar concerns. He asked the others about the savior: "Did he really speak with a woman in private, without our knowledge? Should we all turn and listen to her? Did he prefer her to us?"
>
> Then Mary wept and said to Peter, "My brother Peter, what do you think? Do you think that I made this up by myself or that I am lying about the savior?"
>
> Levi answered and said to Peter, "Peter, you always are angry. Now I see you are arguing against this woman like an adversary. If the savior made her worthy, who are you to reject her? Surely the savior knows her well. That is why he has loved her more than us.
>
> "Rather let us be ashamed and put on the perfect man and acquire him for ourselves as he commanded us, and preach the gospel."[10]

As we can see, the Gospel of Mary, like the Gospel of Thomas, depicts Peter as that chauvinist. But Levi puts him in his place, reminding him that Jesus loved Mary more. Levi emphasizes that they should not make up rules beyond the law

Jesus gave them. The implication is: If Jesus didn't reject women, you shouldn't either.

Some scholars see this conflict between Mary and Peter as symbolic of more than the controversy over the role of women in the Christian community. They believe it represents the fundamental controversy between the orthodox Christians, who supported the apostolic tradition (symbolized in this story by Peter and Andrew), and the Gnostics, who claimed to have access to a higher truth (symbolized here by Mary Magdalene).

Pistis Sophia also depicts a conflict between Peter and Mary Magdalene. Here Mary admits to Jesus that she often desires to come forward and speak about the mysteries that have been imparted to the disciples, "but," she says, "I am afraid of Peter, because he threatened me and hateth our sex."[11] Jesus invites her to come forward and speak, saying: "Every one who shall be filled with the spirit of light to come forward and set forth the solution of what I say—no one shall be able to prevent him."[12]

A Champion of Woman

Upon this conversation of Mary Magdalene and Peter is the turning of Christendom and the way of orthodoxy and the way of the inner walk with God. Upon this conversation is turning Christ's reverence for Woman, for the Divine Mother, and for the feminine aspect of man and woman as that which is the chalice of higher Truth and inspiration.

Jesus gave mysteries to Mary Magdalene. She knew that the disciples would have to ask and humble themselves before her, before her innocence, her femininity and before his reverence for Woman.

We can ask ourselves, "To whom did Jesus entrust the teachings?" And if the one to whom he entrusted the teachings thereby had received the highest portion of himself, then how could one such as Peter, misconstruing his confession of Christ as being the Rock and the living Word,[13] claim the sole authority for doctrine and organization from then to the present?

This is an age of woman's liberation, which means it is the age of the liberation of the soul, because the soul is the feminine potential of being. And in truth, Mary Magdalene represented the soul of all of the twelve disciples, the loving, reverent handmaid of the Lord, the one who was moving on the path of initiation to be the bride of Christ, the one to whom he preferred to reveal himself. Though Peter and the other disciple ran a race to see who would get there first, it was to Mary Magdalene that Jesus appeared at the tomb.[14]

There is no record at all in the New Testament that Jesus ever belittled women, said they were less worthy than men, or banned them from full participation in the future Church hierarchy. Jesus actually started a revolution for Woman. He broke with the traditions that bound the women of his day, and the early Christian community followed Jesus' example.

This attitude is exemplified in Paul's statement:

> *There is neither Jew nor Greek, there is neither bond nor free, there is neither male nor female: for ye are all one in Christ Jesus. And if ye be Christ's, then are ye Abraham's seed, and heirs according to the promise.*

Another way to probe the real meaning of Saying 114 of the Gospel of Thomas is to look at how other Gnostic texts treat women and then see what we can learn from them that make similar statements about females or femaleness.

First: How do Gnostic texts treat women?

While some texts portray Peter as a male chauvinist, they certainly do not portray Jesus in this light. On the contrary, Jesus is depicted as the champion of Woman.

For example, in Pistis Sophia, Mary Magdalene plays a privileged role. It is she who asks the most profound questions of her Lord and replies to his most complex questions. At one point, Mary asks Jesus for permission to discourse on a teaching he has just given, and Jesus replies:

> Mary, thou blessed one, whom I will perfect in all mysteries of those of the height, discourse in openness, thou, whose heart is raised to the kingdom of heaven more than all thy brethren.[15]

While instructing his disciples on "the mystery of the Ineffable," Jesus says:

> Mary Magdalene and John, the virgin, will tower over all my disciples and over all men who shall receive the mysteries in the Ineffable. They will be on my right and on my left. And I am they, and they are I.[16]

We find over and over in Gnostic texts that Jesus emphasizes the idea that "I am they, and they are I." What he is saying is: "The same Christ—the same light essence—that is in me is in you. And when you discover this and realize it, then you will be myself—because that same Christ that is in me will be in you."

Obviously Jesus thought highly of Mary's spiritual prowess. Both the Gospel of Mary and the Gospel of Philip say that the Lord loved Mary more than the other disciples.[17] In the Gospel of Mary, Mary Magdalene is portrayed as the one disciple who holds the disciples together in their time of grief and self-concern. In this text, Jesus' parting words before his ascension are "Do not lay down any rules beyond what I appointed for you."[18] Just imagine if the Roman Church had heeded those two lines, "*Do not lay down any rules beyond what I appointed for you.*"

The Concept of Yin and Yang and Its Application to Male and Female

Now let's examine how other Gnostic texts use the terms female and male, or femininity and masculinity. We can think of this in terms of the *yang* and *yin,* the two opposing but complementary energies, forces or principles in Chinese philosophy whose interactions cause the universe to come into being. The interplay of yang and yin forces governs all formation, movement and change. The yang force in the universe has characteristics that are masculine—active, bright, positive, hot and contracting. The yin force in the universe has characteristics that are feminine—passive, dark, negative, cold and expansive.

The text Zostrianos says, "Flee from the madness and the bondage of femaleness, and choose for yourselves the salvation of maleness."[19] Elsewhere in this text we read about "the femininity of lust."

If you start thinking now about maleness as yangness and femaleness as yinness, things will become clearer.

Frederik Wisse, in his study of antifeminine imagery in Gnostic texts, says that in Zostrianos "the bondage of femininity ... is connected with lust and darkness."[20] Now if we think of yinness as the quality we know it to be as a distendedness, we can see what we are talking about here. We are seeing that the masters have told us that rather than being equally in balance, yang and yin, we should be more yang than yin—5 percent more, 10 percent more depending what the occasion calls for. If we are 90 percent yin and 10 percent yang in our constitution, in our consciousness, in our brains, in our beings, we are very weak. We are subject to decay. We are subject to terminal illnesses.

So we're looking at this concept of the bondage of femininity, the bondage of yinness, when we get in that yin condition being connected with lust and darkness; and we can understand exactly what Jesus was talking about in the Gospel of Thomas. Jesus has spoken in parables that sound exactly like the teachings of Lao Tzu, the great sage of ancient China, who spoke of the Great Tao as the all-embracing First Principle and source of all being.

Wisse continues:

> The preaching of Zostrianos is for "a living generation and to save those who are worthy and to strengthen the elect" (4,15–17). Though this, no doubt, excludes much of humankind, there is no hint that it excludes women. Femininity in the meaning of sexuality and procreation is something that can enslave everyone ...[21]

In other words, yinness can enslave any of us whether we are in a male or female body. That yinness can overtake us and ultimately cause our death. And ultimately, if the soul chooses to remain yin during incarnation after incarnation, it can cause the death of the soul.

And this is Wisse speaking again:

> ... and its opposite, masculinity, does not appear to be a natural quality of males but a state that all must seek in order to be saved.[22]

This is absolutely true. In order to be saved in our actions, our self-discipline, our love, our path, our delivery of the Word, we must have the empowerment of the yangness. And the yangness comes from the Spirit, or the spiritual planes, and the yinness comes from Matter, or the material planes.

In the Book of Thomas the Contender, femininity is also associated with sexuality and not with women per se. It says, "Woe to you who love the practice of femininity and her polluted intercourse."[23]

And so we see the "woe to you" is pronounced upon the squandering of the sacred fire and the life force. The sacred fire is your maleness, your yangness. If you are squandering it in this femininity, this polluted intercourse, then you are going down and down and down into a yin state. And the ultimate degradation of the yin state is death.

In another Gnostic text, the Teachings of Silvanus, the female is associated with the flesh, and the male is associated with the mind:

> Live according to the mind. Do not think about things belonging to the flesh. Acquire strength, for the mind is strong. If you fall from this other, you have become male-female. And if you cast out of yourself the substance of the mind, which is thought, you have cut off the male part and turned yourself to the female part alone.[24]

The mind and the focus of the mind and the ability to concentrate and be intense in our work, in our focus, in our meditation, to not have the mind wandering all over the place—that is maleness. It is yangness. And those who have keen minds and solid minds that are tight are brilliant people in the earth even if they have no spirituality. If they have a yang mind, they have that stability.

Wisse concludes that the meaning of femininity in the texts I just spoke about "appears to focus on sexuality and birth.... Men and women must flee the bondage of femininity and seek the salvation of masculinity."[25]

Origen of Alexandria

Origen of Alexandria frequently used the metaphor of "becoming male" in relation to spiritual progress. Kari Vogt writes that in Origen's works the terms "male" and "female" are used "as metaphors for moral qualities." She says the words *woman* and *the feminine* represent "the flesh and carnal affections," and on occasion they represent "weakness, laziness and dependence. The feminine may also be directly linked with the sphere of sin."[26] When we are yin in the extreme, we are prone to sin. We don't have the tightness of soul or spiritual fire to tether to the mind of God or the Holy Christ Self.

Origen wrote:

> He is a true male who does not know sin, which is the lot of fragile woman.... If our action is female, it is corporeal or carnal.[27]

In another of Origen's works we read:

> Men and women are distinguished according to differences of heart. How many belong to the female sex who before God are strong men, and how many men must be counted weak and indolent women.[28]

Origen understood the principles of yinness and yangness. When men become too yin, they must be counted weak and indolent women. "How many belong to the female sex who before God are strong men?" It is women who have espoused the yang condition at every level of the body who present themselves before God and the community with that strength that we respect.

Vogt explains Origen's teaching in these terms:

> A woman, by virtue of her moral and spiritual qualities, may be turned into a man [into yangness], i.e. may be saved, while man may "become a woman" [become yin], i.e. degenerate and be lost.[29]

Aside from using the term *female* to connote sexuality or lust or a state of degeneracy, some Gnostic texts use this term to connote something that is impermanent and of the earth. Yinness in the extreme is that which is in a state of decay. It is impermanent. It is giving off the atoms of light, and they are going back to the Central Sun.

When we are on a spiritual path, these terms *yinness* and *yangness* are not just tied to conditions of the body or the mind. The yangness that you are putting on when you are on the spiritual path is the spiritual fire, the spiritual energy, the sacred fire on the altar of being, the increase of the threefold flame, the descent around you of your Holy Christ Self.

This spiritual yangness, when you feel it, is an eternal yangness. It is something that is becoming in you an immortal being. You are becoming immortal by the presence of this fire. It is far different from the yangness that comes from extremes of diet. It is a yangness that is the gradual empowerment of three aspects of the male: the Father, the Son and the Holy Spirit—the threefold flame.

Understanding this, when the Bible talks about Jesus' waxing strong, growing in the grace of the Lord, we know that growing in the grace means increasing in the spiritual energy in his being. When Jesus is baptized of John in Jordan, there is that descent of the Holy Spirit that is the increase of the Spirit of the living God dwelling in him bodily. "This is my beloved Son, in whom I am well pleased."[30] That means in whom I dwell. I live in him and I am well pleased to live in him because he has the chalice of the Spirit. He is the Son of God.

Male and Female as Spirit and Matter

Noting the cultural context in which the Gospel of Thomas may have been written, Bentley Layton says, "It was a philosophical cliché that the material constituent of an entity was 'female,' while its form (or ideal form) was 'male.'"[31] In Greek philosophy, the ideal form was the spiritual form. Thus, the Greeks named all that was in the material world "female" and all that remained in Spirit "male." Layton suggests that the last phrase of Saying 114 of the Gospel of Thomas, "every female who makes herself male will enter the kingdom of heaven," could be understood as "Every female (element) that makes itself male will enter the kingdom of heaven."[32]

Bertil Gärtner notes that in the Jewish-Christian texts known as the Pseudo-Clementines, "'the female' is identical with the cosmos, the created world,"[33] Mother Earth. One of these texts says,

> The present world is female, as a mother bringing forth the souls of her children, but the world to come is male, as a father receiving his children.[34]

When we descend to earth, we need the female, or mother, body and condition because we are abiding in her universe, the Matter, or Mater, universe. When we return to God, we must be clothed with the Deathless Solar Body, the seamless garment of Spirit, because now we are going to abide in the Spirit cosmos.

Marvin Meyer,[35] author of several books on the Christian Gnostics and their texts, analyzes Saying 114 in terms of the male-female imagery in other ancient texts. He says:

> Jesus' response to Peter, though shocking to modern sensitivities, is intended to be a statement of liberation. The female principle is saved when all that is earthly (that is, all that is allied with an earth Mother) is transformed into what is heavenly (that is, allied with a heavenly Father). Thus all people on the earth, whether women or men, require such a transformation.[36]

Meyer points out that "the transformation of the female into the male is discussed extensively in ancient literature."[37]

> [Philo of Alexandria, a Jewish philosopher who was a contemporary of Jesus] claims that femaleness is on the side of passivity, corporeality, and *αἴσθησις* [perception by the senses], while maleness is on the side of activity, incorporeality, and *νοῦς* [mind or reason]. So progress, he concludes, "is indeed nothing else than the giving up of the female gender (*γένος*) by changing into the male."[38]

Meyer explains:

> Since for Gnostics femaleness can encompass passion, earthliness, and mortality, it is reasonable to see how they can propose that all humans are involved in femaleness. Such universal participation in femaleness is made even more obvious by virtue of Hellenistic theory on the soul.... The feminine term for "soul" is presented throughout the Greek-speaking world as a female.[39]

The Descent of the Soul and Her Redemption

Let us summarize the previous concepts: The word *male* here does not mean *man* as physical gender but the plus, or masculine, polarity of being. The masculine polarity of being as shown on the Chart of Your Divine Self (see page 80), the upper figure, is the Spirit of the living God, the I AM THAT I AM. Within that plus polarity of that great sphere of light, that Presence of God surrounded by those rainbow rings of light around you, there is contained the plus/minus of androgynous Being, whom we address as our Father-Mother God.

Out of the divine wholeness of the Father-Mother God, your soul descended into form. When she descended into form, she retained the feminine polarity only, because you descended into the Matter cosmos, which, remember, is feminine. The Spirit cosmos is masculine in that great cosmic polarity. So we descended out of that great sphere of cosmic perfection into Matter with a feminine, or minus, charge. And that is why both men and women, the soul in each of us, male or female, is always considered *she*.

Because the Spirit is a masculine polarity, there is this polarity between you and God—you, that feminine soul. And so the magnet of that Presence that is so powerful of the Spirit of God draws you back to itself even as you give devotion to God and draw that Spirit of God down to yourself.

Everything demonstrates the law of opposites. God will draw back to himself the female part of himself—who is the soul. But the "female," that is the portion of the self that is the soul, must be transformed in order to be redeemed. We must be washed of our karma or, in orthodox terms, our sin. We must transmute it. We must be filled with light so that we can enter the planes of Spirit.

Every one of our souls violated the Law of God else we would not be wearing these bodies of flesh. We descended into the karmic condition of this world. *Karma* is not an arcane word; it's a very simple word. *Karma* means causes we have set in motion in previous lifetimes. Those causes have effects that we are reaping today, good positive effects and negative ones also.

There is a path to achieve salvation, reuniting with the Christ and the I AM Presence. *And that is what the ascended masters' teachings are all about.*[40]

Our souls long to be restored to holiness—*holiness* means wholeness—through oneness with the Divine Mother. And the Divine Mother and Jesus Christ are the facilitators that God has given to us to aid us in that accomplishment. We cannot do it without a Saviour. We cannot pull ourselves up by our own bootstraps.

Jesus explained that his goal was to raise up the feminine element of us all, the lost potential of the soul. He said:

Jesus, by Charles Sindelar

> God sent me in my final incarnation for a multifaceted purpose—primary being the raising up of the feminine ray and of the Woman, raising up the light of that feminine as the fallen light in the body temples of all who went forth as twin flames from the heart of the Father-Mother God.
>
> In the course of raising up the light of the Divine Mother within myself [in many prior incarnations], I became the Word incarnate. For truly the Word is Mother—the Shakti, the Shekhinah—origin of light of God known to Hebrew as feminine principle and to Hindu as the same.
>
> All true avataras have declared Woman and have exalted her as the highest aspect of self. Thus the aspiration of man is his feminine nature, and thus it is so that the avatara* does adore the point of the feminine light.
>
> And the point of the adoration is the increase of the light in the temple and in the chakras for the very healing of that feminine gone forth—that lost potential of the soul that is to be found again.
>
> Therefore, in the course of this assignment, male or female body notwithstanding, it is the goal of those who come as revolutionaries of the Spirit, as God's incarnate ones, to go forth after that which is fallen. And that which is fallen by nature is always the fallen feminine [the soul]. For [that portion of the self that is] the divine

* Avatara (Sanskrit): divine incarnation, avatar.

> masculine [the Spirit of the living God, the I AM THAT I AM] does remain ... in the octaves of light.[41]

Reuniting the Elements of the Soul

Thus, the soul who is redeemed is fused to the living Christ and to the I AM THAT I AM. She has rejoined the Father-Mother God, and in the realm of Spirit, the soul is no longer feminine but truly infilled with the masculine being. Entering that wholeness, she too becomes the androgynous one.

The Gnostics also believed that the masculine and feminine elements of being were originally one. Elizabeth Schüssler Fiorenza writes:

> [The masculine and feminine elements] are reunited when the female element becomes male.... Thus the Valentinians [a prominent second-century Gnostic sect] had a very positive image of the marriage union and took it as a symbol and type for salvation that restores the original androgynous unity of humanity.[42]

According to the Gospel of Philip,

> When Eve was in Adam, there was no death.[43]

The reason for this is when male and female parts of the individual or of twin flames are one, there is divine wholeness. When there is wholeness, there is eternal life. The Gospel of Philip continues:

> When she was separated from him, death came.[44]

When Adam and Eve reunite and he receives her to himself, "death will cease to be."[45]

First you unite with your Holy Christ Self and your I AM Presence, and then you reunite with your twin flame.

The two halves of the whole, the plus and the minus, are incomplete without the other. Each one, then, being subject to incompleteness is subject to death, which is a definition of incompleteness. The union of the plus/minus creates the circle of light that can dwell in the realms of immortality.

When you unite the masculine and feminine parts of your being, you will know the wholeness that will enable you to receive the Spirit of God and have everlasting life through Christ. The Gospel of Philip says:

> If the female had not separated from the male, the female and the male would not have died. The separation of male and female was the beginning of death. Christ came to heal the separation that was from the beginning and reunite the two, in order to give life to those who died through separation and unite them.[46]

This is a tremendous prophecy of the reuniting of the masculine and feminine elements within you individually. And it is also a prophecy of the reuniting of you and your twin flame.

Whether your twin flame is in heaven or in another octave or by your side on earth, the union is an inner uniting. When you reunite forces with your twin flame, it's like two halves of the planet coming together, two hemispheres making the Divine Whole. When we are separated as male and female, we do not manifest the fullness of the Divine Whole.

We are separated because of our karma. We reestablish the wholeness of the T'ai Chi through the path of the ascended masters. They teach us how to balance our karma and how to use the science of the spoken Word to that end.[47]

The goal of reunion and the return to the point of origin is also reflected in the Gospel of Thomas. It says:

> Jesus saw some babies nursing. He said to his disciples, "These nursing babies are like those who enter the kingdom."
>
> They said to him, "Then shall we enter the kingdom as babies?"
>
> Jesus said to them, "When you make the two into one, when you make the inner like the outer and the outer like the inner, and the upper like the lower, when you make male and female into a single one, so that the male will not be male and the female will not be female, when you make eyes replacing an eye, a hand replacing a hand, a foot replacing a foot, and an image replacing an image, then you will enter the kingdom."[48]

When male and female become one, what happens? They become *one androgynous whole*. What is Jesus talking about when he says "you make the inner like the outer" and "the upper like the lower"? I believe he means that the "inner" is the Spirit of God, the threefold flame. The "outer" is the Spirit of Mother, the living temple. And "upper" is the Presence of the Spirit of God and "lower" is the soul.

A soul is a mirror and in the pure state reflects fully the Christ and the Father-Mother God, the Holy Spirit. As we are in the Spirit cosmos, so we must become in the Matter cosmos. And the Matter must ascend to the Spirit and the two be fused as one. And then we will know the totality of our Real Being.

I think that we all have the rough spots of our humanness as having been both men and women, cycling back and forth through all these centuries with our karma. I think the strength of Woman is the power of the Word, which was in the Beginning with God. That Word is female, as I stated in chapter 4. It is in the first chapter of John: "In the beginning was the Word, the Word was with God, the Word was God, and without the Word was not any thing made that was made."[49] It is the feminine being of God that created worlds. It is Brahman in the Beginning. It is the light, it is the original Word.

These opening words of the Gospel of John come down to us from the ancient texts of India. John was initiated into these mysteries even when he wrote that gospel.

Underlying it all is the great power of the Buddhas and the bodhisattvas, who are also both male and female.

I would add to this that I believe the subjugation and put-down of Woman for so long has actually molded our Western civilization and brought us to the place of putting Woman not only in an inferior place but a shameful place because of the condemnation of an action supposedly done by Eve. And therefore, Woman, because she does not defend her right to be the sacred repository of the mysteries of Christ and Buddha and of the light of God, must now turn and see that she must defend that right to be the example of the living temple of God to her husband, to her children and to her society—a true pioneer.

I believe that we must defend our right not to have our bodies desecrated whether in rape, whether in pornography, whether in abuse of any kind. And it is only women who can uphold the dignity of Woman that can bring out the most magnificent feminine potential of man.

Some who have been a part of the feminist movement have complained about men not being masculine enough. But you see, it is the female part of man that unlocks his true manhood, the true side of him that is God by polarity, by the divine magnet.

And so, if we as women being in female bodies do not manifest what is natural to us of the true feminine nature of God, then we do not set that example for man to do the same. And only then can both man and woman realize the masculine nature of God. We must realize our feminine nature to draw down by that nature that which is Above—Father, Son and Holy Spirit.

It is up to Woman to reshape her image, her profile and her role and to no longer accept the put-downs that we find in society today, especially in advertising where Woman has become a plaything and a sex symbol. And yet, women of today lend themselves to these images; and therefore, as we have lent ourselves to such images, so we are treated.

We must see to it that this is turned around, and we must do it en masse with the full support of all men, because men truly desire to have the woman of their heart on a pedestal as the aspiring one, the inspiration, the one who has the spiritual kindling and inner direction, even as the man has the outer direction for our life in the physical.

Summary

Let me restate, then, my statements on femaleness and maleness. Our soul is the nonpermanent element of being that is made permanent through her union with Jesus Christ and the Holy Christ Self. When that union is achieved, there is neither male nor female but only androgynous being. The soul who has united with the Christ Self can now declare with Jesus, "I AM Alpha and Omega, the Beginning and the Ending. Neither male nor female, I AM whole. I AM the One. I AM the Knower and the known. With Brahman in the Beginning, I AM the Word."

All that is in the material universe is yin. All that is in the spiritual universe is yang. Spirit and Matter, masculine and feminine. Shakti mirrors Shiva and is the activating principle of Shiva in creation. Shakti is the Word.

When the human female becomes the spiritual male through her soul's fusion with Christ, she is that Christ, that Word. Whoever has the Holy Spirit, who is empowered and infilled with the strength of the Spirit of God, is male in the spiritual sense of the word, whether the soul is clothed in a male or female gender.

Now hear the mystery that Jesus gave to me. All male avatars are the incarnation of the Divine Mother. And the Divine Mother, of course, is the perfect androgynous being, but is the yangness, because this is God, the Divine Mother, manifesting in the physical form. All male avatars are the incarnation of the Divine Mother. All female avatars are the incarnation of the Trinity.

Think of the tenderness of Gautama Buddha and Jesus Christ and Zarathustra and Lao Tzu. Then, think of female incarnations of God who are embodying Father, Son and Holy Spirit, and they are fierce like Kali.[50] They go after all of the injustices against their children. They have that intensity, that yangness that comes from the Trinity, which they embody. All avatars, however, are androgynous spiritual beings who happen to be in material manifestation.

They are the Great Tao[51] fully realized as Above, so below.

Prayer to the World Mother

By Mark L. Prophet

O Mother of the World,
We are all children of thy heart—
Kept apart by triviality,
We remain separate
From thy cosmic ecstasy.

Passions of cosmic freedom, when denied to all,
Bind blind mankind to sensedom, do enthrall.
To fight each other we are pledged—
By dreadful doings, dining
On man's shoddy, senseless spewings
Of aborted patterns charged with hate—
Delusion's senseless, fate confusions.

Do thou now, Great Silent Mother,
Teach thy children how to have no other
Than thyself—to hold our hands from mortal error,
To keep our minds from mortal terror,
To seal our hearts in purpose now supreme,
To forge thy cosmic union—Reality, God-dream.
Long the night has vacant been
From the light of thy radiant Manchild;
Standing in the sun of united Oneness,
We confess to loss of happiness.

Thy office of pure light fears no competition;
Let none doubt thee, but find instead
Attunement with thy blessed head
Of hallowed thoughts;

Thy love, which flows from glowing heart
Of cosmic dreams from God's own musing,

Clears the air from each confusing dream of man
That splits, divides and saws asunder
Many lives until all wonder,
Where's the blunder lying 'neath our feet?
Shall it defeat us evermore—
Never to pause and take our store
With all our reason, wisdom evanescent,
Vanishing to a point of nihilism?

I AM a child of cosmic diligence;
Immaculate is thy concept
Of my willingness to be God-taught,
To learn to love, to shatter matrices of dense desire.
O Cosmic Mother, from thy lofty star position,
Set my heart afire!

May I move by impulse of thy love
To the fount of Brotherhood
Where, washing feet of all my competitors,
I shall serve them all
And see Poseidon rise,
The new Atlantis of our Allness,
Nevermore to sink into the smallness
Of the lesser self that raiseth Cain.
I AM able now to serve and reign
As thy beloved Son.

CHAPTER 6

The Message Is Suppressed

Previous page: Portion of the Gospel of Thomas from the Nag Hammadi Codex II

CHAPTER 6

The Message Is Suppressed

Jesus' Lost Teachings in the Upper Room

Let us talk about the teachings of Jesus that are not written in any book but that Jesus locked in the heart of his disciples and in the hearts of the holy women who were with him in those forty days in the Upper Room, receiving the teaching of the Holy Ghost.

What greater gift could God give us, what greater gift but the gift of eternal life?

God gave us this gift in the Beginning. When he created us to be children of his heart, he endowed us with that very flame, the very same flame that Jesus invoked that passed through his body temple, that restored the fires of life within him[1] so that he could prove that death is not real.

As Hindus see life, we walk the earth embarking on the spiral of death from our birth; fighting every inch of the way the process of disintegration, decay, disease. But this is not what life intended. This is not the way of the Christ. This is not the message of the resurrection. This is not the message of the open tomb.

The message is: I AM come that ye might have life and that more abundantly. I AM the way, the truth and the life.[2] It is the message of the elevation of the true Christ Self within. It is the reception of the Christ by Mary Magdalene. It is the nurturing of the Christ by Mary the Mother. It is the manifestation of the Trinity of the three Marys[3] holding the balance of the Trinity, that Father and Son and Holy Spirit might not remain in heaven but that these might become the flow, the energy, the renewing life within Matter.

We understand the I AM Presence (see the Chart of Your Divine Self, page 80) to be individualized for each of us. But in God, in eternity, in life, that I AM Presence is one, and whether we have the sense of God individualized many times, or in infinity of Oneness, we know that when Jesus ascended, he ascended into the very fiery core of our own individualized I AM Presence. And this is the message that he gave to Mary Magdalene: "Touch me not; for I am not yet ascended to my Father: but go to my brethren, and say unto them, I ascend unto my Father, and your Father; and to my God, and your God."[4] Of course, he said this almost in passing.

"Go and tell the disciples that my ascension is unto the very living Presence of life within you. And because I ascend to my God and your God, to my Father and your Father, we are one; we are one in the victory, and the victory of the one Son of God counts for all."

Can you accept that Jesus has truly ascended into the very Holy of holies of your own God Presence and that when you ascend in meditation into that upper room of the God consciousness that God has given you, you will find there not only your own I AM Presence and your own mansion in the house of the Father,[5] but you will find there sitting on the right hand of your own God flame, the blessed and beloved Saviour of all mankind, Jesus the Christ.

Jesus spoke of ascending to my God and to your God. This wonderful teaching and statement has to do with the fact that when the Christ, the soul in Christ ascends to the mighty

I AM Presence, that one is forevermore a part of the mighty I AM Presence of every living soul. For God is one, and the I AM Presence is a focus of that one in each of us.

The ascension process is to the one God, the eternal God, the Almighty. Therefore, you can understand how the mighty I AM Presence of all of us focuses the collective victory of all saints of all ages. This is a wondrous teaching on resurrection morning.

Why did Jesus say, "my God and your God?" Because he had taught the inner circle of disciples this very teaching, which is in all of the retreats of the Brotherhood, that the I AM Presence individualized is your personal God Presence. Your I AM Presence, my I AM Presence; your permanent atom, my permanent atom. "My God and your God" refers to the witness of the I AM THAT I AM where each of them stood.

Later, when a certain action of the alchemy of the resurrection flame had taken place, he did allow Thomas to touch his hands, his side and his feet[6] to be certain that Thomas would know this was the same body that had hung on the cross and not a heavenly body, not a ghost—that indeed Jesus had paid the price and won eternal life for us all.

We are given to understand that Mary Magdalene had full awareness of this teaching and did not need to have the full explanation. She knew the process. She knew the initiation, and Jesus was reminding her that in her great love for him, it was not the moment to touch him because of the very reason that he was sensitive when someone touched him. And he had felt virtue go out of him as in the healing of the woman.[7]

Touching, therefore, the delicate matrix of the Deathless Solar Body and the resurrected one would also interfere with the divine alchemy of that process. For it was not yet complete, not yet fulfilled.

Teachings Lost or Missing from the New Testament

I would tell you, then, of what I have recorded for those who need to see and understand the proof that there are lost teachings. The clues begin right where they ought to begin—in the New Testament, right where they ought to begin merely because that New Testament has left out a lot.

And if you read with objectivity, you can clearly see where the story leaves off and doesn't pick up again because somebody took it out or maybe it was never there in the first place because it was a mystery or a secret teaching that Jesus only reveals by initiation heart to heart and fire to fire.

A small number of verses in the New Testament actually record Jesus' teaching. At least sixteen passages show him teaching but do not say what he taught.[8] At least ten other passages imply that not all of what he said on a particular occasion is recorded.[9]

Have you ever been frustrated to read that he taught them for many days, but then no teaching is there? What did he say?

There were post-resurrection teachings. The Book of Acts says Jesus taught for forty days of "things pertaining to the kingdom of God"[10] between the resurrection and the ascension. He tutored Paul. He gave John the Book of Revelation after the resurrection.

There is evidence that he spent many years on earth after the resurrection. Church Father Irenaeus wrote (c. A.D. 180) that Jesus lived at least ten to twenty years after the crucifixion and "still fulfilled the office of a Teacher, even as the Gospel and all the elders testify; those who were conversant in Asia with John, the disciple of the Lord, [affirming] that John conveyed to them that information."[11] In other words, Jesus taught until he was forty or fifty years old. The third-century Gnostic gospel Pistis Sophia said that when Jesus had risen from the dead, "he passed eleven years discoursing with his disciples."[12] We have no record and no teaching.

There are missing source documents for the Gospels. Scholars have concluded that the Gospel writers worked from a diverse body of source documents and oral tradition. They have postulated the existence of "Q," "The Little Apocalypse," a "Proto-Mark" and "Proto-Luke," as well as other documents. The oral tradition about Jesus is also missing.

Papias, the bishop of Hieropolis, who lived c. A.D. 70–155 wrote down the words of the apostles and other eyewitnesses to Jesus' life. All but a fragment of his work was destroyed.

There is a lack of literature produced by Jesus' disciples, his close friends and by Jesus himself. It is highly unlikely that they all were illiterate. It is unlikely in light of what we already know about Jesus' journey to the East or in the British Isles or in Egypt that he was illiterate. In the Roman Empire, literacy was common even among the lower classes. And we have the record in Luke's gospel of Jesus reading from the book of Isaiah in the synagogue at Nazareth.[13]

The New Testament was edited and altered—both by its authors (who desired to keep certain teaching from the uninitiated) and by scribes and Church Fathers, who desired to preserve their orthodoxy—in my opinion, to control the people, to control their faith and their knowledge.

We believe that Jesus deliberately kept his inner teachings from the masses, because we read in Mark 4:10–12 that he told his disciples: "Unto you it is given to know the mystery of the kingdom of God: but unto them that are without, all things are done in parables." Mark 4:34 says that "when they were alone, he expounded all things to his disciples."

The Secret Gospel of Mark

A fragment of a secret gospel of Mark was discovered in 1958 by scholar Morton Smith. It was at Mar Saba, a monastery in the Judean desert. This is proof that the inner teachings existed. Smith found the gospel quoted in an ancient letter written by Church Father Clement of Alexandria around A.D. 200.

This letter is a tremendous find for those who understand the personal path of Christhood, who are the mystics of this age. In it, Clement revealed that the apostle Mark had "composed a more spiritual Gospel for the use of those who were being perfected."[14] You remember Jesus said, "Be ye therefore perfect, even as your Father which is in heaven is perfect."[15]

The path of self-perfectionment does not mean a flesh-and-blood perfection. Who of us could pass the test of flesh-and-blood or human perfection? The human consciousness, the human being is not made to be perfect. The perfectionment we are speaking of is the soul, and the qualities of virtue of the soul that God recognizes as perfection are not the virtues that are demanded of the human in this world. Therefore, we can understand that there is a part of us that is being perfected right now, even if the outer self may continue to err and be human.

In Clement's time this gospel was carefully guarded, "being read only to those who are being initiated into the great mysteries."[16]

We have an inkling here of an inner path of initiation transmitted from Master to disciple. It is the Guru-chela or Master-disciple relationship that has existed for tens of thousands of years in the East and on the ancient lost continents of Lemuria, Atlantis and pre-golden ages even before those records. This inner walk with the inner Christ is confirmed in this Secret Gospel of Mark.

Smith's fragment describes a secret baptism and initiation rite that Jesus administers to a youth believed by Smith to be Lazarus. Many scholars accept the authenticity of the Secret Gospel of Mark. The question is: How many other secret gospels like this one existed and are now lost?

One feels no loss, however, because when you are ready, the Master reveals the mysteries. This is the hour of our readiness and of his coming. The true mysteries are not lost. This is the great joy and message I come to deliver to you, for the mysteries themselves and the Christ are your deliverer.

Aside from intentional deletions, some teaching was also deleted over the centuries through the errors of copyists who made mistakes and corrected what they perceived to be mistakes.

Now, if you don't understand something, you think it's a mistake, don't you? So you just correct it so it reads right according to how you think it should be stated. But we know that the ancient mysteries may be a question of a verb, a tense, a pronoun, a very small difference in how something is said or written.

This can be seen in the thousands of New Testament manuscripts we possess and the thousands of Bible quotes preserved in ancient writings that differ from each other in over 250,000 ways.

How can you say this version of the Bible or this copy of the Bible is the absolute Truth? As Mark Prophet[17] used to say, even in our own time we've had so many, many different translations.

The Gospels were also edited for theological reasons. Codex Sinaiticus, one of the oldest Bibles in the world, written about A.D. 340, differs in significant ways from the canonical text we have today. Scholar James Bentley gives an example of the editing. He points out that in the first chapter of Mark's

Gospel we are told of a leper who says to Jesus, "If you will, you can make me clean." Codex Sinaiticus continues: "Jesus, angry, stretched out his hand and touched him, and said, 'I will; be clean.'"[18]

Later manuscripts, perceiving that to attribute anger to Jesus at this point made him appear perhaps too human, alter the word "angry" to the words "moved with compassion." In our scripture today we have, "Jesus, moved with compassion, stretched out his hand." Now if you understand the meaning of divine wrath and divine compassion, they actually are not much different. The anger that Jesus experienced I don't consider to be human, although I believe that Jesus could become humanly angry, and I wouldn't cite him for that.

So, if one does not understand the meaning, one may change the words, but the record is there yet to be read. Everything that Jesus ever did or said is in akasha. That which is secret teaching is veiled and kept sealed by the angels of God until Jesus desires to release it.

Some of the Gnostic writings discovered at Nag Hammadi are at least as old as Matthew, Mark, Luke and John.

It is my opinion and conclusion that they were excluded from our Bible not because they had been proven fraudulent, but simply because the Church Fathers did not like them. The Church Fathers did not like these documents or the truth of Jesus' lost years because it would give to the individual knowledge, and knowledge is independence; and knowledge becomes self-knowledge—gnosis.

When you have self-knowledge, you understand the relationship of yourself to God, to the universe, to your fellow man. And suddenly, you understand that your salvation is not dependent upon organized religion or a priest or a minister or a rabbi. To this day, this enrages organized religion. But I speak it in any case, because I am the champion of your divine rights.

When we realize that this editing and altering of the New Testament happened before Protestantism, then those who are Protestants today, who have this teaching and these lost years and these mysteries denied to them, are still carrying, therefore, the banner of Rome. To be truly liberated from those who keep from you the true teachings, you must recognize that Protestantism inherited the absence of the truth and yet had stripped from it more of the truth in the denial of the saints in heaven, the heavenly hosts, the ascended masters and the angels.

This communion with those saints and heavenly hosts is also your divine right. Christianity today is stripping from us more and more and more of the whole loaf and full-bodied wheat of the message.

Jesus' Teachings on Woman Are Suppressed

Jesus' teaching on the Mother as we find it reflected in the Gnostic texts is conspicuously absent from the Christian scriptures that have come down to us. In both Judaism and Christianity today, God is depicted as Father, in contrast to the teachings of other world religions, ancient and modern, where the Divine Mother figures alongside her masculine counterpart in one or in many guises.

Those who molded orthodox Christian doctrine in later centuries condemned as heretical Gnostic teachings as well as the prominent role of women in Gnostic communities. The orthodox clergy decided that the teachings on the Divine Mother and the feminine principle were not the true teachings of Jesus Christ and therefore should not be included in the Bible. As Elaine Pagels points out:

> By the time the process of sorting the various writings ended—probably as late as the year 200—virtually all the feminine imagery for God had dis-

appeared from orthodox Christian tradition.[19]

This official stance bore consequences for women and their role in the Church. In some Gnostic communities, women shared equally in leadership positions with men, but the Church Fathers vehemently complained that women in Gnostic circles were allowed to do what women were forbidden to do in orthodox churches. They were allowed to prophesy and to share in the celebration of the Eucharist—in effect, to act as priests. Tertullian wrote of female Gnostic Christians:

> These heretical women, how audacious they are. They have no modesty. They are bold enough to teach, to dispute, to enact exorcisms, to undertake cures, and it may be even to baptize.[20]

Result of the Failure of the Church to Include Jesus' Teachings on the Mother

I would like to give you Mother Mary's comments on the failure of the Church to embody the true teachings of Christ on the Mother flame:

> Blessed ones, there are many who do not understand the place of the Mother within the circle of faith, and they speculate that the principle of Mother and the adoration of the Mother flame comes from a sort of oriental philosophy, Hellenism, or even the work of the Gnostics.
>
> Precious ones, the adoration of Mother has ever been at the fount of the ministry of Christ. But the split in Christendom has come about, not because of error in the later Church but because of the destruction of the teachings of my blessed Son concerning the Mother flame within each and every one of you and the Mother flame as the fount of the true Church.

You have understood that the death of the Church* prevents the souls of humanity from approaching the altar of the Father, the Son and the Holy Spirit. For the temple doors are the doors of the Mother. The Mother is the bride of all of these. The Mother is the entrance of that flame to your souls, and thus the fallen ones have torn apart the faith and thus cleaved asunder the Body of God.

The center of the Inner Church is always the Mother light, has ever been from the days of Lemuria and Atlantis. And I tell you, O children of God, that if this civilization is to return to the light of that glory, each one must confess the presence of the Bride of Christ within. Thus, you become the Church within and without. And therefore the gates of hell cannot move against you. For it is the light of God as sacred fire that is the burning of his love in your temple.[21]

The Worship of the Mother as Goddess

Protestants revere and respect Mary as a human being who was Jesus' mother, but they don't see her in the office of the Divine Virgin and the Queen of Heaven, in her rightful place as the divine complement of Raphael, the archangel of the fifth ray of healing and truth. And because she has descended to earth, taken on form and ascended again, she therefore has a higher office than all other archeiai, and thus she is truly called the Queen of Angels and the Queen of Heaven.

Because we know that the level of an archangel and the archeia is the full incarnation of the LORD as the I AM THAT I AM, we can see the God-manifestation of beings of that great light. And we can worship them without having any

* i.e., the failure of the Church to fulfill its mission.

concept that there is more than one God, because they are the manifestation, or the incarnation, of the one God in a certain vibration, a certain frequency on a certain ray.[22]

It's very difficult to speak in Christian churches and circles about gods and goddesses. This must surely be the ultimate blasphemy, many think. But what it means is that that individual has realized the incarnation of God to such an extent that they have received a title or a mantle of god or goddess that signifies that virtue they embody. They are embodying it at the level of the full consciousness of God and have attained that mastery. And so we know that their attainment is very great and that they are an example to this planetary system, if not to many worlds, of the high attainment one can achieve on that ray and on that God-quality. And no one ever thinks that there is more than one God. There is *one God* in many individualizations. The goddess is also in ourselves.

When you get over that hurdle of understanding the mysteries, you can go into ecstasy or, what is a better term, Samadhi, in the very contemplation of God incarnate in a certain manifestation that has a unique quality—hence the gods and goddesses of the Hindu pantheon. And that is how we can understand them.

The Persecution of the Gnostics as Heretics and the Suppression of Their Teaching

At a certain point, when the understanding of the Lord's teaching and the teachings of the Gnostics themselves began to gain popularity, some ecclesiastics decided that the Gnostic version of Christian teaching and practice was not valid or accurate.

As we stated previously, as Gnostic beliefs grew more popular, they presented a challenge to the unity of the Church. The Gnostics refused to recite new creeds written by men or to conform to the emerging doctrines of the Church. They had the teachings of Jesus' inner circle, of his disciples and the holy women. They didn't need dogma and doctrine. These churchmen—whose goal was to consolidate authority and stabilize Christian tradition into a unified and codified set of beliefs—denounced the Gnostic writings as blasphemous forgeries and challenged them in lengthy refutations.

By the fourth century, the ecclesiastical leadership had gained enough power to override the Gnostic alternative: they expelled the Gnostics from the Church as heretics and burned their works. These measures were largely successful; very little of the prolific literature produced by the Gnostics has survived to the present. Until the late nineteenth century, we had to depend solely on secondhand reports of Gnostic teachings preserved in the writings of their enemies.

Joseph N. Sanders observes that in developing an official list of accepted scripture, Christians of the second century felt themselves called

> to conserve the truth then revealed.... The most powerful motive, however,... was the desire to preserve the Church from heresy.... The ostensible criterion was that of authorship by an apostle or the immediate disciple of an apostle, whose authority [the scripture] was deemed to possess: the effective criterion was that of conformity to orthodox teaching....
>
> The Gnostics in particular claimed to derive their teachings from secret traditions entrusted by the Apostles to their favorite disciples, which were accordingly of superior authority to the public tradition to which the Catholics appealed.... In reaction to these, Catholic writers like Irenaeus emphasized not only the apostolic tradition but also the apostolic writings which had been used in the Church from the earliest times.[23]

Listen to these words of the Church Father Irenaeus in his treatise *Against Heresies*. Here he is speaking of the followers of Valentinus, a respected second-century Gnostic teacher in the Christian community.

> Those who are from Valentinus, being . . . altogether reckless, while they put forth their own compositions, boast that they possess more Gospels than there really are. Indeed, they have arrived at such a pitch of audacity, as to entitle their comparatively recent writing "the Gospel of Truth," though it agrees in nothing with the Gospels of the Apostles, so that they have really no Gospel which is not full of blasphemy.[24]

In essence, the criterion of apostolic witness and tradition was a tactic to deny the soul's right to receive progressive revelation from her Lord.

Not only were the Church Fathers then and now bothered by the new gospels the Gnostics were creating but they also did not like the fact that the Gnostics drew upon the Christian scriptures to support their teachings.

Tertullian argues that heretics should not be allowed to cite the scriptures because the scriptures do not belong to them. He says:

> If in these lie their resources, before they can use them, it ought to be clearly seen to whom belongs the possession of the Scriptures, that none may be admitted to the use thereof who has no title at all to the privilege.[25]

A doctrine of privilege, you see, not a doctrine for the poor and the common people who have nothing except the divine spark going for them. And so the divine spark and those of the divine spark who think individually and creatively are pushed back for orthodoxy—a system of law that claims grace but has none because it does not have the capacity to transmit grace.

The Cathars

This same argument was used by the Church in later centuries against the Cathars, a medieval sect with Gnostic beliefs. When the Catholic Church discovered that the Cathars and other so-called heretics were making their own translations of scripture, they proclaimed at the Council of Narbonne in 1229 that laymen were forbidden to possess any part of the Bible except the Psalms and passages in the breviary, and they condemned vernacular translations. To the present day—and perhaps it has changed in the last few years—but to this century Catholics have never been great Bible readers.

In 1208, Christian soldiers were summoned by Pope Innocent III to wage a crusade against the Cathars. In one battle alone, the crusaders murdered 15,000 believers at the town of Béziers. Researcher Arthur Guirdham concludes that Catharism was

> a resurgence of primitive Christianity, and was stamped out for the very reason that it was primitive Christianity. It was a mystical, real, living experience of Christianity as opposed to an avidly theological concept.[26]

The Knights Templar

The suppression of the Knights Templar is another story of unabashed cruelty and horror. The Knights Templar were a military-religious order, founded in 1118, which served valiantly during the Crusades. When they were not on the battlefield, this "militia of Christ," as they were called, lived a disciplined monastic life and took the vows of poverty, chastity and obedience—the same vows that Saint Francis took.

On Friday, October 13, 1307, without warning, all the Knights Templar in France were arrested and their goods confiscated at the order of King Philip IV of France, who was jealous of their influence, independence and wealth (which they held in common). He charged them with heresy, blasphemy and homosexuality. When the knights would not confess to the trumped-up charges against them, they were imprisoned and subjected to such brutal tortures as having sharp splinters driven under their fingernails and flames held under their bare feet. Their grand master and the preceptor of Normandy were slowly roasted to death over a charcoal fire.

Some writers believe the Templars were initiates of a secret, mystery teaching. Helena Blavatsky calls them "the last European secret organization which, as a body, had in its possession some of the mysteries of the East."[27]

In 1312, the Pope, at the insistence of King Philip, officially dissolved the Knights Templar by papal order.[28]

In the mid-sixteenth century, the hammer of orthodoxy fell again. The Council of Trent claimed the infallibility of Catholic dogma and declared that the Church had the sole right to interpret the Bible. In 1564, Pope Pius IV ratified the decrees of the synod in a papal letter (or "bull") that forbade all unauthorized interpretation of scripture under pain of excommunication.

Why Was Gnosticism Suppressed?

Why were the Gnostics such a threat to the orthodox Church? The answer becomes clearer and clearer as the centuries of Christ's enlightenment unfold. The independent, freethinking spirit of the Gnostics challenged the very structure and definition of the Church.

The orthodox demanded allegiance to the Church's creed, rituals, scriptures and clergy. They claimed that God was accessible only through the mediation of the presbyters and bishops, whereas the Gnostics believed that they had direct access to the living Christ through the divine spark within and did not need a mediator in the person of a bishop.

The Gnostics also complained that the ignorant clergy were stifling the spiritual progress of the soul. In the Gnostic text Authoritative Teaching, it is written of the soul's adversaries:

> They did not realize that she has an invisible spiritual body, thinking, "We are her shepherd who feeds her." But they did not realize that she knows another way, which is hidden from them. This her true shepherd taught her in knowledge.[29]

Her "true shepherd" is her Holy Christ Self. To this day these priests do not realize that you have an invisible spiritual body—the body of your I AM Presence, your Holy Christ Self, your Deathless Solar Body.

Summarizing the issue of spiritual authority and its implications for future generations, Pagels writes:

> "Orthodoxy" legitimizes a hierarchy of persons through whose authority in teaching and discipline all others must approach God. Gnostic teaching, as Irenaeus and Tertullian see it, is potentially subversive of this order.[30]

> When the orthodox gained military support, sometime after the Emperor Constantine became Christian in the fourth century, the penalty for heresy escalated.... Christian bishops, previously victimized by the police, now commanded them. Possession of books denounced as heretical was made a criminal offense. Copies of such books were burned and destroyed....
>
> The efforts of the majority to destroy every trace of heretical "blasphemy" proved so successful that, until the discoveries at Nag Hammadi, nearly all of our information concerning alternative forms of early Christianity came from the massive orthodox attacks upon them.[31]

As historian Will Durant wrote:

> Once triumphant, the Church ceased to preach toleration; she looked with the same hostile eye upon individualism in belief as the state upon secession or revolt.[32]

CHAPTER 7

Clerical Celibacy and the Doctrine of Original Sin

Previous page: St. Peter's, Rome

CHAPTER 7

Clerical Celibacy and the Doctrine of Original Sin

The Church's Insistence on Clerical Celibacy

It concerns me that women are not allowed to serve on an equal basis with men in many churches today. And this problem goes hand in hand with the Catholic Church's mandate for celibacy among the clergy. The desire of Catholic women to serve as priests is essentially the same as the desire of priests to be married: It is the desire to celebrate the divine union here below as Above, whether it be in service or in the sacrament of marriage.

As I see it, the requirement of the Catholic Church that a priest has to be celibate denies men and women their proper roles and their true wholeness. The irony of this official position of the Church is that the first Vicar of Christ, Peter himself, was married! The Bible itself tells us of the occasion when Jesus healed Peter's wife's mother.[1]

There are five references by early Christian writers, among them Origen and Clement of Alexandria, that the apostle Paul himself was married.[2] Does that make him less holy? No! The thought that marriage makes anyone less holy is a degradation of the role of man and woman to marry and out of that union to bring forth the children of God.

The Bible itself records no directive of Jesus or his apostles that the clergy had to be celibate. In fact, according to Hebrew scriptures all priests *had* to be married.[3] Rabbis have always been married. Who should be better qualified to bring forth children and raise them up according to the traditions of Church and State than rabbis, priests and ministers?

During the first three centuries of Christianity, clerical celibacy was widely practiced but it was not obligatory. In about A.D. 306, the Council of Elvira decreed that all priests and bishops, whether married or not, should abstain from sexual relations. It wasn't until 1123 and 1139 that the first and second Lateran Councils put an end to clerical marriages in which the couples agreed to be celibate and declared that priests could not be married at all. How far removed is this from the early traditions of Christianity!

The Doctrine of Original Sin

This put-down of marriage goes back to the Church Father Augustine, who associated original sin with lust and the sexual act. The doctrine of original sin as it is currently taught states that as a result of the fall of Adam, every member of the human race is born with an hereditary moral defect and therefore is subject to death. There is barely a trace of the concept of original sin among the early apostolic fathers. They believed that no sin could prevent man from choosing good over evil by his own free will.

It wasn't until the fifth century that a controversy over the doctrine of original sin erupted. Augustine, a major advocate of this doctrine, taught that the stain of original sin was transmitted by the sexual act from generation to generation. And because the sexual act was accompanied by lust, it was inherently sinful.

Augustine, by Pinturicchio

You would be amazed if you could realize what a weight of world condemnation there is upon every human being because of this doctrine and this consciousness. We all carry it around at subconscious levels—that there is condemnation connected with the sexual act—so much so that we are born sinners because of it.

It is highly important that we challenge this weight and burden upon ourselves.

Elaine Pagels writes in *Adam, Eve, and the Serpent:*

> That semen itself, Augustine argues,... transmits the damage incurred by sin. Hence, Augustine concludes, every human being ever conceived through semen already is born contaminated with sin.[4]

This makes unholy the seed of life that God has prepared to transmit the genes, the light, even the Holy Spirit for a new soul or an old soul to come forth.

Pagels says:

> Through this astonishing argument, Augustine intends to prove that every human being is in bondage not only from birth but indeed from the moment of conception.... Augustine applies his account of Adam's experience, disrupted by the first sin, to every one of his offspring (except, of course, to Christ, conceived, Augustine ingeniously argued, without semen).[5]

There is nothing whatsoever in scripture to support this conclusion. But this is what Augustine convinced his fellow Christians. He wrote:

> Everyone, arising as he does from a condemned stock, is from the first necessarily evil and carnal through Adam.[6]

> It is of indispensable importance that we should say that the soul and God are not of one and the self-same nature.[7]

Bad things happen to good people because all people are bad by nature, Augustine argued, and the only chance for them to overcome this natural wickedness is to access God's grace through the Church. As Augustine wrote, "No one will be good who was not first of all wicked."[8]

Jerome, by Carpaccio

Although the Church has since rejected some of Augustine's arguments, the Catholic catechism still tells us: "We cannot tamper with the revelation of original sin without undermining the mystery of Christ."[9] Original sin is linked so closely with Christ, the Church argues, because it is Christ who liberates us from original sin.

Perhaps Jerome, another Church father, summarized the orthodox position most concisely when he wrote, "We are black by nature."[10]

Augustine and Jerome are both doctors of the Church.*

The controversy over original sin within the doctrine of the Catholic Church was settled in A.D. 529 when the Council of Orange accepted Augustine's doctrine of original sin. The council decreed that Adam's sin corrupted the body and soul

---

* Doctor of the Church is a title that has been bestowed by the Catholic Church on thirty-three saints whose teaching has been influential in the development of the doctrines of the Church.

of the whole human race and that sin and death are a result of Adam's disobedience.

The synod also declared that because of sin, man's free will is so weakened that "no one is able to love God as he ought, or believe in God, or do anything for God which is good, except the grace of divine mercy comes first to him."[11] Thus, grace and not human merit was primary to salvation.

There was much at stake in the outcome of the debate on original sin. The controversy threatened to undermine the role of the Church in the life of the communicant. The Church taught that baptism was the way in which the faithful were initiated into the Church and introduced to grace, and that a life of grace was sustained by the sacraments. If the sacrament of baptism was no longer necessary to wash away original sin and to attain salvation, then the Church and its clergy would be expendable.

I believe the doctrines of Augustine and Jerome are doctrines of Satan, to perpetually cast upon the entire human race the sense of guilt, of sin, of imperfection that disqualifies all of us from walking in the footsteps of Jesus Christ in fulfillment of the Gnostic principles and teachings.

It is amazing to me, and it was amazing to me when as a child I was first taught this doctrine, that the body of believers of Christendom ever thereafter could actually accept the lie that we are all stained by a supposed act of Adam.

Jesus did not teach original sin. I believe that the real original sin is the sin of the fallen angels[12] who rebelled against God, challenged the Divine Mother and her Son. And these fallen ones have perpetrated the lie of the sinfulness of God's children ever since they fell from grace.

They have led the children of God into paths of sinfulness in order to convince them that they are "sinners" and hence, unworthy to follow in the footsteps of Jesus Christ. The fallen angels have kept from the children of God the true understanding that God has endowed each of them with the Divine Image; instead they have taught them that they are forever stained by "original sin" and can never become Christ-like or realize their own Christ potential. The fallen angels have thus promulgated the false doctrine that because the children of God are sinners, they can only be saved by grace, thereby denying the necessity for each one to "work the works of him that sent me,"[13] as Jesus declared of his own mission.

I believe the violation of the light of God and its misuse is a sin, but I do not believe there is anything sinful about the procreation of life upon earth or that the means for procreation given to us is an indelible mark that has stained you forever and made you to be helpless sinners. And I believe that this concept has been degrading to man and to woman, and therefore the denial of that true sense of being instruments of God in bringing forth holy children is not there in the true teachings of the Church.

At the time of the birth of Jesus Christ, many Jewish women were waiting for the birth of the Messiah, were preparing themselves, were fasting and praying. In the mystical communities such as the Essenes and throughout the Old Testament, fathers and mothers who gave birth to great lights had prepared themselves to receive those lights; all looked forward to being the mother of the Messiah. No one knew when or where he would come. This shows the Jewish concept of the sacredness of the body of man and woman to be the instruments of the descent of the living God.

And each couple longed to be those called to have the incarnation of the Christ. But the truth of the matter is that as Jesus Christ came to Joseph and Mary, so the Christ comes to every parent, because the Christ exists as potential and divine spark in all of us. And our true calling is to give birth to the Messiah.

What is the Messiah? The Messiah is bringing into incarnation the fusion of the Divine Mother and the Divine Father. Where do we see the oneness of father and mother? Why, of course, in children. We say, "He's got his dad's hair and his mother's eyes," and we take apart the child and we look and see how he came together, but he is one person.

That is why marriage is sacred and sanctified. It is sanctified and sealed in a circle of light because we want that blessing from the altar of our temples and churches. We want to consecrate the circle of our union and our love to making a home of light into which God may descend.

We go to the altar of God to be married. We seek the sanctification of our love and the consecration of our lives to God's service. And we affirm the sealing of the sacred fire unto God and one another in the circle of our love.

When you think of it, this entire argument of Augustine and original sin, which also leads to the doctrine of the virgin birth,* hinges on the fact that this act makes it impossible for the Son of God to embody in the sinful body. Yet are we made perfected by the flesh? No! We are perfected in the Spirit. To me, the entire argument that Jesus had to be born of a virgin is based on the sense that the flesh itself is inherently sinful by this creative act. Therefore Jesus had to be born independently of it. But what we see here is that God has never taught us that we would be perfected in the flesh but that we would be perfected in our souls through Christ our Lord.

Now the teaching of original sin may be Church doctrine, but it's not the words of Jesus Christ! This is condemnation at the very root of our life. Jesus came into this world not to condemn the world but that the world through him might have eternal life.[14] And that's why God sent him.

---

* See pages 257–66 for a more complete discussion of the virgin birth.

The Doctrine of the Immaculate Conception

In the eyes of the Catholic Church, the *only* exception, apart from Jesus, to the universal condemnation of mankind because of original sin is Mary, the mother of Jesus. In 1854 in a papal bull (a written mandate of the pope), Pope Pius IX stated that "by a unique grace and privilege" the Blessed Virgin Mary was preserved from "the stain of original sin."[15] According to the theologians, this special grace—a privilege that no other human being has ever received—qualified Mary to be a suitable mother for Jesus.

They had to invent this doctrine if they were going to live with Augustine. Our Lord could not have been born with the stain of original sin. The doctrine of the Immaculate Conception of the Virgin Mary means that she also was not conceived by normal means, or if so, that sin was wiped from her.

In my estimation, the consequence of this proclamation doesn't make Mother Mary better—we already give her our highest veneration and our highest love. The consequence is to make *us worse!* It elevates the Blessed Mother far beyond our reach. It makes her totally unlike us. She is no longer human. She no longer has gone through what we have gone through. This papal bull is degrading you and me and the rest of the human race. It makes Mother Mary and Mother Mary alone worthy to give birth to the Christ. But God sent us into this world to give birth to children that they might realize their individual Christhood.

Jesus Sanctifies Marriage

The official stance of the Roman Church today is that the state of celibacy is holier and higher than that of marriage. The fact of the matter is that Jesus consecrated human marriage. He performed his first public miracle in Palestine at the marriage feast in Cana of Galilee.[16] He changed the water into wine. By this he taught us that the water of human consciousness is not adequate, that we must go through the alchemy of the Holy Spirit and that the wine of the Spirit must be a higher level of consciousness.

He sanctified human marriage by his presence at that feast. To deny the holiness of the married state is to deny Jesus' sanctification of marriage—and Saint Paul's, for that matter—although Paul pointed out that celibacy was to be preferred if it could be kept.[17]

So the Church's view that celibacy is holier than marriage denies the very heart of the sacrament of marriage celebrated by the Church.

Out of Elohim, our Father-Mother God, came forth male and female. You and your twin flame were created in the beginning by God out of the white-fire body. Together you were in the realms of light in the beginning, and you were destined to be together in the ending—unto your resurrection and ascension into the light whence you came.

The Results of the Doctrines of Mandatory Celibacy and Original Sin

I believe that the doctrine of mandatory celibacy for priests and nuns and the doctrine of original sin are destroying the Church to its very core today.

These doctrines are the Devil's undoing of the Church by dividing the masculine and feminine principles of the

Godhead. They deny priests and nuns the strength and protection that would be afforded them in their service by their union in holy matrimony. Thus they must leave their Holy Orders and break their vows if they want to be married.

Mother Mary said that the requirement of celibacy in the Church is at the root of many of its problems. She said that when celibacy is forced on the clergy without an understanding of the true spiritual teaching behind it, how to maintain it, or how to raise up the sacred fire on the altar of the spine of the temple of being, the results can be heinous.

She said:

> Blessed ones, do you not find it strange that the original Vicar of Christ, Peter, was married and yet all others who followed have been given the law of celibacy? Do you understand, beloved, that the rabbis who came before were married and are to this hour? And do you understand that the nature of wholeness found in the balance of Alpha and Omega is a security and a protection to the path of spirituality when complementary ones may serve together in holy matrimony?
>
> You find, then, that where the spiritual teaching as practiced in the Far East is not a part of the goal of celibacy, the end of that celibacy is far more heinous than the lawful marriage that is also ordained for those clergy outside of the Roman Church. Thus, today homosexuality is rampant in the Church with high percentages of my priests so engaged. The misuse of the sacred fire, unlawfully [according to the laws of God], does place those priests outside of their vows, outside of a sense of personal dignity and truly outside of the holiness of the altar.

These burdens upon the religious in holy orders have, as you know, in times long ago resulted in pregnancies and often the abortion or the death [killing] of the child at birth in an attempt to conceal and remove the evidence of the infraction of that code of ethics and conduct.

Blessed hearts, it is good to place before oneself goals and self-discipline. Even the path of celibacy may be put on by married couples for a season of devotion, fasting and prayer [voluntarily, by mutual consent]. These cycles, then, of conjugal love side by side with an acceleration of the marriage to the living Christ can therefore allow the individual to be balanced, to retain dignity, to know the beauty of family life yet not to be deprived of the priesthood of holy orders.

Even so, the ancient prophets were married. Even so, some who later became saints and came apart from the world were married in the beginning, such as Siddhartha.[18] And you know, beloved, that my own Son shared a beautiful love with his twin flame,[19]... who held the balance for him, even as I did, as he pursued a mission of immensity, holding the sacred fire of the Divine Mother in the full mastery of his chakras.[20]

The doctrine of celibacy is not only hurting the Catholic Church but it's hurting society. In the United States, reports of priests sexually abusing young boys and having sexual relations with adult men and women have been increasing.

The Shortage of Priests

Psychotherapist and former monk Richard Sipe estimates that 50 percent of the Catholic priests in the United States are breaking their vows of celibacy,[21] although Church officials disagree. The celibacy requirement is also contributing to the grave shortage of priests.

According to Dean Hoge, a sociologist at Catholic University in Washington, D.C., for every hundred priests who leave active ministry, only fifty-nine are taking their place. Mandatory celibacy and the refusal to allow women to be ordained are the main reasons for the shortage, he says. "Because of the loneliness and isolation [priests] feel, the alcoholism rate is just enormous."[22]

This insistence on compulsory celibacy is far from universal. Marriage is permitted for clergy in almost all Protestant sects and in some Catholic rites not under the authority of the Roman Magisterium. These include the Eastern Orthodox churches, the Old Catholic Church and the Brazilian Catholic Apostolic Church.

The results of compulsory celibacy can be serious for clergy who do not understand the true spiritual teaching behind it and who are not instructed how to maintain it, as Mother Mary stated. Where the celibate is not wholeheartedly dedicated to the mystical union of the soul with God, the end of that celibacy can be far worse than marriage.

And what does the Vatican have to say about this crisis? Well, when a synod of bishops gathered in Rome in October 1990 to study problems in the priesthood, the bishops were told that Pope John Paul II had forbidden all discussion on allowing the clergy to be married.[23]

The Solution to the Lack of Priests: Ordain Women as Priests

Of course, the synod never considered the most obvious solution to the lack of priests: *opening the priesthood to women!*

As I stated previously, God has ordained women in the ministry from the beginning. This is my conviction and this is what I know from my research into the records. On the ancient continents of Atlantis and Lemuria, both men and women served in the priesthood.

I myself am an ordained minister. I believe with all my heart that our Lord respected women and gave female disciples equal opportunity and equal status to that of male disciples. And I believe, as every good Christian should, in the imitation of Christ.

I believe that if it is your calling from God to serve in any office of the Church, you should be allowed to do so if you study to show yourself approved unto God—rightly dividing the word of Truth[24]—regardless of your sex.

There is nothing wrong with a woman being a priest! The right women would make fine priests!

When I am at the altar, I don't identify myself as male or female. I remember the words of Saint Paul, *"There is neither Jew nor Greek, there is neither bond nor free, there is neither male nor female: for ye are all one in Christ Jesus."*

CHAPTER 8

The Forgiveness of Mary Magdalene

Previous page: *Mary Magdalen,* by Carlo Dolci

CHAPTER 8

The Forgiveness of Mary Magdalene

Mary Magdalene: Personification of the Soul

In Mary Magdalene, we see all aspects of our own soul awareness. We see that feminine potential all the way from the point of Eve—I, *Eva*—"the mother of all living,"[1] to Mary who became the Mother of God. We see Woman's consciousness from her descent to the testings and temptations of Eve to her ascent through the initiations of Mary.

It is the blessed Mother who summons women of the twenty-first century to their own revolution in higher consciousness. By following in her footsteps, women set the standards for a way of life that protects the rights of the soul within the family and the community to pursue the path of a creative Self-realization. She teaches Woman to mother the Christ consciousness in her children and in her beloved. For it is the privilege of every woman to give birth to the potential of the Real Self first in herself, second in her husband, third in her children and fourth in her community.

And so the soul moves from that point of Eve's creating anything and everything, releasing any kind of vibration whatsoever, to that point of Mother Mary's Christly discrimination, creating only after the inner blueprint of that only begotten Son of God, that Christ-potential that is the gift not to one but to all sons and daughters of God.

The Need for Forgiveness

In defining love, the love that must be realized through the soul, we consider three episodes in the life of Mary Magdalene. These three episodes can be described as: (1) "Mary Magdalene washes the feet of Jesus"—to believe on the Lord Christ who lives in one another and serve him by lovingly serving each other, (2) "Go and sin no more"—the remorseful soul calls upon the law of forgiveness, accepts the grace of God through the indwelling Christ and must now assume greater responsibility to integrate with the Law, (3) "The recognition of the risen Christ"—that development of the feminine principle that enables the soul to recognize and acknowledge the Christ as her teacher and master.

And they represent three episodes in our own life that we also must experience as individuals. To get from the place of Eve's soul awareness to the soul awareness of Mary the Mother, we must reinstate within ourselves conformity to the inner blueprint. In order to do this, we require forgiveness.

We have forgotten the meaning of grace. We know not the scientific use of the law of Christ: the law of forgiveness. Without it we cannot pursue our fiery destiny. We cannot define our individual and national goals. We don't know where we're going because we don't know where we've come from. We are not correctly defining our policies within or our policies without. We do not know how to release the flow of love because love, as pure love, cannot come forth until we are cleansed by Christ.

There has been a great rejection of organized religion. The concept of confession and forgiveness of sins is repugnant to many. Some say, "Why should we go through a human being to experience forgiveness? We can go directly to God. How can a man and a mortal who is a sinner himself be the instrument of forgiveness?" We experience many dilemmas—the challenging of the authority of Church and State and the demand for greater standards of morality, honor and integration in both.

"Come now, and let us reason together, saith the LORD."[2] We have much to consider. We find that many of our woes and our wants concerning authority around us are resolved in the teachings of the Great White Brotherhood. Let us consider the law of forgiveness as Jesus taught and demonstrated it, for this is the point of beginning.

Christ, the Forgiver

Who is the great forgiver of all? It is Christ. We must know, then, who is Christ. Christ is not Jesus alone; Christ is the potential of the Real Self in us all. It is the potential toward which the soul is moving. And therefore, we have a priest of the sacred fire within ourselves—our own Christ Self. And to that Christ Self we run for forgiveness. In this, the Beloved's name, we cry out to the Father and he answers us through his Son.

Let us consider, then, how Jesus defined what the Father would forgive and what the Father would not forgive. It is made very clear in the teachings that are set forth in the New Testament—forgive us our trespasses against the law of thy being in the same manner in which we forgive (or do not forgive) those who trespass against the law of our own being.[3]

Three Episodes in the Life of Mary Magdalene: The First Episode: Mary Magdalene Washes the Feet of Jesus

The law of forgiveness first is taught by Jesus at the house of Simon, a Pharisee.

And one of the Pharisees desired him that he would eat with him. And he went into the Pharisee's house, and sat down to meat. And, behold, a woman in the city, which was a sinner, when she knew that Jesus sat at meat in the Pharisee's house, brought an alabaster box of ointment, and stood at his feet behind him weeping, and began to wash his feet with tears, and did wipe them with the hairs of her head, and kissed his feet, and anointed them with the ointment.

Now when the Pharisee which had bidden him saw it, he spake within himself, saying, "This man, if he were a prophet, would have known who and what manner of woman this is that toucheth him: for she is a sinner." And Jesus answering said unto him, "Simon, I have somewhat to say unto thee." And he saith, "Master, say on."

"There was a certain creditor which had two debtors: the one owed five hundred pence, and the other fifty. And when they had nothing to pay, he frankly forgave them both. Tell me therefore, which of them will love him most?"

Simon answered and said, "I suppose that he, to whom he forgave most." And he said unto him, "Thou hast rightly judged."

And he turned to the woman, and said unto Simon, "Seest thou this woman? I entered into thine house, thou gavest me no water for my feet: but she hath washed my feet with tears, and wiped them with the hairs of her head. Thou gavest me no kiss: but this woman since the time I came in hath not ceased to kiss my feet. My head with oil thou didst not anoint: but this woman hath anointed my feet with ointment. Wherefore I say unto thee, Her sins, which are many, are forgiven; for she loved much: but to whom little is forgiven, the

The Penitence of the Magdalen, by Giovanni da Milano

same loveth little."

And he said unto her, "Thy sins are forgiven."

And they that sat at meat with him began to say within themselves, "Who is this that forgiveth sins also?"

And he said to the woman, "Thy faith hath saved thee; go in peace."[4]

This weeping at the feet of Jesus is the soul in remorse, in a state of penance for the misuse of energy. It is the soul, the feminine part of being, who has recognized her lord and master, her Guru in her twin flame.

When in his heart Simon challenged Jesus' authority because he allowed the sinner to touch him, Jesus taught him the Law: She who loves much is forgiven much; she who loves little is forgiven little.

The Law is plain. The penitent heart of society's condemned sinner was moved to intense love for Christ. This love became a prayer of deeds. Her first deed—an act of faith—was her unconditional acceptance of the one sent, the Messiah come, as her personal Saviour (Guru). Her second deed—an act of loving obedience—was personal service to the Master. Her devotion to the Person of Christ was her way of calling upon the law of forgiveness; she understood that Jesus was the embodiment of the Law come in the person of the Teacher.

In this instance, Jesus clarifies the requirements of the law of forgiveness—the law of grace that is sent by the Father and mediated by the Son. He gives the teaching embodying the principle of the will of the Father by faith in and obedience to his living Word. Here faith has become love and love has increased faith.

The Master pronounces his benediction upon Woman's first initiation: "Thy faith hath saved thee; go in peace." Believe on the Lord Christ who lives in one another and serve him by serving each other in love according to the greatest needs of the hour.

The Second Episode: "Go and Sin No More"

> *The scribes and Pharisees brought unto him a woman taken in adultery.*[5]

The scribes and the Pharisees represent the previous two-thousand-year dispensation under the cycle of Aries.[6] They had received the law from Moses. They were in the consciousness of the law and the interpretation of the law. They did not understand the identity of their prophets and teachers in Christ. They didn't see the Christ in their teachers; therefore they could not accept the Christ in themselves or in Jesus. They did not understand grace, the grace of the Person of the Son of God that is the mitigating factor of the law.

And so they challenged him:

> *This woman was taken in adultery, in the very act.*[7]

Jesus and the Woman Taken in Adultery, by Gustave Doré

They sought to trap Jesus. They wanted to be sure he understood the law.

> *"Now Moses in the law commanded us, that such should be stoned: but what sayest thou?" This they said, tempting him, that they might have to accuse him. But Jesus stooped down, and with his finger wrote on the ground as though he heard them not.*
>
> *So when they continued asking him, he lifted up himself, and said unto them, "He that is without sin among you, let him first cast a stone at her." And again he stooped down, and wrote on the ground.*[8]

What was he writing on the ground? He was writing the higher Law. He was writing the record of their own adulterous consciousness and their own sin and the sins committed in previous incarnations. They saw what he wrote on the ground.

They saw that he knew the Law, that he perceived the record of their sins that he read in akasha.

> *And they which heard it, being convicted by their own conscience, went out one by one, beginning at the eldest, even unto the last: and Jesus was left alone, and the woman standing in the midst.*[9]

Jesus *the Christ,* the Christ Self of Jesus and the Christ as your Real Self, is the Great Mediator of the Law. Without the Christ as the Saviour of us all, nothing stands between us and the absolute Law of the absolute Lawgiver. We are under the absolute Law; and if we sin against that Law, without him we have no recourse. Because we stepped out of the way of the Garden of cosmic consciousness, God provided that intermediary, that Christ Self. And so the Christ Self becomes the interpreter of the Law. The Christ Self, then, is the aspect of the Great God Self that can extend forgiveness.

Jesus Christ was a priest after the order of Melchizedek.[10] He came to reestablish the Melchizedekian order. He has ordained your own Christ Self as the representative of his own priesthood. You may therefore in his name confess your sins before the inner priest, the hidden man of the heart who dwells forever in your own Holy of holies.

> *When Jesus had lifted up himself, and saw none but the woman, he said unto her, "Woman, where are those thine accusers? hath no man condemned thee?" She said, "No man, Lord." And Jesus said unto her, "Neither do I condemn thee: Go, and sin no more."*[11]

Jesus was also aware of the vulnerability of the lesser self to err. He was aware of his own past incarnations when he manifested less than the totality of the Christ consciousness. How could he condemn in another what he himself could be subject to or may have been subject to? Furthermore it is written: "For God sent not his Son into the world to condemn the world; but that the world through him might be saved."[12] Jesus is much more concerned with the saving of the soul than with her condemnation. So should we be.

This is the illumination of the Great Law that comes to the disciples of the enlightened ones—Jesus, Gautama, Maitreya, Kuthumi, Lanto, Confucius, Meru and Padma Sambhava, to name a few—who have taught that the law of forgiveness necessitates the forsaking of sin through understanding the lower self and the Higher Self. This episode illustrates the teaching of the World Teachers and avatars that embodies the principle of the wisdom of the Son.

Just after this episode recorded by John, Jesus makes the revolutionary statement: "I AM the light of the world: he that followeth me shall not walk in darkness, but shall have the light of life."[13]

His teaching to Mary Magdalene is this: "Because I have realized the I AM He consciousness, because the I AM THAT I AM is where I AM—as Above, so below, Being is congruent where I AM—this Word incarnate in me is the I AM who sustains the light of God on behalf of all of earth's evolutions. Therefore, I AM the embodied authority of the Law, hence the forgiver of sin—i.e., the one who transmutes the law of sin that you yourself have set in motion and that now binds you. You may retain this forgiveness only so long as you maintain that level of my Christ consciousness that is required of my disciples. In the heightened awareness of your Real Self, go and sin no more."

In this initiation, the individual assumes greater responsibility to personify the Law. To retain the grace of the Guru, he must be willing to make the sacrifices necessary to embody a portion of that grace. No longer does he walk by faith alone or simply by trusting, loving obedience. Now he must integrate with the Law and the Lawgiver through understanding and through acceptance of a personal commitment to witness both to his Teacher and to the teaching by his words and his works.

The Bible speaks about the casting of the seven devils out of Mary Magdalene.[14] The seven devils represent the seven deadly sins, or compromises of the energy of the seven chakras (see page 83). We as individual souls have sinned also. We have misused the light of the seven rays of God, the seven planes of the Christ consciousness, that are intended to be anchored in these chakras.

Paul said: "All have sinned, and come short of the glory of God."[15] This is not condemnation. This is not the wrath of God. This is a necessary understanding of our present state of evolution—so self-limiting—in order that we may take the necessary steps for our soul's restoration to the state of grace—i.e., oneness with God through Christ Jesus, the Mediator of our personal Christhood.

The very first step, then, on the path of initiation—unless you are a perfected one, unless you have balanced one hundred percent of your karma—is the call for forgiveness. The soul must be rescued from the self-made laws of sin and death by the Christ or she cannot begin the Path.

Forgiveness is the setting aside by the law of individual Christhood of the energies misqualified in the misuse of the sacred fire that is God. When that energy is set aside, then the soul is free to move Godward, to move toward the Christ consciousness. When the soul grows in stature and in the wisdom of the Christ, then with that self-mastery, she is free to balance the karma that has been temporarily set aside by the grace of our Lord. And our Lord is our Christ Self, personified in Jesus and many other ascended masters who have walked in his footsteps and fulfilled the requirement for personal Christhood and the ascension.

Forgiveness, then, is not the wiping out of sin (karma); it is the setting aside of sin (karma) for the purpose of allowing our souls to expand in grace and understanding of the law of transmutation. When we reach a certain level of soul attainment, we are required to stand, face and conquer the weight of karma that has been temporarily held in abeyance while we attained a certain spiritual maturity.

The great gift of salvation through Jesus Christ is that he, as the Piscean avatar, took upon himself the sins of the world— i.e., world karma—until the world through him might accept the Christ within as the individual redeemer. Through that inner Christ—or Logos, the creative Word incarnate in all sons and daughters of God—the individual invokes the sacred fire of the Holy Ghost, which now consumes the sin set aside, transmuting the darkness of the misqualified energy of previous incarnations into the illuminating light that now becomes the Word made flesh[16] in us all.

The Third Episode: The Recognition of the Risen Christ

The third episode of Mary Magdalene is the initiation embodying the principle of the love of the Holy Spirit. It is the meeting on Easter morning of Mary, the chela, with her Guru. She is the first to see him out of the tomb because she has, at this point, that development of the feminine principle that enables her to see the risen Christ.

> *In the end of the sabbath, as it began to dawn toward the first day of the week, came Mary Magdalene and the other Mary to see the sepulchre.*
>
> *And, behold, there was a great earthquake: for the angel of the Lord descended from heaven, and came and rolled back the stone from the door, and sat upon it.*
>
> *His countenance was like lightning, and his raiment white as snow: and for fear of him the keepers did*

The Resurrection, by Gustave Doré

shake, and became as dead men.

And the angel answered and said unto the women, "Fear not ye: for I know that ye seek Jesus, which was crucified. He is not here: for he is risen, as he said. Come, see the place where the Lord lay. And go quickly, and tell his disciples that he is risen from the dead; and, behold, he goeth before you into Galilee; there shall ye see him: lo, I have told you."[17]

Then she runneth, and cometh to Simon Peter, and to the other disciple, whom Jesus loved, and saith unto them, "They have taken away the Lord out of the sepulchre, and we know not where they have laid him."

Peter therefore went forth, and that other disciple, and came to the sepulchre. So they ran both together: and the other disciple did outrun Peter, and came first to the sepulchre. And he stooping down, and looking in, saw the linen clothes lying; yet went he not in.

Then cometh Simon Peter following him, and went into the sepulchre, and seeth the linen clothes lie, and the napkin, that was about his head, not lying with the linen clothes, but wrapped together in a place by itself.

Then went in also that other disciple, which came first to the sepulchre, and he saw, and believed. For as yet they knew not the scripture, that he must rise again from the dead.

Then the disciples went away again unto their own home. But Mary stood without at the sepulchre weeping: and as she wept, she stooped down, and looked into the sepulchre, and seeth two angels in white sitting, the one at the head, and the other at the feet, where the body of Jesus had lain.

And they say unto her, "Woman, why weepest thou?" She saith unto them, "Because they have taken away my Lord, and I know not where they have laid him."

And when she had thus said, she turned herself back, and saw Jesus standing, and knew not that it was Jesus.

Jesus saith unto her, "Woman, why weepest thou? whom seekest thou?" She, supposing him to be the gardener, saith unto him, "Sir, if thou have borne him hence, tell me where thou hast laid him, and I will take him away."

Jesus saith unto her, "Mary." She turned herself, and saith unto him, "Rabboni"; which is to say, Master.

Jesus saith unto her, "Touch me not; for I am not

> *yet ascended to my Father: but go to my brethren, and say unto them, I ascend unto my Father, and your Father; and to my God, and your God."*
>
> *Mary Magdalene came and told the disciples that she had seen the Lord, and that he had spoken these things unto her.*[18]

Mary is weeping. She is looking for her Lord. He comes forth and he says unto her, "Mary." And with that word, he calls her "Mother ray"—*Ma-ray*. And when he ignites in her the flame of Mother, she then has the awareness to exclaim in profound recognition of his person, "Rabboni"—to acknowledge him as her teacher and her master. As we ourselves define love and the action of love, we will come to an understanding of these relationships.

Noli Me Tangere, mural by Fra Angelico

Here we see Jesus, now representing the risen Christ, his soul risen to the plane of Christ Self-awareness about to ascend to "my Father and your Father," to "my God and your God"—to the one God individualized as your I AM Presence and my I AM Presence.

In this painting of this event, we see depicted here our soul's relationship to the Spirit. Here is the soul kneeling before the Spirit. The soul has come to the threefold embodiment of the virtues of the Trinity: faith, enlightened hope and love. The soul will no longer be part of the adulterous generation, but she will be the manifestation of the abundant regeneration, giving birth to the Christ light.

What we must do, then, is to call upon the law of forgiveness. It is a legitimate law. We understand that in asking for forgiveness, we are asking for a cleansing—the cleansing of the chakras of the individual and the cleansing of the chakras of the nation. Until Christ has forgiven us, we constantly stand in fear of our accusers. Who are our accusers? Our accusers are the nations of the world and individuals within our own society, those who do not understand grace. They are still in the consciousness of the Pharisees.

We must accept the grace of God through the indwelling Christ. Hear his Word spoken unto thee: "'Thy faith hath saved thee; go in peace … Neither do I condemn thee, Go and sin no more'… Mother ray of the world, Enter into the abundant life and heal thyself and the nations of the earth as I have healed thee!"

Saint Germain,
by Charles Sindelar

We have to realize that the Christ consciousness—the Christ Self whom we see personified in Jesus and in Saint Germain[19]—in order to forgive, must "unsee" the wrong, must realize that every misqualification of energy can be transmuted by the sacred fire of the Holy Ghost, whose very Person appears to us in the violet flame. This transmutation can take place—which means that all that is created in time and space, when it is passed through the violet flame[20] (the veritable flame of forgiveness) can be transmuted into love and into the Christ consciousness by the release of that sacred fire of the heart.

The Acceptance of Forgiveness

We, then, must begin with forgiveness so that we can get on with self-mastery in the levels of the chakras, so we can anoint the feet and the head of Christ—i.e., prepare the blessed sons and daughters of God for their initiations of the crucifixion, the resurrection and the ascension. We must walk this path as Mary Magdalene. We must believe that we can be purified, that we can become whole, that we can be restored and be regenerated.

And what is the key to this? It is the acceptance of forgiveness and the fact that there is a Principle, a Person, a God, a Christ, a flame, an energy—the Holy Spirit. It is a mathematics and it is a science. It is a consciousness. And when we make contact with it, the Holy Spirit releases the light of God for the clearing and the cleansing. And this, too, is the fulfillment of prophecy that "though your sins be as scarlet, they shall be as white as snow; though they be red like crimson, they shall be as wool."[21] White as snow, white as wool, white as the sacred fire of the noonday sun—this is the promise of the prophets of the Old Testament to us today.

We cannot rise, we cannot hold our heads high, we cannot look ahead to define love until we get through this crux, this nexus, of the law of forgiveness. Because we have rejected mortals as the instruments of forgiveness, we have failed to seek forgiveness. But beyond the mortal is the immortal, the Shining One.

Do you know how good it feels when you go to a friend and tell that friend that you have done something wrong that you are ashamed of, and the friend says to you, "That's all right; we're still friends"? That's the action of the Christ in that friend. And when you can confide something that is of great shame and a source of great self-condemnation to someone that you love and that someone can still love you, it makes you feel that there is hope, that God still loves you, and you can pick up the pieces and you can carry on. So the Christ of each of us is able to forgive not only sin in ourselves but in all, when we appeal to that Christ.

I find that it is a tremendous experience for me to look at the life of Mary Magdalene, because until we come into the love of Christ, there is yet the carnal-minded side of us that takes the side of the Pharisees, that sees her as a woman of ill-repute, that does not equate her with Mary, the Mother of Jesus, or other holy women. And we tend to tie into the mass consciousness of condemnation—and of course, that condemnation is then heaped upon our own heads.

And so in order for us even to experience the forgiveness of Mary Magdalene, we have to grow in love. We have to realize that she was worthy to be equal with the Christ—yes, this position of co-equality he gave to her as a soul, as a woman and as his disciple and dear friend. Because she accepted the Christ in him, he acknowledged the Mother flame in her as not only the soul forgiven but now as the initiate on the same Path that he was walking. We have to realize that we can rise as Mary Magdalene. We can rise in the name of the Lord who is risen within us.

CHAPTER 9

A Revolution of Theology in the Making

CHAPTER 9

A Revolution of Theology in the Making

Was Jesus Married?

As we previously said, there have emerged in best-selling books many theories that could start a revolution in theology. While we neither affirm nor deny this research, we feel we should present these theories to the reader for your meditation.

These authors say that Jesus may have been taken down from the cross before he was dead, wrapped in myrrh and aloes and laid in a tomb, and that he survived the ordeal with the assistance of healers in the Essene community. They have proposed that Jesus arranged events so that there would be the appearance that he had died, and he could thereby make his exit from the scene by this means—by going through the crucifixion and then disappearing from Palestine.

Their theory is that Jesus may have been married to Mary Magdalene, and that after the crucifixion, his wife and off-spring, and perhaps Jesus himself, were smuggled by ship out of the Holy Land, traveled to Marseilles, found refuge in a Jewish community in southern France in the vicinity of

Languedoc, and there preserved the Saviour's bloodline, which has survived to the present.[1]

Interestingly, Islamic and Indian sources assert that Jesus survived the crucifixion, lived a long life and died in Kashmir or somewhere in the East.[2] We have other evidence that Jesus taught for many years after the crucifixion, went to Kashmir, and ascended at the age of eighty-one.[3]

In addition, there is historical evidence that some of Jesus' disciples traveled to France after the crucifixion. According to the apocryphal Acts of Magdalene and local traditions, Lazarus settled in Marseilles, Mary Magdalene went to Aix-en-Provence, and Martha lived in Tarascon. A church of St. Martha that stands today in Tarascon bears witness to the long-standing belief that she had a ministry there. Marseilles, Aix, and Tarascon are all about 140 miles from the hamlet of Rennes-le-Château, where some traditions claim Jesus' tomb is located.*

While these theories may or may not be true, we *can* attest to the fact that Jesus and Mary Magdalene were twin flames—in heaven and in earth.[4] Whatever happened between them may not be written in the history books, and I don't profess to know myself, but it wouldn't matter to me. It wouldn't in any way detract from the Saviour if he had married Mary Magdalene and had children, because his power and magnitude is not based on how he chose to have his relationship with her.

A Flesh-and-Blood Concept of Christianity

If it were true that Jesus was taken down from the cross before he died, it would make no difference to our understanding of the crucifixion, the resurrection and the ascension.

---

* However, other sources say Jesus' tomb is in Kashmir.

Take care that you do not indulge in a flesh-and-blood religion. You need to understand that one day all of us will lay down this physical temple. And if you are a true disciple of God and have walked in his ways and fulfilled the requirements of the Law, you, too, can be resurrected—which simply means that your soul in the etheric body, now your soul wed to Christ, is infilled with the spiraling of the resurrection flame. It means the threefold flame expands, and you are the living presence of that threefold flame bodily. It is no longer one-sixteenth of an inch in height within your heart. It fills your entire temple.

You need to understand that your etheric body is more solid, more real, more vibrant, more fiery than the physical body you wear. This is a mere vehicle for a time. Your sense of immortality and of everlasting life is not wed to the flesh, nor is your attainment, nor is the ascension process. In the process of the ascension, the physical body dissolves and the etheric body appears, and the Christ Self is one with the etheric body as you are one with that Christ Self (see Chart of Your Divine Self, page 80). And you live forevermore with not a vestige of the clay vessel.

The resurrection, the ascension and the transfiguration, as well as the crucifixion, are all spiritual initiations. To some they happen physically; to some people they happen on a spiritual level. Mark Prophet did not ascend physically. He was not resurrected physically. It is the soul within the finer body that resurrects.

Paul says, "flesh and blood cannot inherit the kingdom of God.... This corruptible must put on incorruption, and this mortal must put on immortality."[5]

Mark L. Prophet

We wear bodies of clay that were designed for this octave. Remember that, because otherwise, if the physical body of the messengers or of yourself or your friend or someone you think is holy doesn't do what you think it should do, you can be disillusioned. Some of the greatest saints died of cancer, and there was nothing particularly sinful about them. They took upon their bodies world karma.

The orthodox concepts—of Matthew and Luke especially and the early apostles such as Peter—have wed Christendom to a very physical religion. Everything becomes very physical. The virgin birth becomes very physical. And all of the proofs of the sanctity and the sainthood of Mother Mary and Jesus are given physical explanations. Orthodoxy cannot accept the law of reincarnation. They cannot see the evolution of the soul of the Son of man when he was David, king of Israel, or Joseph, the eleventh son of Jacob, and later Jesus. They cannot accept the Holy Spirit flowing through him and the Word itself as the mark and the sign of the Son of God.

From its very roots the concepts of Christianity, which we have accepted from childhood, wed us to a flesh-and-blood concept. They sing on Easter morning "Up From the Grave He Arose" with a mighty triumph. We should say that the victory is that he did not die again thirty or fifty years later or forty days later. He had demonstrated that the Son of God may call the threefold flame back to the physical temple and the heart may beat again.[6]

Reports of Jesus' Second Journey to the East

When you think of the very logic of what Jesus would accomplish in his life, would he not go to every corner of the earth? What about other years that we know nothing about? We previously said that the Catholic theologian Irenaeus says that Jesus was teaching well beyond his resurrection. This is in Catholic writings. It is nothing that we have invented. The ancient text Pistis Sophia says the same: he was with his disciples after his resurrection.

Some say also that Jesus returned to the East and specifically to Kashmir after his crucifixion. The Acts of Thomas tell us that Jesus sent his apostle Thomas to India, and ancient tradition credits Thomas for the conversion of India and Mesopotamia to Christianity.[7]

There may also be truth in the legends that after the crucifixion and after his healing by the Essenes and his many appearances to his disciples, Jesus left with a small band of companions and again journeyed East, eventually settling in Kashmir.* Scholars in Kashmir have explored the historical records of a first-century holy man named Yuzu Asaph who came from Palestine and whose tomb at Anzimar can still be visited, and they agree that he may well be Jesus.[8]

We do not know the breadth and the extent of the work of Jesus or in what state he was. Was he in the resurrected state, the ascended state, as he gave the revelation to John the Beloved on the isle of Patmos, as he talked with the apostle Paul? When does it ever end?

Well, the truth of it is that it never ends. Jesus has never left off being the World Teacher. He is continuing to teach you and me to this very hour. Open your heart and know that

---

* These legends conflict with the theories that Jesus and his disciples sailed to France and ministered there. We leave it to the reader to draw your own conclusion from your meditations.

through your own Holy Christ Self, the voice of God is speaking to you. This Son of God, Jesus, who is the great Master of the age, desires you to know all of the truth that he spoke in those brief years in Palestine, that he gave during forty days with his disciples in the Upper Room. Were they not written down or have we just not found them yet? What are those mystery teachings to the inner circle? Could those twelve disciples really be the only ones that Jesus ever wanted to have his teaching directly?

Jesus is your teacher. And he even told you he would always be your teacher because he promised to send another Comforter,[9] and that Comforter is the descent of the Spirit and the Person of the Holy Ghost. He said that this Comforter would bring to our remembrance "all things whatsoever I have said unto you."[10] Well, he was speaking to us all. Jesus has been teaching us for two thousand years.

He is the great exemplar who embodied in his life and work the highest manifestation of God, looked to and long awaited by all the world's religions.

That is why I am come only to awaken you to what you already know inside of your heart and soul, connecting you with your higher consciousness where the record is of your union with the Master.

And there are also many
other things which Jesus did,
the which, if they should be
written every one, I suppose
that even the world itself
could not contain the books
that should be written…

John

EPILOGUE

The Universal Divine Feminine

Whether man elects to probe the far reaches of interplanetary and intergalactic life or to traverse the forcefields of atoms, molecules and cells within the heart of the earth, he must understand that the exploration of the material universe is the exploration of the body of the Divine Mother. Matter in all her glory is revealed through telescopic and microscopic probes and through journeys in consciousness to the uttermost parts of creation. Though he traverse the heavens and the earth from subconscious to superconscious realms, man cannot escape the folds of her consciousness. Wherever he goes, he is caught in the vast network of her sentient Being, and he discovers more of the eternal Father through her compelling ministration.

Lack of contact with the divine Mother, resulting in an unbalanced manifestation of her flame, is the underlying cause of all functional disorders occurring at physical, mental, emotional and etheric levels of man's experience. As the superconscious mind governs the spiritual aspect of man's being through the father image, so the subconscious mind (including the etheric body and the electronic belt)[1] governs the material aspect through the mother image. Since man's subconscious is preeminently feminine (in that it is the passive receiver of the active impressions of man's being), the soul, or psyche, which evolves through man's subconscious (which contains all of the records of his conscious and superconscious experiences) is likewise polarized to the Matter principle.

Just as the worship of God as Father has dominated religious thought for many centuries, so in the next cycle, the appreciation of God as both Father and Mother will provide the theme on an ascended master philosophy and way of life. This promises to be an era of perfecting the precipitation of Spirit in and as Matter, as man takes dominion over the four elements—fire, air, water and earth—which represent the four planes of God's androgynous consciousness whose cycles man must master prior to his reunion with the God Self.

Through the worship of the Motherhood of God and the elevation in society of the functions of the feminine aspect of the Deity, science and religion will reach the apex, and man will discover the Spirit of God as the flame enshrined upon the altar of his own being even as he discovers the Matter of God in the cradle of nature. Moreover, through the enlightenment of the Divine Theosophia, he will accept his role as the living Christ—the seed of the Divine Woman.

Civilization remains on a downward spiral today because we have not realized that we have lost the flame of Mother and without it we have no cohesive force, no central nucleus whereby to draw the tremendous momentum of Spirit that is required to rebuild a new order of the ages.

The separation we feel from God is only by our neglect to realize that God is right here in the person who is nearest us. And it is the flame within that being, it is the soul within that being, it is the consciousness and the evolving self that we adore as the element of God's own expanding consciousness. This truly is the message of the ascended masters.

The symbol of God as a person is most essential, because as we meditate upon the personal personality of God, which the Mother is, we then put on the characteristics, the virtues of that person. As we meditate upon these many manifestations, regardless of their names or their attributes, we realize that one and all they represent to us that God is Mother—that God has taken a portion of himself, placed that portion in flesh, into the Matter universe, to mother our souls.

Mother is the personification, then, of primal elements that are named in the second verse of Genesis, "the Spirit of God moving upon the face of the waters." The Universal Divine Feminine appears in a multitude of guises, for the possibilities of Matter creation are innumerable. The many guises of the Mother become the testing of our souls.

One of these guises is Mother Mary, the daughter of God who realized the supreme Motherhood of God in her communion with Father, Son and Holy Spirit. Mother Mary is the daughter of the Father, the Mother of the Son and the bride of the Holy Spirit. She then becomes the *Shakti,* the active principle in the Matter plane of the Trinity that is represented in Spirit. She becomes the Mother of Quadrants—through her heart flow the energies of the four seasons.

If we can say with complete love and purity and adoration, "I accept Mother Mary as the incarnation of God as Mother," then we can begin the path of our own initiation to say, "And I too can become God as Mother."

This is the healing that we require in the West. Until we as a part of Western civilization can become the Mother, we see that the Mother flame will be missing from our government, from our economy, from our education. All of the religion and the science and the communion with the Trinity that she teaches will be absent. Without the Mother flame as the center spiral of every area of life, that life crumbles, that life decays, because it has not the cohesive power of the Mother flame to endure.

The Mother in the Matter cosmos is the focal point of the Trinity. She, then, carries the energies of Spirit. Unless she becomes the center of our life, we do not have that permanent energy, that permanent atom of God made manifest so that we, too, can realize the Selfhood as Mother and go on to become the Trinity. The Mother, then, is known in the Catholic Church as the intercessor. She intercedes for us before Father, Son and Holy Spirit because she is closest to us. She is the direct link between us and our God consciousness. She is even closer than the Son because she is the Mother of the Son.

The Buddha's teaching to us is actually the religion of the Mother. And so is the teaching of Jesus Christ. It is the religion of Mother, the religion of compassionate regard for one another and compassionate regard for God incarnate. That is the entire basis of Christianity. It is the way Mother would have us relate to one another—as God, as Christ.

By contrast to this dichotomy that we find in the West, in the East the Mother holds an equal position with the Trinity of Brahma, Vishnu and Shiva as she manifests herself as the consort or the complement of each one. We find, then, that the equality of the sexes has been inherent in Hinduism and in Buddhism for thousands upon thousands of years, whereas in the religion of the West we find that the male figure still has predominance; and our clear-cut understanding of what the Mother is and what she can become, what is her potential, is not clearly defined.

It would be clearly defined if we would change our understanding of Mother Mary. She is the archetype of the twenty-first-century woman. She is the archetype of the practical woman, of the scientist, of the priestess, of the mother, of the one who understands our innermost being; but we have Mother Mary pocketed into a doctrine and a dogma of a religion that may not necessarily be our own. Mother Mary is not unique to Catholicism. She is unique only to the cosmos. She belongs to each and every one of us, and she cares for us and nourishes the Mother flame within us.

I have written this book in the hope of calling all souls back to the altar of God within our hearts, both as supplicants and as priests. The gender of the body we wear does not determine the fitness of our souls to be a servant at the altar of God. But the quality of our spirit, our heart and our mind does. I am and have been for forty years a priest at the altar of my own church. But when I am at the altar, I don't identify myself as male or female. I remember the words of Saint Paul, *"There is neither Jew nor Greek, there is neither bond nor free, there is neither male nor female: for ye are all one in Christ Jesus."*

Elizabeth Clare Prophet

Mary Magdalene's Memorial

Verily I say unto you, Wheresoever this gospel shall be preached throughout the whole world, this also that she hath done shall be spoken of for a memorial of her. Mark 14:9

These words of Jesus have certainly been fulfilled in the last two thousand years. In fact, writes Edith Filliette, "The giants of Christian literature have remembered her with infinite love and reverence in their writings. St. Gregory the Great, St. Jerome, St. Augustine, St. Teresa of Avila, St. Bernard, St. Bonaventure, St. Peter Chrysologus, Blessed Rabanus Maurus, and numerous others have left testimonials to her greatness.

"The painters and sculptors, commissioned by Popes, Bishops and Kings to adorn their palaces and churches, have immortalized Mary Magdalene in masterpieces that can be admired in our time. The extraordinary events of her life have been unforgettably portrayed by Giotto, Fra Angelico, Michelangelo, Botticelli, Veronese, Rubens, Titian, Caravaggio, El Greco, and dozens more. And her name graces poems, hymns and prayers, and the splendid oratorios that fill the halls of music and Cathedrals throughout the world."[1]

Questions and Answers

Questions and Answers

The discoveries of the Gnostic texts found at Nag Hammadi in 1945 and the Dead Sea Scrolls found at Qumran in 1947 have opened new perspectives on Christianity that are radically different from what is presented in the New Testament. You have read in the earlier pages of this book author and theologian Elizabeth Clare Prophet's interpretations of Jesus' lost teaching on Woman and of some of the fundamental issues that helped to shape Christianity and the early Church. Her views may seem questionable or even heretical to some; however, we present them with the hope that the reader will ponder them with an open heart and mind.

Mrs. Prophet does not stand alone in reinterpreting Christianity, Mary Magdalene and Jesus' teaching on Woman. If you have been seeking Mary Magdalene amidst today's best sellers, you may already be familiar with authors such as Margaret Starbird, Lynn Picknett, Ean Begg, Laurence Gardner, Karen King, Susan Haskins and others.

While this author and her editors do not necessarily endorse or support the views of these or other authors, we present excerpts of their work here as we offer answers to questions often asked about some of the mysteries of history: Joseph of Arimathea and the Grail legends, the Black Madonna and the two Marys. And the reader may find an extraordinary question and answer or two about Jesus.

The texts discovered in the last century have given new insights into the origins of Christianity. Who knows what else may be awaiting discovery, buried beneath the shifting sands of the desert, deep in caves, in forgotten libraries—or in the very heart of man?

Let us be willing to build upon the evidence as we know it, and yet leave space for progressive revelation as we proceed on this fascinating quest for Truth.

The Editors

I

Following the Grail

What Part Does Joseph of Arimathea Play in the Grail Legends and the Life of Mary Magdalene?

While many recent sources chronicle Mary Magdalene in France, we offer this unique account of Joseph of Arimathea transporting her to France.

After his resurrection, Jesus had commissioned the apostles: "Ye shall be witnesses unto me both in Jerusalem, and in all Judaea, and in Samaria, and unto the uttermost part of the earth."[1] How did they fulfill this calling? Where did the inner circle go? The Bible is largely silent about any of the apostles other than Peter and Paul. However, other sources enable us to piece together some of the lost history of Mary Magdalene and those early followers of Jesus.

Central to many of these sources is Joseph of Arimathea, who appears only briefly in the New Testament, but who plays a crucial role in the events of the Passion Week.

Glastonbury is 3,300 miles from Jerusalem, yet according to the legacy of Arthurian tales, Joseph of Arimathea traveled the distance soon after the crucifixion, carrying the Holy Grail. Joseph is something of a mystery man in the New

Testament. After the crucifixion of Jesus, he suddenly appears on the scene, boldly asks Pilate for Jesus' body, winds it in linen cloth, lays it in what may be his own tomb and disappears. There are stories about him, not found in the Gospels, that only add to the mystery. Legend has it that Joseph took the cup from which Jesus drank at the Last Supper and brought it to Glastonbury, which was then an island in southwest England. Thus begins the legend of the Holy Grail.

There is a body of evidence surrounding the Grail—archaeological fact, ancient legend and tradition being brought to the forefront by contemporary scholars and authors—which is hard to dismiss. Even if this material be only partially true, the questions it raises, the assertions it makes are hard to ignore.

Whether fact or fantasy, the Holy Grail has been a persistent thread in our psyche, an archetypal image finally ensconced as a modern-day metaphor.

It is worth our while to trace the concept of the fabled Grail as carried by Joseph of Arimathea back to its earliest origins, to pick up one end of the cord—like a miner's clue—that leads into the mists of time to the mysteries surrounding the fabled Isle of Avalon ... and follow the Grail.

We have a brief sketch of Joseph of Arimathea from the Gospels. He was a rich man and a respected member of the Sanhedrin who refused to consent to the condemnation of Jesus. He was also "a disciple of Jesus, but secretly for fear of the Jews."[2]

A number of the legends agree that Joseph received the vessel that was later to be known as the Holy Grail and after a certain period of time, either he or his relations took it to England. But they differ on key points, including how Joseph obtained the Grail.

The Journey to Glastonbury

Ancient and deep-rooted traditions say that Joseph came to Glastonbury.

In his Ecclesiastical Annals, a sixteenth-century work, Cardinal Caesar Baronius, an historian and librarian to the Vatican, stated that those who accompanied Joseph were "the two Bethany sisters, Mary and Martha; their brother Lazarus; Saint Eutropius; Saint Salome; Saint Cleon; Saint Saturninus; Saint Mary Magdalene; Marcella, the maid of the Bethany sisters; Saint Maxim or Maximin; Saint Martial; Saint Trophimus; Restitutus, the man who was born blind." And he also says that "Mary the mother of Jesus undoubtedly was not left behind."*

These disciples, with Joseph, left Palestine during the period of persecution that followed the crucifixion.

According to tradition, Joseph and his band were cast adrift by the Sanhedrin without sail or oars, near Caesarea, a city north of Jerusalem. They came ashore safely at the North African city of Cyrene. There the group of disciples obtained sails and oars. Following Phoenician trade routes, they traveled to Marseilles, France. Crossing France to the Atlantic coast, they continued onward by the trade routes to Cornwall.

They then, by one account, traveled overland from Cornwall or, by another, sailed around Land's End on the southwestern tip of England, followed the west coast of Britain north to the Severn sea, entered the estuaries of the Parrett and Brue rivers, and sailed twelve miles inward on the Brue, arriving at a cluster of islands, which, according to tradition, was Joseph's destination—Glastonbury. The weary

---

* We also have conflicting research that says that Mary the Mother of Jesus went with John, the Beloved apostle, to Ephesus and was buried there. Additional reports say that she went to Kashmir with Jesus and show pictures of her tomb at Murree.

Mary Magdalene Traveling to France

pilgrims were welcomed to Glastonbury by King Arviragus, a first-century king of the Silurian dynasty in Britain. They began building huts for themselves on the island to which Arviragus gave them title.

According to Hardynge's Chronicle (a fifteenth-century document based on a much earlier work), Arviragus granted "twelve hides" of land—somewhere around 1,900 acres—tax-free to Joseph and his company in a place called Yniswitrin, a marshy tract later called the Isle of Avalon.

Partial confirmation of this royal charter was found in the official Domesday Book, the record of a massive economic survey made for tax purposes by order of William the Conqueror in 1086. It says, "The Domus Dei, in the great monastery of Glastonbury, called the Secret of the Lord. This Glastonbury Church possesses in its own villa XII hides of land which have never paid tax."

The First Christian Church in Britain

In his 1983 *Traditions of Glastonbury,* archaeologist and anthropologist E. Raymond Capt wrote that these pilgrims "erected what must have been the first Christian Church above ground. These early hutments would have been made from wattle daubed with mud and built in a circular form. From studies made by the late F. Bligh Bond, F.R.I.B.A. (member of the Somerset Archaeological Society and formerly director of excavations at Glastonbury Abbey), the first church was circular, having a diameter of 25 feet, with the twelve huts of the other disciples forming a circle around it."

In about A.D. 540, historian Maelgwyn of Avalon wrote in his *Historia de Rubus Britannicus,* "in this church they worshipped and taught the people the true Christian faith. After about fifteen years, Mary died and was buried at Glastonbury. The disciples died in succession and were buried in the cemetery."

By local tradition, Mary is buried in the old cemetery at Glastonbury Abbey beside the Lady Chapel dedicated to her. Through the centuries, the cemetery has been called variously the "holiest ground in earth," "the most hallowed spot in Christendom" and "the burial place of the saints."

After Mary's death, the tradition continues, a wattle church was built over her home. It was sixty feet long and twenty-six feet wide—dimensions that are said to approximate those of the Tabernacle. It was called the "Vetusta Ecclesia," or the "Old Church."

Was the journey even possible in those days? Can these traditions be confirmed by any other sources?

The search begins in Palestine where we pick up the thread of Joseph of Arimathea. A second-century document places him in Caesarea, his legendary point of departure. Reverend Lewis wrote:

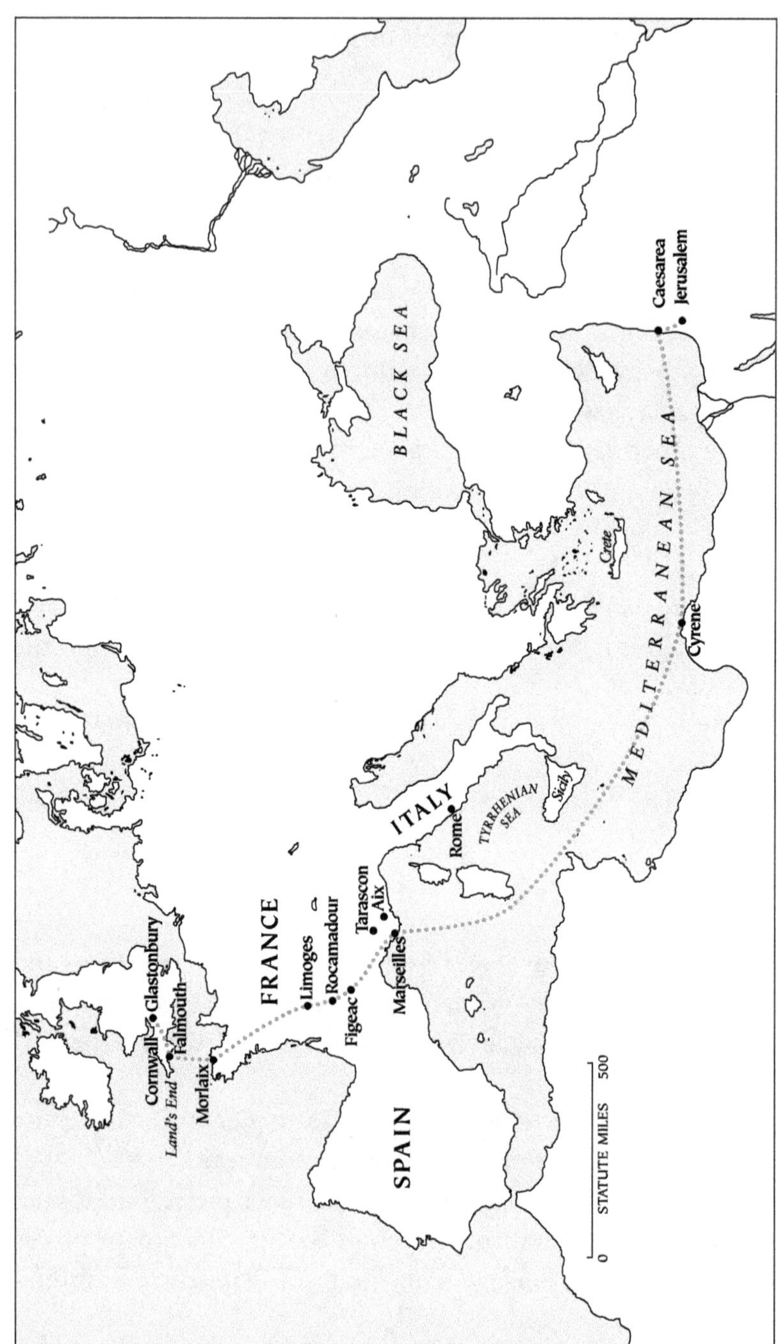
BLACK SEA
MEDITERRANEAN SEA
Caesarea
Jerusalem
Crete
Cyrene
Sicily
TYRRHENIAN SEA
ITALY
Rome
Tarascon
Aix
Marseilles
FRANCE
Limoges
Rocamadour
Figeac
Glastonbury
Falmouth
Cornwall
Land's End
Morlaix
SPAIN
0
STATUTE MILES
500

> The Recognitions of Clement—a second-century document tainted with Ebionite errors, probably based on an account by St. Clement of Rome (so Rufinus, who translated it in A.D. 410, thought) describes St. Barnabus and St. Clement going to Caesarea and finding there, among others, SS. Peter, Lazarus, the Holy Women, and St. Joseph of Arimathea! Here we find not only St. Joseph but some of the group whom we find later in the boat.

We may surmise that Joseph's influential position and devotion to the cause probably made him a leader in the early Church. Members of the church were forced to flee the "great persecution against the church which was at Jerusalem" recorded in Acts,[3] which followed the martyrdom of St. Stephen, about A.D. 35. "They were all scattered abroad throughout the regions of Judaea and Samaria, except the apostles," Acts continues. "Therefore they that were scattered abroad went every where preaching the word."[4]

The Ministry of the Saints

If the apostles were not the ones scattered, then who was? Traditions from Britain to the Mediterranean to India say it was the early saints—those who had been close to the Lord and part of his mission. A local tradition in Provence, France, tells of the scattering of a small group, among them Joseph of Arimathea. It says they sailed to Marseilles.

Their journey was possible in the historical framework of the time. Marseilles was a prosperous port under Roman protection. In fact, John William Taylor, author of *The Coming of the Saints: Imaginations and Studies in Early Church History and Tradition,* says that Marseilles and the provinces around it "became the favourite emigration ground of Rome, and generation after generation of Romans traded here, lived here, made their fortunes here, and died here." Doubtless, ships regularly made the journey from the flourishing port of Caesarea to Marseilles.

The apocryphal Acts of Magdalen, or Life of St. Mary Magdalene, compiled in the eighth or ninth century by Rabanus Maurus, archbishop of Mainz, gives confirmation to the story.

> Leaving the shores of Asia ... they came near to the city of Marseilles, in the Viennoise province of the Gauls, where the River Rhone is received by the sea. There, having called upon God, the great King of all the world, they parted; each company going to the province where the Holy Spirit had directed them; presently preaching everywhere, "the Lord working with them, and confirming the word with signs following."

There is evidence of the saints' ministry in France. According to the Acts of Magdalen, Lazarus stayed in Marseilles, Mary Magdalene went to Aix with St. Maximin, and Martha went to Tarascon. This is corroborated by local tradition. Beneath the old church of St. Victor in Marseilles is a natural cave that is reputed to be Lazarus' refuge. At Aix, a relic of Mary Magdalene is preserved in the church of St. Maximin.

Relics believed to be St. Martha's are preserved in the town of Tarascon. A church of St. Martha and numerous traditions bear witness to the long-standing belief that her ministry was there. One story tells of the cure of King Clovis around A.D. 500 after a pilgrimage to St. Martha's tomb at Tarascon, and of his consequent gift to the church. Marseilles, Aix and Tarascon are all about 140 miles from the hamlet of Rennes-le-Château, where some traditions claim Jesus' tomb is located.*

---

* We also have reports of Jesus' tomb being located in Kashmir (see p. 281).

Tin Mining in Roman Times

Archaeological excavations at Glastonbury show that a village flourished there from 50 B.C. to about A.D. 80, a village whose inhabitants, according to Capt, "possessed the most advanced civilization of their time in Britain." The people "were highly cultured, and skillful in various kinds of work." They were expert carpenters, used canoes for coastal trading, built wheeled carts and worked lead, tin and copper.

The Glastonbury village was probably related to the tin trade. Capt says that metal mined in the Mendip Hills above Glastonbury was placed on small boats to be floated down the river Brue. Therefore "the lake villages of Glastonbury would have been a natural stop-over for trading."

Thus, it is within the realm of possibility that Joseph came to Glastonbury by following well-worn trade routes and that he and his band took up residence on an island there, choosing an isolated, beautiful spot whose civilized inhabitants would be a natural choice for their first ministry.

Traditions of the other saints are scattered along the Rhône valley, but nowhere is there an account of Joseph's settling there. The traditions place him in Britain. They also give a reason for his continuing the journey after his companions had settled in France.

They say that he had been to England many times before—on business—that he was a tin merchant. The tradition is strongest in Cornwall, a mining county in the extreme southwest of England. It lingers also in the Mendip Hills not far from Glastonbury, in Gloucester and in the west of Ireland.

We know that for hundreds of years prior to the first century A.D. there was a well-established tin trade between Cornwall and Phoenicia. Herodotus, the fifth-century B.C. Greek historian, calls the British Isles the Cassiterides, or Tin Islands. The fourth-century B.C. navigator Pytheas visited the

British Islands and mentions the tin trade. In his *History of England,* Sir Edward Creasey writes: "The British mines mainly supplied the glorious adornment of Solomon's Temple."

That the Roman Empire mined lead in England during Joseph's time is shown by a bar of lead found near the Mendip mines in Somerset. It was dated A.D. 49 and stamped with "Britannicus," the name of the son of Emperor Claudius.

What Was the Grail?

What was the Grail? Was it, as is commonly assumed, the cup from which Jesus drank at the Last Supper? Or was it a serving dish? Was it a physical object at all, or just a Jungian archetypal image? Or was it, as some stories suggest, Christ himself? Or as some best sellers theorize, was the Grail the womb of Mary Magdalene herself, who was carrying the living blood of the Christ?[5] From what did the current conception of the Grail evolve?

Apparently, the Grail has become all things to all people. One explanation for the diversity is expressed by Geoffrey Ashe. He says that "the mystical romancers came to conceive the Grail as something ineffable, the source of a stream of visionary enlightenment and mysterious life. Christ's chalice was a medium through which the senses could apprehend a deeper reality, which might, however, be apprehended through other media."

Regardless of what it was, we can trace its spiritual linkage with Britain, to Joseph of Arimathea and to Glastonbury,* believed to be the holiest and most magical place in England and the original home of Christianity in the British Isles.

---

* Glastonbury is located in Somerset, England, 130 miles west of London.

Historical Records of the Grail Destroyed

If evidence providing historical authenticity to the Grail romances did exist, it may have perished in the great fire of 1184 that burned most of Glastonbury Abbey, including the magnificent library. This structure, according to Capt, housed "the finest collection of books of the period, including records covering a thousand years of Glastonbury Abbey history."

The persecution of Christians under the emperor Diocletian in A.D. 303, which according to one source killed 889 communicants in Britain, could easily have destroyed all written record of Joseph of Arimathea, leaving him alone in the memories of the Britons.

In any event, many authors give Joseph the strongest claim to the title of earliest Christianizer in Britain.

Whether the tradition is true or not will probably never be known unless the British equivalent of the Dead Sea Scrolls is found by some Somerset shepherd.

In any case, it is easier to believe that Joseph was in England than that he was not, because something must account for the deep-rooted tales of him and the Grail. For the Grail, too, has its Glastonbury traditions.

A reputed sarcophagus of Joseph of Arimathea does exist today in Glastonbury. A fourteenth-century monk, Roget of Boston, recorded an epitaph attached to it found after it was exhumed in 1345. It read in Latin, "To the Britons I came after I buried the Christ. I taught, I have entered my rest."

Today Glastonbury is an emerald plain with majestic ruins of a twelfth-century abbey dissolved by Henry VIII in 1539. Walls and columns bereft of their roof, and halves of arches reaching out to each other like lovers divided by an uncrossable gulf still stand on the grassy expanse.

But it was once an island—perhaps the fabled island of Avalon where Arthur is said to have died. Through the sixth century, it was surrounded by water, but gradually, according

Ruins of the Abbey Church, Glastonbury

to Capt, the swampy lake surrounding the island was filled in with layers of peat, clay and gravel "as the estuary retreated to the sea." By the early 1500s, there were still six lakes in the area.

What Happened to the Grail?

If Joseph indeed brought the Grail to Glastonbury, what happened to it? Several fates are conjectured. One is that "the holy cup was caught away to Heaven, and disappear'd," as Tennyson said. Another is that it still exists somewhere in England.

Another possible resting place for the Grail is an ancient spring. At the foot of Chalice Hill in Glastonbury, there is a well that for centuries has been called "Chalice Well" and "Holy Well." Fed by an underground river, its water is reported to have miraculous healing powers. One Glastonbury tradition says that Joseph of Arimathea hid the Grail in this well.

The Mystical Grail Presence

The myths, legends and traditions of Joseph are many and widespread. So are those of the Grail. There are links between Britain and Palestine, making it possible that the Grail did find its way to Glastonbury to form the heart of Arthur's kingdom.

It is not clear from the mass of conflicting legends what exactly the Grail was or is. It is clear that no single physical object could fulfill all the preceding specifications.

Most probable is that the mystical Grail presence takes on different forms in the minds of those who see it, or desire to—as a crystal chalice or brilliant light or the Buddha's begging bowl—according to their capacity for understanding.

But it would seem that the singular explanation that encompasses all the legends is that the Grail can be seen only by those who already contain its inner matrix. As a man with a treasure map inevitably finds the treasure, if motivated, so those who have woven the Grail into their tapestry of life will, as like attracts like (as inner causes eventuate in outer effects), magnetize it to themselves.

The legendary Galahad could not be kept from seeing the Grail because it was an inseparable, preexistent part of him. Some call it destiny.

Conversely, as the treasure eludes the one who is minus the map, so those knights who had not internalized the mystery of the Grail could never find it. It was not a part of them. They could not see it though it feed them a magical banquet.

But the Grail can be forged and won. Those who do not have its formula "written in their foreheads"[6] can apprentice themselves to the Master Craftsman who does—and fashion the chalice. Take Percival, for example, who did not see it at the feast of Pentecost. After arduous journeying, questing, fasting and prayer, he finally saw the Grail unveiled.

Perhaps the Grail is the golden mystery that will not die, the archetypal image that endures the centuries because it is the inner goal that in all our strivings beckons us on.

Perhaps it strikes an inner sound, heard as a crystal bell—a chalice ringing—because it is the chalice we are meant to become, a repository of God's gifts, a dispenser of his light unending.

The concept of the physical cup, the tangible Grail that the mind and hand can grasp, is the magnet that rallies souls to take up the spiritual quest—lifetime after lifetime—of discovering and becoming the inner light and the Holy Grail.

II

Did Jesus Go to School in Britain?

Glastonbury tradition says that the boy Jesus accompanied Joseph of Arimathea on one of his business trips to England and lived there for several years, studying and preparing for his mission.

Let us review the evidence. The belief that Jesus went to England is a persistent one. William Blake, the English poet (1757–1827), conveys this belief in a poem that caught men's imaginations, has been sung as a hymn, and was heard in the sound track of the Academy Award–winning *Chariots of Fire*.

> And did those feet in ancient time
> Walk upon England's mountains green:
> And was the holy Lamb of God,
> On England's pleasant pastures seen!
>
> And did the Countenance Divine,
> Shine forth upon our clouded hills?
> And was Jerusalem builded here,
> Among these dark Satanic Mills?
>
> Bring me my Bow of burning gold:
> Bring me my Arrows of desire:
> Bring me my Spear: O clouds unfold!
> Bring me my Chariot of fire!

I will not cease from Mental Fight,
Nor shall my Sword sleep in my hand:
Till we have built Jerusalem,
In England's green and pleasant Land.

In a pamphlet, *Did Our Lord Visit Britain As They Say in Cornwall and Somerset?,* Reverend C. C. Dobson, MA, recounts four separate and independent traditions that say Jesus came to Britain.

The first of these is found in Cornwall. In his *Book of Cornwall,* Baring-Gould reports a "Cornish story ... to the effect that Joseph of Arimathea came in a boat to Cornwall, and brought the Child Jesus with him, and the latter taught him how to extract the tin and purge it of its [ore] wolfram[ite].... When the tin is flashed then the tinner shouts, 'Joseph was in the tin trade.'"

The second is a Somerset County tradition describing how Jesus and Joseph came to Summerland on a ship from Tarshish and stayed in Paradise (a place name for areas around Burnham and Glastonbury).

The third says that Jesus and Joseph of Arimathea stayed in the mining village of Priddy, north of Glastonbury, in the Mendip Hills of Somerset County. An old saying there is: "As sure as Our Lord was at Priddy...."

The fourth tradition places Jesus and Joseph in Glastonbury.

Summarizing the beliefs, Dobson says, "[Joseph] gained his wealth as an importer in the tin trade, which existed between Cornwall and Phoenicia. On one of his voyages he took Our Lord with him when a boy. Our Lord either remained in Britain or returned later as a young man, and stayed in quiet retirement at Glastonbury.* Here he erected for himself a small house of mud and wattle. Later Joseph of Arimathea,

---

* See *The Lost Years of Jesus* by Elizabeth Clare Prophet.

fleeing from Palestine, settled in the same place and erected a mud and wattle church."

The evidence that Joseph came to Glastonbury soon after the crucifixion, reviewed in the foregoing "Following the Grail," says that Joseph was in the tin trade. If so, it is likely that he went to Britain periodically and stopped at different mining centers. Thus, it is logical that each of the four traditions could be valid.

But why would Joseph bring Jesus? Ancient traditions in the Eastern Orthodox Church say that Joseph of Arimathea was the great-uncle of Jesus. The Jewish Talmud says he was the younger brother of Mary's father.

Indirect support for this relationship can be found in the Gospels: Joseph was given Jesus' body after the crucifixion.[7] The vigilant Sanhedrin were unlikely to allow anyone to claim it who did not have a legal right. Jewish and Roman law permitted only next of kin to claim the body of executed criminals. Joseph asked Pilate for Jesus' body, and when he received it, laid it in his own tomb—also suggesting he was related to Jesus.

If Joseph of Arimathea had been Mary's uncle, it is possible that he would have become Jesus' legal guardian upon the passing of Joseph, his father. If Joseph of Arimathea had been Jesus' guardian and also an official in the Roman-British tin trade, it is certainly possible he would have taken his nephew with him when he traveled on business.

Sixth-century writings also suggest that Jesus visited Glastonbury.

Around A.D. 550, Taliesin, the Prince-Bard Druid, wrote: "Christ, the Word from the beginning, was from the beginning our Teacher, and we never lost His teaching."

In A.D. 597, Saint Augustine traveled to Britain, thinking the entire island was pagan. The eastern half was as he expected, but the western portion had a well-developed

Christian church, complete with its own bishops and holidays.

And this church, as Augustine wrote to Pope Gregory, had unexpected origins:

> In the Western confines of Britain there is a certain royal island of large extent, surrounded by water, abounding in all the beauties of nature and necessaries of life. In it the first Neophites of Catholic Law, God beforehand acquainting them, found a Church constructed by no human art, but by the hands of Christ Himself, for the salvation of His people. The Almighty has made it manifest by many miracles and mysterious visitations that He continues to watch over it as sacred to Himself, and to Mary, the Mother of God.

Analyzing this account, Dobson asks, "Are we precluded from taking this [statement regarding the church] literally?... The statement in any case makes it clear that a church of some sort was already standing on the arrival of Joseph and his companions. Who erected it? The use of the word constructed shows that it is as a material not a spiritual church that is referred to."

If [young] Jesus did go to Britain, what did he do there? A logical explanation is that he was studying, perhaps under his mother or Joseph, or taking the opportunity to absorb the knowledge of his neighbors. We can infer from the Gospels that he did study somewhere and not in his neighborhood synagogue.

John 7:15 says: "And the Jews marvelled, saying, How knoweth this man letters, having never learned?"

It has been conjectured that he studied under the Druids—about whom little objective evidence survives. Our perception of the Druids has been shaped by their chroniclers, who were also their conquerors—the Romans.

The Romans, considering the Druids their greatest religious opponents, forbade their religion. According to Dobson, there is little doubt that the Roman invasions under Julius Caesar and Claudius were largely influenced by their desire to exterminate the cult that had for too long been a successful rival of the Roman civilization.

The Roman historian Tacitus described the Druids as "a band of females and fanatics" clad in "robes of deathly black and with dishevelled hair," who considered it "a pious duty to slake the altars with captive blood."

However, it is now believed that at the time of Joseph of Arimathea, the Druids were not nearly so uncivilized. Although some of those living in Gaul, divorced from their ancient heritage, may have practiced human sacrifice, there is little to suggest it was a tenet of the faith.

Little unbiased information survives about the Druids, partly because they kept no written records but passed their knowledge down orally from generation to generation. Nevertheless, we know they played an important role in educating the young. It took twenty years to master the full Druidic curriculum, which included astronomy, arithmetic, geometry, medicine, poetry, law, natural philosophy and public speaking. There were forty Druidic universities in Britain at the time of Christ. Their total enrollment was as high as sixty thousand students and included the British nobility as well as the sons of important men from all over Europe.

Situated forty miles from Stonehenge, the ancient astronomical observatory, Glastonbury is said to have been a prominent center of Druidism. Archaeological excavation at Glastonbury Lake Village has not provided evidence that the inhabitants were idol worshipers or pagans, leaving it quite possible that they were Druids.

Nothing is certain about Druidic theology, yet some have asserted that it possessed numerous similarities to Christianity. Although the Romans eventually broke their power, the Druids yielded only to Christianity. Historian David Hume said, "No religion has ever swayed the minds of men like the Druidic."

Dobson concludes that "Druidism thus anticipated Christianity and pointed to the coming Saviour under the very name by which Christ was called."

Druidism has been connected with another mystical school—Pythagoras' academy. Over the years, scholars and seers such as Manly Palmer Hall have noted the similarities in the teachings on the afterlife. Geoffrey Ashe writes, "The doctrine of transmigration fascinated the Greeks particularly, because the same had been taught by their own arch-mystic Pythagoras. They speculated as to whether the Druids had learnt from him."

Dobson does not think it unlikely that Jesus studied Druidism. He writes:

> May it not have been that Our Lord, bringing with Him the Mosaic law, and studying it in conjunction with the oral secrets of Druidism, prepared to give forth His message, which occasioned so much wonderment among the Jewish elders?
>
> In Britain He would be free from the tyranny of Roman oppression, the superstition of Rabbinical misinterpretation, and the grossness of pagan idolatry, and its bestial, immoral customs. In Druid Britain He would live among people dominated by the highest and purest ideals, the very ideals He had come to proclaim.

One can imagine Jesus as a youth traveling by ship to Glastonbury. We can see the young Christ at the bow, facing the fresh wind and the fine salt spray, his mind enthralled with the wonder of the future that lay before him—the golden-fire halo of the avatar upon him. With Palestine and the ages-old controversy between pagans, Rabbis and Romans far behind him, he would see ahead the unfoldment of his life and mission—with worlds to conquer on the horizon.[8]

III

Was Jesus Really Born of a Virgin? An Analysis of the Concept of the Virgin Birth

"The concept of the Virgin Birth of Jesus sits at the very heart of the orthodox Christian tradition. Even so, it is mentioned in only two of the four Gospels, and nowhere else in the New Testament," writes Laurence Gardner in *Bloodline of the Holy Grail: The Hidden Lineage of Jesus Revealed.*

It was a common practice in Israel to compile genealogical records, especially since succession to high priest and to leadership of tribe, of tribal family and of father's house depended on lineage. However, biblical genealogies were seldom concerned with purely biological descent, and generation was only one way of getting a son. A man could adopt a child simply by declaring him to be his son or, posthumously, by the law of the levirate marriage wherein the brother of the deceased was required to marry his childless widow and raise up seed in his name (Deut. 25:5–10). Members of a tribe or clan traced their lineage from a common ancestor by fact or legal fiction, i.e., those who were not of natural descent were effectively amalgamated into the group by the adoption of its ancestors.

Remarkably different genealogies for Jesus appear in the

Gospels of Matthew and Luke. Matthew's genealogy (1:1–17) contains forty-two names listed in descending order from Abraham to Jesus, artificially grouped into three fourteen-generation periods: the pre-monarchical period, Abraham to David (750 years); the monarchical period, David to the Babylonian Exile (400 years); the post-monarchical period, Babylonian Exile to Jesus (575 years). The genealogy of Luke (3:23–38) moves in ascending order from Jesus back to Adam.

There are other important differences between the two texts. Matthew intends to demonstrate that Jesus is the Davidic Messiah; Luke to show he is the Son of God. Luke's line contains fifty-six names from Abraham to Jesus; Matthew's, forty-one. Since both Gospel writers are trying to establish by their genealogies a claim to legitimate Davidic ancestry, some have argued that Matthew's table contains the legal successors to the throne of David while Luke's contains the paternal ancestors of Joseph. Another solution is that Matthew gives Joseph's genealogy while Luke gives Mary's. (There is also minor support for the reverse.)

Both genealogies are intimately related to the concept of the virginal conception—i.e., the doctrine that Jesus was conceived by the Holy Ghost without the agency of his father, Joseph, and hence was born of a virgin—usually referred to as the *virgin birth*.

It is not the purpose of the genealogies to defend the virginal conception of Jesus; that is its presupposition—at least in the case of Matthew. Immediately after the genealogy Matthew includes a short passage that explains how Jesus was conceived (Matt. 1:18–25). "Now the birth of Jesus Christ was on this wise: When as his mother Mary was espoused to Joseph, before they came together, she was found with child of the Holy Ghost" (Matt. 1:18),* which occurred in fulfillment

---

* All quotes from the Bible are from the King James Version (KJV) unless otherwise noted. RSV: Revised Standard Version; JB: Jerusalem Bible.

of that "which was spoken of the Lord by the prophet, saying, Behold, a virgin shall be with child, and shall bring forth a son, and they shall call his name Emmanuel, which being interpreted is, God with us" (Matt. 1:22, 23).

One purpose of this passage is to show that Jesus was incorporated by divine command into the house of David, which occurred when Joseph named his son—an exercise that would have been unnecessary if Joseph had been Jesus' natural father. Joseph's act of naming the child, which is the prerogative of the father, is also an act of adoption and thus inclusion into the Davidic line.

It is likely that the author of this part of Matthew had a "Messianic proof text"—that is, a list of passages lifted from the Old Testament to demonstrate that Jesus was the Messiah, used as a preaching aid by early Christians—and took from it a mistranslated version of Isaiah 7:14 and incorporated it into the infancy narrative (Matt. 1:22, 23). The passage in Isaiah reads in the King James Version: "Therefore the Lord himself shall give you a sign; Behold, a virgin shall conceive, and bear a son, and shall call his name Immanuel." Any discussion of the virginal conception, particularly with reference to Matthew, must take into consideration Isaiah 7:10–17, particularly verse 14.

Examination of Isaiah 7:14 (and whether it prophesied the birth of the Messiah) and of the use and meaning of the word "virgin"—especially as it forecast the virginal conception as a Messianic sign—has given rise to some of the most famous debates in theological history.

Some versions of the Old Testament use the words "a young woman" (RSV) or "maiden" (JB) rather than "virgin." The text of the Isaiah scroll found at Qumran library has made it clear that the original Hebrew word used to describe the woman was *almâ,* which means "young woman." Since the verse in the original says "*the* young woman," it is likely the young girl was someone known to Isaiah and King Ahaz. The *almâ* is certainly a young girl who has reached puberty and is thus marriageable if not already married and, given the context, may be referring to the wife of the king or the wife of Isaiah. But it is not clear whether she is a virgin and, if not, if she was already pregnant.

When the Hebrew Masoretic text of the Old Testament was translated into Greek in the Septuagint, the word *almâ* was translated (for reasons that are not clear) into the word *parthenos,* which means "virgin," rather than *neanis,* literally "a young woman." Some scholars believe this was done in the last century before the birth of Jesus. But there is no existing Greek manuscript that was taken from the Hebrew prior to Christian times to show that. Consequently, it is impossible to determine who changed the word, and thus the interpretation of Isaiah 7:14, and whether it was done by Jews *prior* to the birth of Jesus or by Christians *after* the time of Jesus tampering with the Septuagint text in order to bring the translation into line with the virgin doctrine. (Later editors of the Septuagint deleted *parthenos* and reverted to *neanis* to bring the Greek text into conformity with the Hebrew original.) In any event, the Greek translation *parthenos* (virgin) still would have meant that a woman who is now a virgin will, by natural means, once she has united with her husband, conceive the child Immanuel.

While scholars do not agree on the identity of the child, *at most* it may refer to a Davidic prince who would deliver Judah from her enemies. What is really at issue in Isaiah 7:14 is not the manner of conception, nor the prophecy of the Messiah—messianism had not yet developed to the point of expecting a single future king—but rather the timing of the birth of the providential child vis-à-vis events in the Fertile Crescent.

Thus, in the final analysis, neither the Hebrew nor Greek of Isaiah 7:14 refers to the virginal conception about which

Matthew writes; nor was there anything in the Jewish understanding of the verse that would give rise either to the idea of conception through the Holy Spirit or to the Christian belief in the virginal conception of Jesus. In the opinion of Jesuit scholar Raymond Brown, an expert on the infancy narratives, at most, reflection on Isaiah 7:14 colored the expression of an already existing Christian belief in the virginal conception of Jesus.[9]

Further analysis of the infancy narratives (Matt. 1–2; Luke 1–2) and of Luke's genealogy (the latter thought to have been inserted into the third chapter of the Gospel when the first two chapters were composed) in relation to the rest of the New Testament casts doubt on the historicity of the virginal conception. The Messiah was anticipated as the fulfillment of Jewish history. Nevertheless, there was no expectation of a virgin birth in Israel, nor was there any indication in the New Testament literature (outside of the infancy narratives) that anyone was aware that Jesus was born without the agency of a human father. The Gospels were preached for years without any mention of the virginal conception, and it is never touched upon in the writings of Paul.

The baptism of Jesus is the starting point of the earliest preaching of the Church as seen in the Pauline Epistles and Acts. Mark begins there and so does John, following a brief introductory passage on the preexistence of the Word. Matthew and Luke deal with Jesus' birth in the infancy narratives, but do not mention his birth again in their Gospels. If the infancy narratives (which were probably composed after the narratives of Jesus' ministry) are taken as a foreword to the Gospels of Matthew and Luke, then these Gospels are seen to also begin with the baptism of Jesus.

Apart from their introductory placement, the events of the infancy narratives seem disconnected from Matthew and Luke and none of the characters in their writings appears to have any knowledge of the miraculous circumstances of Jesus' birth; even his sisters, brothers and mother appear unaware of Jesus' virginal conception. Furthermore, Mark 3:21–31, especially Mark 3:20, 21, suggests that they saw him more like themselves: "He went home again, and once more such a crowd collected that they could not even have a meal. When his relatives heard of this, they set out to take charge of him, convinced he was out of his mind" (JB). If they were aware of his miraculous conception, it seems unlikely they would have thought his behavior out of character with his mission.

There are no statements in the New Testament indicating that Joseph was a foster father or a legal guardian. When giving the Matthew genealogy, the old Sinaitic Syriac version of the New Testament (an important Greek manuscript based on early source material from the late second or early third century) says, "... Jacob begat Joseph; Joseph to whom was betrothed Mary the virgin, begat Jesus who is called the Messiah." In the next section referring to Joseph (Matt. 1:18–25) the Sinaitic Syriac version reads, "She will bear you a son ... and he took his wife and she bore a son and he called his name Jesus." Shortly thereafter the same text reads, "but knew her not until...," referring to the Matthew assertion that Joseph and Mary did not have sexual relations until after she brought forth her firstborn son.

This has led some scholars to argue that this passage in the Sinaitic Syriac text does indeed speak of a virginal conception —an assertion, which for some theologians is not entirely convincing, especially in light of Matthew 13:55, 56 (KJV), which discloses Jesus to be the son of Joseph: "Is not this the carpenter's son? is not his mother called Mary? and his brethren, James, and Joses, and Simon, and Judas? And his sisters, are they not all with us?" *A New Catholic Commentary on Holy Scripture* notes that regarding "the problem of the historicity of the [infancy] stories in Matt.," which often have a legendary or 'apocryphal' nature, "it is impossible to be dogmatic."[10]

If Jesus were conceived by the normal means, there still remains the question of why Joseph and Mary would have had sexual relations prior to their marriage. Assuming the accuracy of the report in Matthew that Mary was with child after she and Joseph were betrothed but before their marriage, prevailing customs of the day would not make that such an unusual situation.

Betrothal at the time of Jesus legally effected a marital relationship as attested to in both the Old Testament and the Talmud. It was sealed when the husband-to-be paid the future bride's father or guardian a "bride price" as compensation for his loss. Thereafter she was in his power and considered him her "Baal," i.e., lord, master, husband. The betrothal could only be repudiated by a bill of divorce. If the woman lay with another man, it was considered adultery. If the man died, the woman was considered a widow and subject to the levirate. Thus marriage and betrothal carried similar rights and responsibilities.

"Within a short time after the betrothal covenant was completed the boy had the privilege and obligation of cohabitation with his spouse. In the case of the earliest tradition pertaining to Hebrew marriage customs, there appears to have been only a few days lapse between the betrothal transaction and the cohabitation. The girl remained at the home of her father until the husband was ready to receive her. At that time there was usually a nuptial drinking party to celebrate the bride's transference to the groom's home. Intimate relations by betrothed couples were not prohibited in Jewish Scriptures. The Mishnah and the Talmud indicate that Palestinian Judaism showed considerable tolerance towards prenuptial unions in the era of the New Testament, and children conceived as a result were not stigmatized as illegitimate."[11]

A review of Hebrew attitudes toward procreation may help to clarify the controversy over the virginal conception. For some time prior to the birth of Jesus, the Hebrews assumed that God was active in the generation of each individual—that Yahweh creates when parents procreate—something that biblical scholar William E. Phipps says might be called a theory of dual paternity: "This double sonship outlook became established in Jewish tradition. One ancient rabbi said that human creation occurs in this manner: 'Neither man without woman nor woman without man, and neither of them without the Divine Spirit.'

"In the first birth account of the Bible, Eve exclaims: 'I have brought a child into being with the help of YHWH.' ["I have gotten a man from the LORD."] This was interpreted by a rabbi: 'There are three partners in the production of a man: the Holy One, blessed be he, the father, and the mother.' In that Talmudic assertion 'the rabbinic theory of marital intercourse is summed up.'"[12]

The concept of dual paternity, Phipps points out, was not a uniquely Jewish idea. Confucius wrote: "The female alone cannot procreate; the man alone cannot propagate; and Heaven alone cannot produce a man. The three collaborating, man is born. Hence anyone may be called the son of his mother or the son of Heaven."[13]

Phipps argues that the doctrine of the virginal conception, at least in Luke, depends upon two Greek words in Luke 3 and four words in Luke 1 that were probably added by a scribe who misunderstood the Hebrew doctrine of dual paternity. Luke 3:23 contains an obvious scribal insertion: "And Jesus himself began to be about thirty years of age, being (as was supposed) the son of Joseph, which was the son of Heli." Phipps declares that the words "as was supposed" render irrelevant the aim that the genealogical compiler had in mind, which was to trace Jesus' descent through Joseph.

Luke 1:34 contains a less obvious scribal insertion. "Then said Mary unto the angel, How shall this be, seeing I know not a man?" The statement is incongruous when the words "seeing I know not a man" remain in the text. Phipps points out that an intelligent bride would hardly be puzzled by the means by which she would become pregnant. But if "seeing I know not a man" is deleted, then Mary's puzzlement refers to the magnificent destiny for a carpenter's son prophesied by Gabriel in the preceding verses, not the method of fertilization. Some scholars suggest that an old Latin version of this passage, without reference to the virginal conception, may be the way Luke wrote it.[14]

Considering this and other scribal insertions, Dr. John C. Trever, head of the Dead Sea Scrolls Project at the Claremont School of Theology, believes that it is not necessary to assume that the author of the Gospel of Luke ever referred to the virginal conception; it seems that Luke was doctored to harmonize with Matthew. Trever concludes: "We might say with considerable support that the Gospel of Matthew may be the origin of the doctrine of virgin birth."[15]

Phipps notes that there is no way to prove or disprove that the original texts of Matthew and Luke were tampered with, because the earliest existing manuscripts are several centuries later than the lost originals. However, it was in the second and third centuries that the virginal conception became exalted among Gentile Christians as the only fitting way for the Divine Logos to have become enfleshed.[16] Today it is the position of the Roman Catholic church, the Eastern Orthodox church, and the Coptic church that Jesus was the product of a virginal conception.

It is important to draw a distinction between the virginal conception and the virgin birth, which deals with the way Jesus actually passed out of Mary's womb. Christian traditions of the second century hold that Jesus was born miraculously, without pain to his mother and leaving her physically intact.

As Raymond Brown points out, Matthew is concerned only with showing Mary's virginity before Jesus' birth so that the Isaiahan prophecy will be fulfilled. As time passed, however, the notion of the virginal conception grew, and by the second century traditions of the virgin birth developed, followed by the idea that Joseph and Mary never had normal sexual relations, finally concluding that Joseph, too, was a virgin!

Jesus' brothers and sisters are sometimes held to be children of Joseph by a previous marriage. "In antiquity there were debates whether these were half-brothers of Jesus (sons of Joseph by a previous marriage—*Protevangelium of James;* Epiphanius), or cousins (sons of either Joseph's brother or of Mary's sister—Jerome), or blood brothers (children of Joseph and Mary—Helvidius)."[17]

Mrs. Prophet says, "I do not believe that the conception of Jesus by his father Joseph, as the agent of the Holy Spirit, in any way detracts from the divinity of his soul or the magnitude of the incarnate Word within him; rather does it enhance the availability of the fullness of God through his chosen and anointed human instruments."

Sources: John D. Davis, *A Dictionary of the Bible,* 4th rev. ed. (Grand Rapids, Mich.: Baker Book House, 1954); Matthew Black and H. H. Rowley, eds., *Peake's Commentary on the Bible* (Walton-on-Thames, Surrey: Nelson, 1962); *New Catholic Encyclopedia,* s.v. "Genealogy," and "Luke, Gospel According to St."; Isaac Asimov, *Asimov's Guide to the Bible—Volume Two: The New Testament* (New York: Avon, 1969); D. Guthrie and J. A. Motyer, eds., *The New Bible Commentary Revised,* 3rd ed. (Grand Rapids, Mich.: Wm. B. Eerdmans Publishing Co., 1970); *The Anchor Bible: Matthew* (Garden City, N.Y.: Doubleday & Co., 1971); Fuller, *A New Catholic Commentary on Holy Scripture;* and *The Anchor Bible: The Gospel According to Luke (I–IX)* (Garden City, N.Y.: Doubleday & Co., 1981).

IV

Are Mary Magdalene and Mary of Bethany the Same Woman, as So Many Authors Believe?

There has been much controversy over the identity of these two women, who are mentioned often throughout the scriptures of the New Testament. The prevailing belief among authors and church historians (at least in the Western Church) is that they are the same woman—Mary of Magdala is Mary of Bethany. However, the Eastern Orthodox Church has always held the view that Mary Magdalene and Mary of Bethany are two different women.

And Elizabeth Clare Prophet has her own interpretation of these two, which we shall present after we have discussed the prevailing concept of the Western Church.

In *Mary Magdalene: Myth and Metaphor,* Susan Haskins describes the controversy:

> Until the later sixth century there was no fixed tradition concerning the unity or plurality of the women. Some had identified Mary Magdalen with Luke's sinner, others with Mary of Bethany; still others identified the latter two with each other, but not with

> Mary Magdalen. But with Gregory the Great's homily on Luke's gospel, delivered probably in 591, the identity of Mary Magdalen was finally settled for nearly fourteen hundred years.[18]

"According to a very old tradition (accepted by such writers and fathers of the Church as Tertullian, St. Ambrose, St. Jerome, St. Augustine, St. Gregory, the Venerable Bede, Rabanus, St. Odo, St. Bernard and St. Thomas Aquinas), St. Mary Magdalene was none other than St. Mary of Bethany," summarizes John William Taylor in *The Coming of the Saints.*"[19]

Haskins writes:

> From the time of Gregory the Great until 1969, when changes were made to the Roman calendar, the western Church tended to treat the three as one, celebrating them as Mary Magdalen on 22 July. This despite the fact that the sixteenth century Jacques Lefèvre d'Etaples ruffled the until-then untroubled waters of consensus by daring to suggest that Mary Magdalen was a separate character from Mary of Bethany and Luke's sinner, and was duly excommunicated for his pains. The eastern Church, however, followed St. John Chrysostom in distinguishing the two different Marys of Bethany and Magdala, and Luke's sinner, and celebrates their feasts on separate days.[20]

Mrs. Prophet's view on the subject of Mary Magdalene and Mary of Bethany as being two separate women is substantiated by her meditations on the ascended masters. And thus, she also confirms that Mary Magdalene was the scripture's woman with the alabaster box:

> Modern scholars have challenged the traditional view that the sinful woman who anointed Jesus' feet in

> Luke 7:37–38 was Mary Magdalene because Luke does not give the woman's name. However, the ascended master Jesus Christ has confirmed that the woman who figured in this episode was Mary Magdalene. Jesus has also confirmed that the accounts of the woman anointing Jesus with spikenard in Matthew 26:6–13; Mark 14:3–9; and John 12:1–8 are all referring to the same event that was recorded in Luke 7. This incident took place at the home of Simon the leper in Bethany; Jesus gives the identity of the woman as Mary Magdalene. In addition, Jesus has confirmed that Mary Magdalene was the woman taken in adultery (John 8:1–11) whom the scribes and Pharisees wanted to stone and whom Jesus forgave, saying, "Go, and sin no more."[21]

Mrs. Prophet has also received revelations that Mary Magdalene was the twin flame of Jesus and that she ascended two thousand years after him and is now known as the ascended lady master Magda.

It has also been revealed by the ascended masters to Mrs. Prophet that Mary of Bethany was indeed another Mary. Mary Baker Eddy (1812–1910) was embodied as Mary of Bethany and now is the ascended lady master Theosophia, upholding the office of the Goddess of Wisdom.

V

Who Was the Black Madonna?
Was She Mary Magdalene?

> *I am black—but beautiful ... Do not stare at me because I am swarthy, because the sun has burned me... (Cant. 1:6).*

The Black Madonna, the Black Virgin. She is found in the humble shrines and great cathedrals of Europe, in ancient statues that survived the Inquisition, in the heart of Pope John Paul II. Her mystique rivals her veneration. Her great age was the twelfth century; but contemporary authors trace her legacy to the legendary Isis, to the "bride" in Solomon's Song of Songs and, always, to Mary Magdalene.

In the abodes of the Black Madonna we find clues to the real nature of Mary Magdalene, writes Lynn Picknett in *Mary Magdalene: Christianity's Hidden Goddess.*

> Scattered across Europe are little cult centres that blur the line between pagan and Christian, and which contain clues not only to the true origins of Christianity, but also to the real nature of the Magdalene. These are the homes of the Black Madonnas or Black Virgins.... Wherever they are found, they are the focus of

> enormous veneration, real passion, among the local people, who regard them as something other than the usual array of pale-faced Christian saints—even as something quite different from the usual Virgin and Child.[22]

Picknett connects Mary Magdalene with the mysterious Black Madonna of the Middle Ages. She writes that an unorthodox cult (which may have included the Cathars and the Templars) dedicated to Mary Magdalene was "connected with the mysterious Black Madonnas . . . that flourished in the Languedoc and Provence. . . ." This enduring fervor of devotion to Mary Magdalene, albeit it now be the *Catholic* cult, "shows how deeply engrained she is in the hearts and minds of the people there," writes Picknett.[23]

The Black Madonna of Montserrat

What is the origin of such devotion? Laurence Gardner, in *Bloodline of the Holy Grail,* portrays the Black Madonna in the tradition of the ancient Isis:

> The early orthodox Church was struggling with the veneration for the Universal Goddess, especially in the Mediterranean world. From prehistoric times she had been known by many names, but especially that of Isis, who was identified as the Universal Mother.
>
> To the ancient Egyptians, Isis was the sister-wife of Osiris, who was the founder of civilization and the

> judge of souls after death. Isis was the Universal Goddess, specifically a maternal protectress, and her cult spread far and wide. She was frequently portrayed holding her child, Horus, whose incarnations were the pharaohs themselves....
>
> In some cases [the statues of the Black Madonna] are black all over, but many have only black faces, hands and feet. It is not a question of discoloration, as some disconcerted clerics have suggested. A few have been overpainted in pale flesh tones to conform with the standard Madonna representation; some have simply been removed from the public gaze altogether. The features of the Black Madonna are in no way negroid in racial characteristics, but are quite simply black in colour.[24]

"The controversial texts, known as the *Dossiers secrets (Secret Files)* deposited by the Priory of Sion in the Bibliothèque Nationale in Paris, make repeated references to the Magdalene, whom they associate (without explanation) with Isis and the Black Madonnas," writes Picknett.[25]

Are the Black Madonna and Mary Magdalene the archetypal "bride" of the Old Testament poem, Song of Solomon—"I am black—but beautiful"? Does it explain why the Song of Songs is read in Catholic churches on the feast day of Saint Mary Magdalene?[26]

Margaret Starbird says that Christians in the early Church readily identified Mary Magdalene with the dark Sister-Bride in the Song of Songs.[27] She writes:

> The Song of Songs was understood in antiquity to have been a wedding song of the archetypal bride and bridegroom. It was retained in the Hebrew Bible and later adopted by Christianity, where, in the earliest centuries, the dark bride of the Song was widely under-

> stood to represent Mary Magdalene—the acknowledged sister-counterpart of Jesus. She was understood to bear the archetype of the entire community as *ekklesia* (church).[28]

Picknett adds that "the earliest Christian commentary—dating from the second century ... associates the central character of the legendary Queen of Sheba, Queen of Ethiopia (which means 'burnt faces') with Mary Magdalene."[29]

Why Is She Black?

Some answers are symbolic.

Gardner states, "She is black because Wisdom (*Sophia)* is black, having existed in the darkness of Chaos before the Creation."[30]

And Starbird says:

> Her "blackness" would have been symbolic of her hidden state; she was the unknown queen—unacknowledged, repudiated, and vilified by the church through the centuries in an attempt to deny the legitimate bloodline and to maintain its own doctrines of the divinity and celibacy of Jesus. Her blackness is also a direct reference to the deposed Davidic princes of Jerusalem: 'Brighter than snow were her princes, whiter than milk ... now their appearance is blacker than soot, they are unrecognized on the streets. (Lam. 4:8).[31]

And others offer reasons for the actual appearance of her icons and statues.

Ean Begg in *The Cult of the Black Virgin* proposes a few explanations that have been given for her blackness:

> Spokesmen for the Church, when asked to explain the origin of Black Virgins, tend to invoke candle smoke or general exposure to the elements. After a time, they

> would say, as at Einsiedeln, the faithful become accustomed to a sooty image, and the clergy pander to their prejudice by the use of paint where necessary. Apart from the considerable contrary evidence of clerical antipathy to Black Virgins and disregard for parishioners' wishes, this rationalistic hypothesis raises two important questions. If the presumed polychrome faces and hands of the Virgin and Child have been blackened by the elements, why has their polychrome clothing not been similarly discoloured? Secondly, why has a similar process not occurred in the case of other venerated images?[32]

However, Begg submits a more plausible theory. He says that

> at the time of the Crusades, original pagan statues, or images based on them, were brought back from the east by returning warriors, as Madonnas.
>
> Apart from the candle-smoke theory, this is the simplest and most widely held explanation for the existence of Black Virgins under a new name and a new religion of goddesses from the classical world....
>
> The contention, then, of the Catholic Church is that most such statues were not originally intended to be black, and only became so by accident later. The fact remains that they are black and to discuss the phenomenon in visual terms only is to disguise their deepest significance....
>
> From whatever viewpoint one examines the subject, however, and whatever the causes of the phenomenon may be, it is indisputable that some of the most famous statues of the Madonna in Western Europe have faces and hands that are black, by intention, and are known to have been so for many centuries.[33]

Picknett and Prince offer yet another theory in *The Templar Revelation: Secret Guardians of the True Identity of Christ:*

> Black Madonnas are almost always associated with much more ancient *pagan* sites. And whereas the Christianization of such places has been a common enough phenomenon in Europe, the very blackness of these images suggests that they represent the continuation of pagan goddess worship that is dressed up as Christianity. This is, presumably, why the Church treats them with disdain, although the fervour accorded to them makes such worship nigh on impossible to ban. Besides, in order for a ban to take effect—certainly these days—reasons would have to be given which would merely draw attention to what has been going on for nearly 2000 years.[34]

Since "most of these statues were deliberately painted black or made of black material such as ebony," Picknett and Prince conclude, "one may reasonably suppose, they were intended to be black."

The Black Madonna of Czestochowa

The Black Madonna of Czestochowa, distinguished by the scar on her cheek, is revered as patroness, preserver and liberator by the Polish people—including Pope John Paul II.

Why is she wounded? Starbird cites to two Scripture passages to explain:

> One is from the fourth chapter of Micah, only a few verses after the reference to the Magdal-eder, the "stronghold of the daughter of Sion," through whom dominion (of the House of David) will one day be restored (Mic. 4:8–10). It says, "With a rod they strike

on the cheek of the ruler of Israel" (Mic. 5:1).

The second Scripture reference of which we are reminded by the Black Madonna's wound is found in the Song of Songs. The Bride speaks of her search for her lover who has departed: "The watchmen came upon me as they made their rounds; they struck me and wounded me ..." (Cant. 5:7).[35]

Starbird brings the story of the Black Madonna into the twentieth century:

Our Lady of Czestochowa

> The biblical text from Isaiah 45 read on the day of Pope John Paul II's anointing is astounding in its prophetic message: "thus says the Lord to his anointed Cyrus, whose right hand I grasp, subduing nations before him, and disarming kings, opening doors before him and leaving the gates unbarred: I will go before you and level the mountains; bronze doors I will shatter and *iron bars I will snap*" (emphasis mine).
>
> Contemplating the iron bars snapping before Cyrus, the 'anointed of God,' we are reminded specifically of the Iron Curtain—the guarded walls and rolls of barbed wire—that turned to dust in 1989 and 1990 in the wake of the freedom movements in Eastern Europe. These freedom movements received their encouragement from the Solidarity movement in Poland, whose members' formidable strength was derived from an unshakable

> faith that God was with them. The attributes of the Black Madonna universally include compassion, strength, and an ability to break chains and to bring down walls. She is very often identified with the oppressed and freedom-fighters.[36]

The scarred Black Madonna as the feminine archetype of God's people is eulogized by Starbird:

> In the image of the dark Madonna, we encounter not just the human Mary who was the Jewish mother of Jesus, but rather the scorned and neglected "other face of God"—the entire feminine archetype that must be acknowledged before we can be whole.[37]

VI

Did Jesus Survive the Crucifixion and Continue His Teachings until Age 81?

There is much of Jesus' life following the resurrection about which we know very little. There are few post-resurrection appearances of Jesus chronicled in the New Testament. We see his appearance to Mary Magdalene and later Peter and John at the tomb. The Gospels provide accounts of his appearances and discourses with the disciples in the Upper Room, on the way to Emmaus, in Galilee at the sea of Tiberias, at Jerusalem and Bethany—prior to "being carried up into heaven."[38]

For additional information concerning his later life we need to look to the writings of the Gnostics, to Eastern writers and historians and to revelations of the ascended masters through Elizabeth Clare Prophet.

Mrs. Prophet said:

> Jesus lived many lifetimes, just as we all have. And India was home for him in one of those lifetimes thousands of years ago.[39] He went to Kashmir after the resurrection because if he had remained in the Middle East, his enemies would have sought him out and killed

> him again. It was as though he played out a drama, and for all intents and purposes, that Palestinian drama was finished. The world accepted that Jesus died for our sins, and he wanted it to be that way. He didn't want to be pursued by his enemies of Rome and the Jews, and he wanted to be free to continue his mission....
>
> It is widely believed in India that Jesus spent the rest of his life in Kashmir, that he was married and that he had children. And I have spoken to people in India, when I was in Kashmir, who talk about descendants of Jesus, members of his family who are alive today in India.[40]
>
> Jesus lived to the age of 81. He spent many years of his life in Kashmir and passed on there in A.D. 77. He ascended from the temple of light, Shamballa, from the etheric octave....
>
> Jesus has never ceased to be with his disciples as the ascended master since the hour of his ascension. And even before his ascension, in his resurrected light body, he communed with Paul and many of those who were his disciples. The Gnostic Gospels tell of his interaction with his disciples when he was in the resurrected state, following the crucifixion but before his ascension.[41]

Now let us see what other authors say happened to Jesus after the crucifixion. Holger Kersten (author of *Jesus Lived in India)*, Andreas Faber-Kaiser (author of *Jesus Died in Kashmir)* and the Ahmadiyya movement all say he went to Kashmir. Baigent and his co-authors think he may have gone to Egypt, but they are not sure.

Jesus in Heaven on Earth by Kwaja Nazir Ahmad describes the journey of Jesus to Kashmir, his preaching to the lost tribes of Israel and his death and burial in Srinagar. He says:

> Except in *Actae Thomae [the Acts of Thomas]*, no reference is to be found in Occidental literature as to what became of Jesus after he reached Nisibis,[42] and we have to look for this information to Oriental writers....
>
> Josephus in his *Antiquities* mentioned that Jesus knew that some of the lost tribes of Israel were at Nisibis: (Josephus, *Antiquities*, 18, 9:1–8.) Since the people of Nisibis were out to kill Jesus, and he could not travel far in a few days, Jesus traveled incognito under the name of *Yuz Asaf*, and the books and local traditions of the countries he visited or passed through speak of him as *Yuz Asaf*. It has been said that Yuz stood for Yusu (Jesus) and Asaf in Hebrew means gatherer.[43]

Ahmad says that the best proof of the presence of Jesus in Kashmir is the existence of his tomb in Mohalla Khaniyar, Srinagar,[44] and he shows many pictures of Jesus' tomb. He closes by saying:

> As for Jesus, he went in search of the 'lost sheep of Israel,' found and preached to them in Kashmir and elsewhere, and ultimately he died a natural death and was buried there. His soul was 'taken up' to meet his Creator.[45]

Mrs. Prophet says, we are determined that the true story of Jesus' life and his message shall be made plain and shall be published abroad for the freeing of the individual disciple to follow him all the way Home—not only to Golgotha but to India, to Nepal, to Tibet, to every nation and to the high and holy light of Kashmir and the ascension in the light.

Discussion Questions

1. The Christian Gnostics had a very different view of religion from that proposed by Church hierarchies of their time. Do you think that the Gnostic approach to religious experience is one that is viable in today's society?

2. The Gnostic path has been criticized as being dangerous in that without some sort of boundaries, its adherents may find themselves following false paths. The modern New Age movement has been criticized on the same grounds. Do you think it is possible to discern the path of true Gnosticism? What guidelines would be necessary to do this?

3. Augustine's doctrine of original sin became a foundation for Christian theology from his time to the present. What effects do you think it has had on western society and its views on women and marriage?

4. The last century has seen dramatic changes in woman's role in the societies of the West. However, the women's liberation movement has been criticized for promoting an

image for woman that is based on current male stereotypes. To what extent do you think this is valid? What would a balanced expression of the Divine Feminine look like?

5. Male archetypes portrayed in popular culture are often unbalanced or extremes. Two opposites are the action-movie hero (unbalanced masculine) and the effeminate male (unbalanced feminine). An archetype frequently shown in advertising is the weak or ineffective masculine who is dominated by woman. What would a balanced expression of the Divine Masculine look like?

6. If conclusive proof were somehow found that Jesus was married to Mary Magdalene, how would this change your views of him and his mission?

7. Protestant denominations allow (and often require) ministers to be married. The Catholic Church does not. If you were called to be a priest or minister, do you think that marriage would assist or hinder your service?

8. Religions of the East have manifestations of the Deity in both masculine and feminine form. The religions of the West (Judaism, Christianity and Islam) see God as masculine. How is this reflected in the development of culture and spirituality in these different societies?

9. While affirming an exclusively masculine Godhead, Catholicism does provide a path of devotion to the feminine principle through the rosary and devotion to Mary and female saints. One of the most significant effects of the Reformation was removal of the Mother principle from this branch of Christianity. How has this affected the development of religion and spirituality in predominantly Protestant societies?

10. Mary Magdalene as the Divine Spouse is a very different archetype and role model from Mary, the Virgin Mother. How might religion and society have evolved differently in the last two thousand years if Mary Magdalene had been a more prominent feminine image in Christian thought?

11. The Gnostics saw the soul of both man and woman as a feminine polarity in relation to the masculine Spirit. As we integrate more fully with our soul and its true nature, how would this feminine manifest? How can we integrate the masculine of Spirit with this feminine nature to bring balance to our spiritual path?

12. What new understanding of Mary Magdalene and the feminine aspect of God have you gained from reading this book? Has this changed your attitude toward Jesus and the path of Christianity? In what ways? In what ways will it change or enhance your pursuit of a spiritual path?

Notes

INTRODUCTION

1. Gnosticism is a term applied to a diverse group of sects within Christianity that flourished in the second century A.D. before the canon, doctrine and creeds of the Church were solidified. Gnosticism comes from the Greek word *gnosis,* meaning "knowledge" or "understanding." While Gnostic groups differed in many ways, they shared a common belief that the means to salvation was through knowledge—knowledge of God, knowledge of the True Self as God and knowledge of the universe in which they lived.
2. The Dialogue of the Savior III 139.12–13, in Elaine Pagels, *The Gnostic Gospels* (New York: Vintage Books, 1979), p. 22.
3. In the Gospel of Mary, the apostle Levi says, "Surely the Savior knows her very well. That is why he loved her more than us." 18.12–15, in James M. Robinson, *The Nag Hammadi Library in English* (San Francisco: Harper & Row, 1988), p. 527. The Gospel of Philip says: "And the companion of the [...] Mary Magdalene. [... loved] her more than [all] the disciples [and used to] kiss her [often] on her [...]. The rest of [the disciples ...]. They said to him, 'Why do you love her more than all of us?'" 63.32–64.2, in *Nag Hammadi Library,* p. 148.
4. See Michael Baigent, Richard Leigh, and Henry Lincoln, *Holy Blood, Holy Grail* (New York: Delacorte Press, 1982); Laurence

Gardner, *Bloodline of the Holy Grail: The Hidden Lineage of Jesus Revealed* (Shaftesbury, Dorset; Boston, Mass.: Element, 1998); Margaret Starbird, *The Woman with the Alabaster Jar: Mary Magdalen and the Holy Grail* (Santa Fe, N.M.: Bear & Co., 1993); Margaret Starbird, *Magdalene's Lost Legacy: Symbolic Numbers and the Sacred Union in Christianity* (Rochester, Vt.: Bear & Co., 2003); and Margaret Starbird, *The Goddess in the Gospels: Reclaiming the Sacred Feminine* (Santa Fe, N.M.: Bear & Co., 1998).

5. *The Two Marys: The Madonna and the Magdalene,* a one-hour documentary produced by CNN, discusses the historical evidence about Mary Magdalene and Mary the Mother of Jesus. *Jesus, Mary, and DaVinci,* a one-hour documentary produced by ABC News and hosted by Peter Jennings, discusses the claims about Mary Magdalene that are made by Dan Brown in his best-selling novel *The Da Vinci Code.*
6. John 8:11.
7. See pages 267–69.
8. Twin flames are two souls who were born out of the same "white-fire ovoid." They share the same blueprint of identity. When twin flames descend into form, one assumes the masculine polarity and one assumes the feminine polarity.
9. See upcoming book, *Jesus and Magda,* to be published by Summit Lighthouse Library in July 2006.
10. The gospels of Mark and John both say that Mary Magdalene was the first of the disciples to see Jesus after his resurrection. Matthew has "the other Mary" also present. See Matt. 28:1–10, Mark 16:9; John 20:1–18.
11. The Bible itself is silent on whether Jesus was married. However, it is important to remember that the gospels were not intended to be biographical in the modern sense, but rather encapsulations of the message that Jesus brought. For example, Mark and John provide no information at all about Jesus' birth or childhood, and none of the gospels provide any information about his education.

    For a discussion of the scriptural and historical evidence for and against Jesus being married, see William Phipps, *Was Jesus Married? The Distortion of Sexuality in the Christian Tradition* (New York: Harper & Row, 1970).
12. Heb. 13:8.

13. Many commentators conclude that Mary Magdalene and Mary of Bethany were the same person. This has also been the view of the Catholic Church. See pp. 267–69 for a discussion of this issue and Elizabeth Clare Prophet's views.
14. Irenaeus writes: "On completing His thirtieth year He suffered, being in fact still a young man, and who had by no means attained to advanced age. Now, that the first stage of early life embraces thirty years, and that this extends onwards to the fortieth year, every one will admit; but from the fortieth and fiftieth year a man begins to decline towards old age, which our Lord possessed while He still fulfilled the office of a Teacher, even as the Gospel and all the elders testify; those who were conversant in Asia with John, the disciple of the Lord, [affirming] that John conveyed to them that information." Irenaeus, *Against Heresies* 2.22.5, in Alexander Roberts and James Donaldson, eds., *The Ante-Nicene Fathers,* American reprint of the Edinburgh ed., 9 vols. (Grand Rapids, Mich.: Wm. B. Eerdmans Publishing Co., 1981), 1:391–92.
15. G. R. S. Mead, *Pistis Sophia: A Gnostic Gospel* (New York: Spiritual Science Library, 1984), p. 1.
16. Gal. 1:11–12.
17. Rev. 12:1.

CHAPTER 1
JESUS PREPARES FOR HIS MISSION

1. Elizabeth Clare Prophet, *The Lost Years of Jesus* (1987), is available from Summit University Press, P.O. Box 5000, Gardiner, MT 59030, USA. Tel.: (406) 848-9500. www.summituniversitypress.com.
2. Luke 2:42–52.
3. Matt. 3:13; Mark 1:9.
4. Dr. Caspari, a Swiss musician and professor of music pedagogy. and her husband, Charles, were members of a pilgrimage to Mount Kailas organized by Mrs. Clarence Gasque, head of the World Fellowship of Faith and Mother Superior of the Western Zoroastrian movement. See chapter 5 of Prophet's *The Lost Years of Jesus* for a description of the pilgrimage and Dr. Caspari's testimony on the texts at Himis.
5. William O. Douglas, *Beyond the High Himalayas* (Garden City,

N.Y.: Doubleday & Co., 1952), p. 152.

6. *The Life of Saint Issa* 4:13, in Prophet, *The Lost Years of Jesus,* p. 218.
7. Luke 2:40.
8. Luke 2:52.
9. John 14:12.
10. John 9:4; John 5:17.
11. Mark L. Prophet and Elizabeth Clare Prophet, *The Lost Teachings of Jesus* (1994), 4 vols., is available from Summit University Press, P.O. Box 5000, Gardiner, MT 59030, USA. Tel.: (406) 848-9500.
12. *The Life of Saint Issa* 5:11, in Prophet, *The Lost Years of Jesus,* p. 220.
13. Nicholas Roerich, "Banners of the East," in Frances R. Grant et al., *Himalaya* (New York: Brentano's, 1926), p. 149. In this writing, Nicholas Roerich quotes an unnamed Tibetan manuscript with "the antiquity of about 1500 years" that has striking similarities to portions of the manuscripts found by Notovitch at Himis in Ladakh. The parallel passage in Notovitch's *Life of Saint Issa,* 5:11, reads: "He inveighed against the act of a man arrogating to himself the power to deprive his fellow beings of their rights of humanity." (Prophet, *The Lost Years of Jesus,* p. 220.
14. In the introductory material for his book *The Unknown Life of Jesus Christ,* Nicolas Notovitch recounts a conversation with an unnamed cardinal, who told him that "the Vatican Library possesses sixty-three complete or incomplete manuscripts in various Oriental languages referring to this matter, which have been brought to Rome by missionaries from India, China, Egypt, and Arabia." Prophet, *The Lost Years of Jesus,* p. 107.
15. The date of Jesus' birth is not given in the Bible and has been the subject of much debate. Margaret Starbird comments that "according to the Gospel of Matthew, Magi (astrologers) from the East had noticed the unusual 'star of Bethlehem' in the sky at the time of the birth of Jesus. Some astronomers have identified this celestial configuration as the conjunction of Jupiter and Saturn in the sign of Pisces, which occurred from May to December in 7 B.C., an event probably perceived by many to herald the Age of Pisces and announce the birth of the long-awaited Messiah of the Jewish people." Starbird, *Magdalene's*

Lost Legacy, p. 113. While the terms C.E. (Current Era) and B.C.E. (Before Current Era) are preferred by Bible scholars, we have chosen to use the more traditional B.C. and A.D., which are universally understood.

16. Matt. 2:15.
17. See Lionel Smithett Lewis, *St. Joseph of Arimathea at Glastonbury* (Cambridge: James Clarke & Co., 1955); George F. Jowett, *The Drama of the Lost Disciples* (London: Covenant Publishing Co., 1980); and E. Raymond Capt, *The Traditions of Glastonbury* (Thousand Oaks, Calif.: Artisan Sales, 1983). Laurence Gardner comments on the importance of the tin trade in the Roman Empire in this era: "Tin is essential to the production of bronze—and the most important tin mines were in southwestern England, an area also rich in copper and lead, for which there was a great market in the expanding Roman Empire. The British Museum contains two splendid examples of lead from the Mendip mines near Glastonbury, dated AD 49 and AD 60 respectively. One bears the name of 'Britannicus, son of the Emperor Claudius', and the other is inscribed (in Latin) 'British lead: property of the emperor Nero'." Gardner, *Bloodline of the Holy Grail,* p. 370, note 7.
18. *The Life of Saint Issa* 4:10–13, in Prophet, *The Lost Years of Jesus,* p. 218.
19. Ibid. 5:3, 4, in Prophet, *The Lost Years of Jesus,* p. 219.
20. Jesus is the man and Christ is the universal second person of the Trinity.
21. John 14:12.
22. "By the beginning of the Christian era, a fusing and blending of traditions had already been in progress for some centuries in the great mixing bowl of Alexandria," writes Ean Begg. "The vast Jewish population, worshipping one masculine, invisible God, and abhorring graven images, was surrounded on every hand by the deities and philosophies of Greece and Egypt." Ean Begg, *The Cult of the Black Virgin* (London: Penguin Books, 1996), p. 93.

    Yahweh had not always been the pre-eminent deity. "The original religion of the Hebrews was, like that of all other ancient cultures, polytheistic—venerating *both gods and goddesses,*" write Lynn Picknett and Clive Prince in *The Templar Revelation: Secret Guardians of the True Identity of*

Christ (New York: Simon & Schuster, 1998), p. 295.

The people of Israel trace their origin to Abraham, who left the city of Ur to journey to the land that God would give to him and his descendants. The religion that we know today as Judaism was not all given to Abraham, but was received in a series of revelations over a period of hundreds of years. The five books of the Law, a key element of this new dispensation, date from many hundreds of years after Moses, and the teachings of the prophets led to further evolution of the religion and social customs of the people.

Evidence from the Bible and from archaeology shows that the Hebrews continued to practice elements of the old religions for many hundreds of years. For example, Judges 2:13 records that after their entry into the promised land and the death of Joshua, the children of Israel "served Baal and Ashteroth" (the primary male and female gods of the Canaanites). Throughout the Old Testament, we find evidence of the prophets continually exhorting the Israelites to discontinue their worship of these "strange gods" and to return to the worship of the one true God, Yahweh. (See Gen 35:2–4; Judg 10:6–16; I Sam. 7:3–4; II Chron. 33:14–17.)

Susan Haskins writes that "the fertility cults, and the goddesses who presided over them, which had co-existed with Yahweh in the early days, vanished from the land of Canaan sometime after the Exile [586–538 B.C.]. Yahweh, the one true God, became universal creator, transcendent beyond, and superior to, the sphere of nature." Susan Haskins, *Mary Magdalen: Myth and Metaphor* (New York: Riverhead Books, 1995), p. 46.

23. John Temple Bristow, *What Paul Really Said about Women: An Apostle's Liberating Views on Equality in Marriage, Leadership, and Love* (1988; reprint, Harper, San Francisco, 1991), p. 12.
24. Matt. 3:17.
25. Roerich, "Banners of the East," pp. 149–50.
26. Ibid., p. 150.
27. Ibid.
28. Ibid.
29. Gloria Steinem and Betty Friedan were prominent leaders of the feminist movement in the twentieth century.
30. Elizabeth Clare Prophet teaches that we have all reembodied

many times, as man and woman, in many different roles and circumstances, and we will continue to do so until we return to God having fulfilled our reason for being here.

31. Jesus was embodied as Abel, as Joseph (one of the twelve sons of Jacob), as Joshua (who led the children of Israel into the Promised Land) and as King David.

32. Atlantis was the island continent that existed where the Atlantic Ocean now is and that sank in cataclysm (the Flood of Noah) approximately 11,600 years ago as calculated by James Churchward. Vividly depicted by Plato; "seen" and described by Edgar Cayce in his readings; recalled in scenes from Taylor Caldwell's *Romance of Atlantis;* and described in great detail in *A Dweller on Two Planets,* by Phylos the Thibetan.

    In his dialogues, Plato recounts that on "the island of Atlantis there was a great and wonderful empire" that ruled Africa as far as Egypt, Europe as far as Italy, and "parts of the continent" (thought to be a reference to America, specifically Central America, Peru and the Valley of the Mississippi). It has been postulated that Atlantis and the small islands to its east and west formed a continuous bridge of land from America to Europe and Africa.

    See Otto Muck, *The Secret of Atlantis* (New York: Pocket Books, 1979); Ignatius Donnelly, *Atlantis: The Antediluvian World* (New York: Dover Publications, 1976), pp. 11, 23, 173, 473.

33. Rev. 7:9.

34. Climbing the mountain is a symbol of the trek of the soul, who seeks to rise from the valleys of the worldly consciousness to the heights of God consciousness. The highest mountain is symbolically the I AM Presence, the highest point of individual God awareness. This trek of the soul is outlined in the thirty-three chapters of the Climb the Highest Mountain series, by Mark L. Prophet and Elizabeth Clare Prophet. The first six volumes, which contain the first nineteen chapters of the series, are *The Path of the Higher Self, The Path of Self-Transformation, The Masters and the Spiritual Path, The Path of Brotherhood, The Path of the Universal Christ* and *Paths of Light and Darkness*.

35. Matt. 3:13–17.

36. The ascended masters are those who, like Jesus, have mastered

time and space, balanced their karma and fulfilled their destiny in the ritual of the ascension. Many of the saints of East and West have demonstrated this as the goal of life, including Elijah, Zarathustra, Confucius, Gautama Buddha and Mary the mother of Jesus.

CHAPTER 2
JESUS' REVOLUTION FOR WOMAN

1. Karen Jo Torjesen, *When Women Were Priests: Women's Leadership in the Early Church and the Scandal of their Subordination in the Rise of Christianity* (New York: HarperSanFrancisco, 1993), pp. 68–69.
2. Tosephta, *Megilla,* iv.II. 226, quoted in Torjesen, *When Women Were Priests,* p. 40.
3. Ruth A. Tucker and Walter L. Liefeld, *Daughters of the Church: Women and Ministry from New Testament Times to the Present* (Grand Rapids, Mich.: Zondervan Publishing House, Academic Books, 1987), p. 61.
4. Luke 10:42.
5. John 11:23.
6. Matt. 16:18.
7. Matt. 16:16.
8. Mark 16:9; John 20:14–17.
9. Pagels, *The Gnostic Gospels*, p. 9.
10. John 20:17.
11. Mark 16:9; Luke 8:2.
12. Gal. 3:27–29.
13. Acts 1:14; 2:1–4. Some commentators propose that the "each of them" referred to in Acts 2:3 are only the twelve apostles, citing to support this conclusion that 2:14 mentions the twelve as being present. However, while it would certainly have been expected in the Jewish community at that time that public preaching would have been limited to the male apostles, this does not limit the descent of the Holy Spirit on that occasion to only these twelve.

    Luke's use of the words "they were all with one accord in one place" (2:1) echoes his description of the community in Acts 1:14–15, "These all continued with one accord in prayer and supplication, with the women, and Mary the mother of Jesus, and with his brethren . . . about an hundred and twenty." Many commentators conclude that it was the 120 who were together on Pentecost and were the recipients of the Holy Ghost.

In Peter's sermon on Pentecost, he speaks of the occasion as being the fulfillment of the prophecy of Joel: "This is that which was spoken by the prophet Joel; And it shall come to pass in the last days, saith God, I will pour out of my Spirit upon all flesh: and your sons and your daughters shall prophesy, and your young men shall see visions, and your old men shall dream dreams: and on my servants and on my handmaidens I will pour out in those days of my Spirit; and they shall prophesy" (2:16–18). This certainly implies that both men and women were present as recipients of the Spirit. Other passages also indicate that the Holy Spirit was given to all (Acts 2:37–39, 8:12–17, 10:24–48), and that women prophesied, thus manifesting one of the gifts of the Spirit (Acts 21:8–9; I Cor. 11:5).

14. Howard Clark Kee and Franklin W. Young, *Understanding the New Testament* (Englewood Cliffs, N.J.: Prentice-Hall, 1957), p. 342.
15. *Pseudepigrapha* is a term used to describe pseudonymous or anonymous Jewish and Christian religious writings that are not included in any canon of biblical Scripture.
16. Ralph P. Martin's introduction to the Pastoral Letters, in James L. Mays, ed., *Harper's Bible Commentary* (San Francisco: Harper & Row, 1988), p. 1237.
17. D. Guthrie and J. A. Motyer, eds., *The New Bible Commentary Revised* (Grand Rapids, Mich.: Wm. B. Eerdmans Publishing, 1970), p. 1070.
18. Ibid., p. 1065.
19. Ibid.
20. Pagels, *The Gnostic Gospels,* pp. 60–61.
21. Uta Ranke-Heinemann, *Eunuchs for the Kingdom of Heaven,* trans. Peter Heinegg (New York: Bantam Doubleday Dell Publishing Group, Doubleday, 1990), p. 132.
22. Ibid., p. 133.
23. Ibid., p. 131.
24. Ibid., p. 133.
25. Tucker and Liefeld, *Daughters of the Church,* pp. 46–47.
26. Pagels, *The Gnostic Gospels,* p. 69.
27. Pope John Paul II, *World News Tonight,* ABC, September 30,

1988.

28. Elaine Pagels, "Visions, Appearances, and Apostolic Authority: Gnostic and Orthodox Traditions," in Aland, B., ed., *Gnosis: Festschrift für Hans Jonas* (Gottingen: Vandenhoeck and Ruprecht, 1978), p. 417, 422.
29. Tertullian, *On the Veiling of Virgins* 9, quoted in Pagels, *The Gnostic Gospels,* p. 69.
30. Matt. 16:15–18.
31. G. Campbell Morgan, *The Gospel According to Matthew* (New York: Revell, 1929), p. 211.
32. Mother Mary, August 15, 1981, "Divine Wholeness," in *Pearls of Wisdom,* vol. 24, no. 71, August 1981.
33. "And then [God] made man, who was not a man before, of different parts, giving to him a soul made out of nothing." *Apostolic Constitutions* 5:1:7 (A.D. 400). "For you did create heaven and earth, not out of thyself, for then they would be equal to your only-begotten [Son], and thereby even to you; and in no wise would it be right that anything should be equal to you which was not of you." Augustine, *Confessions* 12:7 (A.D. 400). "Though God formed man of the dust of the earth, yet the earth itself, and every earthly material, is absolutely created out of nothing; and man's soul, too, God created out of nothing, and joined to the body, when he made man." Augustine, *The City of God* 14:11 (A.D. 419).

CHAPTER 3
THE GNOSTICS

1. Helmut Koester points out: "It has become more and more evident that the rise of Gnosticism must be dated earlier than the second century and that it cannot be viewed as a relatively late Christian phenomenon. Among the tractates discovered at Nag Hammadi, one finds a number of texts which unfold a rich legacy of Jewish Gnosticism which likely predates the beginnings of Christianity." *Ancient Christian Gospels: Their History and Development* (Philadelphia: Trinity Press International, 1990), pp. 83–84.
2. G. R. S. Mead, *Fragments of a Faith Forgotten* (New Hyde Park, N.Y.: University Books, 1960), p. 32.
3. Hans Jonas, *The Gnostic Religion,* 2d ed., rev. (Boston: Beacon

Press, 1963), pp. 34–35.

4. The original Coptic text reads "her sister" here, but in the next sentence reads "his sister." The text does not provide any other evidence to indicate which of these is correct. Matt. 13:56 and Mark 6:3 speak of Jesus' sisters, without giving their names. Epiphanius of Salamis (A.D. 4th cent.) gives their names as Mary or Anna and Salome. "Her sister" could refer to the sister of Jesus' mother, Mary the wife of Cleophas, who is mentioned in John 19:25. See Marvin Meyer, *The Gospels of Mary: The Secret Tradition of Mary Magdalene, the Companion of Jesus* (New York: HarperSanFrancisco, 2004), p. 108, n. 18.
5. The Gospel of Philip 59.6–11, in Robinson, *The Nag Hammadi Library,* p. 145.
6. The Dialogue of the Savior III 139.12–13, in Pagels, *The Gnostic Gospels,* p. 22.
7. While most commentators interpret Paul's writings as being anti-Gnostic (for example, his preaching against the pursuit of "wisdom" in I Cor. 1), there are Gnostic elements in Paul's writings, and some later Gnostic writers claimed him as the source of their teachings. Perhaps most significantly, Paul claimed that he did not receive Jesus' teaching from the other apostles, but by direct revelation from Jesus (Gal. 1:1–2:10). This was the claim of the Gnostics, and it was one of the most important differences between them and the orthodox, who claimed that legitimate spiritual authority only derived from those who had been with Jesus during his earthly ministry (the twelve apostles) and those who were their successors in the Church. See Elaine Pagels, *The Gnostic Paul: Gnostic Exegesis of the Pauline Letters* (Philadelphia: Fortress Press, 1975).
8. Acts 9:1–19.
9. For a description of Jesus' retreats in Arabia and over the Holy Land, see Mark L. Prophet and Elizabeth Clare Prophet, *The Masters and Their Retreats* (2003).
10. See also Mark L. Prophet and Elizabeth Clare Prophet, *The Lords of the Seven Rays* (1986). The lords of the seven rays are masters, spiritual brothers of Jesus, servant-sons in heaven who assist Jesus in teaching the path of personal Christhood. *Lords of the Seven Rays* tells us how each of these masters prepares us to receive the nine gifts of the Holy Spirit through the sacred heart of Jesus.

11. I Cor. 2:6–7. In his exegesis of I Cor. 2:6–9 in *The Interpreter's Bible* (10:36–37), New Testament scholar Clarence Tucker Craig states: "Those who believe that this section is dominated by ideas from the mysteries think that the word [perfect (KJV) or mature (RSV)] should be rendered 'initiates.'"
12. John 12:32.
13. I Kings 4:25; Mic. 4:4; Zech. 3:10. The vine is the Holy Christ Self, the fig tree is the I AM Presence and the causal body bearing the fruits of God consciousness through good works.
14. Exod. 3:14.
15. James 4:8.
16. Rev. 14:6. See also the Climb the Highest Mountain series, by Mark L. Prophet and Elizabeth Clare Prophet.
17. Rev. 10:2.
18. Heb. 13:2.
19. Phil. 3:14.
20. I Cor. 3:16, 17; 6:19, 20; II Cor. 6:16.
21. The Gospel of Thomas, logia 49, 50, in Marvin Meyer, *The Secret Teachings of Jesus: Four Gnostic Gospels* (New York: Vintage Books, 1986), pp. 27–28.
22. Irenaeus, *Against Heresies,* in *Ante-Nicene Fathers*, 1:324.
23. Werner Foerster, *Gnosis: A Selection of Gnostic Texts,* 2 vols., trans. R. McL. Wilson (Oxford: Clarendon Press, 1972), 1:5.
24. Ibid.
25. Mal. 3:1–3.
26. Mal. 3:2.
27. Foerster, *Gnosis,* 1:5, 2–3.
28. The First Apocalypse of James 28.11–20, in Robinson, *Nag Hammadi Library,* pp. 263–64.
29. The Gospel of Thomas, logion 18, in Meyer, *The Secret Teachings of Jesus,* p. 22.
30. Rev. 1:8, 11.
31. A number of I AM affirmations of Jesus are recorded in the Bible, among them the following: "I AM the resurrection and the life" (John 11:25); "I AM the way, the truth, and the life" (John 14:6); "I AM the light of the world" (John 8:12); "I AM come that they might have life, and that they might have it more abundantly" (John 10:10). These affirmations use the name of God, "I AM" (see Exod. 3:14). They are not used to claim that our lower self has these qualities, but rather to affirm that God

can manifest the qualities of the Christ in and through us. The affirmation of "I AM . . ." means "God in me is . . ." Jesus' I AM affirmations may be used by disciples who wish to put on his consciousness and follow in his footsteps.

32. I Cor. 15:53.
33. The Gospel of Thomas, logion 50, in Robinson, *Nag Hammadi Library,* p. 132.
34. The Gospel of Truth 42, in Marvin Meyer, *The Gnostic Gospels of Jesus: The Definitive Collection of Mystical Gospels and Secret Books about Jesus of Nazareth* (New York: HarperSanFrancisco, 2005), p. 112.
35. For more information about the inner temples and retreats of the ascended masters, see Prophet, *The Masters and Their Retreats.*
36. The Gospel of Truth 42, 43, in Meyer, *The Gnostic Gospels of Jesus,* p. 112.
37. Exod. 3:14, 15.
38. Matt. 22:11–14.
39. Exod. 3:15.
40. John 11:25.
41. For more information about dynamic decrees and the use of the Science of the Spoken Word as it is taught by the ascended masters, see Mark L. Prophet and Elizabeth Clare Prophet, *The Science of the Spoken Word* (2004). For an introduction to the Teachings of the Ascended Masters, see Mark L. Prophet and Elizabeth Clare Prophet, *Keys to the Kingdom and New Dimensions of Being* (2003).
42. The enemy within has been known in esoteric tradition as the "dweller-on-the-threshold." This term is used to designate the anti-self, the not-self, the synthetic self, the antithesis of the Real Self, the conglomerate of the self-created ego, ill-conceived through the inordinate use of the gift of free will. It consists of the carnal mind and a constellation of misqualified energies, forcefields, focuses and animal magnetism comprising the subconscious mind. For more information about the dweller-on-the-threshold and how to meet the challenge of this internal enemy, see Mark L. Prophet and Elizabeth Clare Prophet, *The Enemy Within: Encountering and Conquering the Dark Side* (2004).
43. Foerster, *Gnosis,* 1:2.

44. Luke 19:10; Matt. 18:11.
45. John 10:1–16.
46. The Gospel of Truth 22, 24, 25, in Meyer, *The Gnostic Gospels of Jesus*, pp. 99, 101.
47. Ezek. 18:4.
48. Mark 8:36.

CHAPTER 4
THE DIVINE FEMININE—EAST AND WEST

1. Lemuria was the lost continent of the Pacific which, according to the findings of James Churchward, archaeologist and author of *The Lost Continent of Mu,* extended from north of Hawaii three thousand miles south to Easter Island and the Fijis and was made up of three areas of land stretching more than five thousand miles from east to west. Churchward's history of the ancient Motherland is based on records inscribed on sacred tablets he claims to have discovered in India. With the help of the high priest of an Indian temple he deciphered the tablets, and during fifty years of research confirmed their contents in further writings, inscriptions and legends he came upon in Southeast Asia, the Yucatan, Central America, the Pacific Islands, Mexico, North America, ancient Egypt and other civilizations. He estimates that Lemuria was destroyed approximately twelve thousand years ago by the collapse of the gas chambers that upheld the continent.

   See Mark and Elizabeth Prophet, *The Path of the Higher Self*, pp. 61–82. See also James Churchward, *The Lost Continent of Mu* (1931; reprint, New York: Paperback Library Edition, 1968), p. 226.
2. According to esoteric tradition, there are seven primary aggregations of souls—that is, the first to the seventh root races. The first three root races lived in purity and innocence upon earth in three golden ages before the fall of Adam and Eve. Through obedience to cosmic law and total identification with the Real Self, these three root races won their immortal freedom and ascended from earth.

   It was during the time of the fourth root race, on the continent of Lemuria, that the allegorical Fall took place under the influence of the fallen angels known as Serpents (because they used the serpentine spinal energies to beguile the soul, or female principle in mankind, as a means to their end of lowering the masculine potential, thereby emasculating the Sons of God). The fourth, fifth and sixth root races (the latter soul group not having entirely descended into physical incarnation) remain in embodiment on earth today.

3. Logos. (Gk. for "word," "speech," "reason"—the divine wisdom manifest in the creation.) According to ancient Greek philosophy, it is the controlling principle in the universe. The Book of John identifies the Word, or Logos, with Jesus Christ: "And the Word was made flesh and dwelt among us." Hence, Jesus Christ is seen as the embodiment of divine reason, the Word Incarnate.
4. Rev. 17:1–6.
5. Rev. 12:1.
6. The fallen angels are those who followed Lucifer in the Great Rebellion and whose consciousness therefore "fell" to lower levels of vibration and awareness as they were by law "cast out into the earth" at the hand of Archangel Michael—constrained, by the karma of their disobedience to God and his Christ and their blasphemy of his children, to take on and evolve through dense physical bodies. Here they walk about, as Peter said, seeking whosesoever souls and minds and bodies they may devour, sowing seeds of unrest and the Luciferian rebellion among the people through the subculture of rock music and drugs, the media and their Babylonian cult of idolatry. They are known variously as the fallen ones, Luciferians, Watchers, Nephilim, "giants in the earth," Satanists, Serpents, sons of Belial, etc. See Rev. 12:9; Gen. 6:1–7; and Elizabeth Clare Prophet, *Fallen Angels and the Origins of Evil: Why Church Fathers Suppressed the Book of Enoch and Its Startling Revelations* (2000).
7. Great Guru of the seed of Christ throughout cosmos; Hierarch of Venus; the Ancient of Days spoken of in Daniel 7:9, 13, 22, Sanat Kumara (from the Sanskrit, meaning "always a youth") is one of the Seven Holy Kumaras. Long ago he came to planet Earth in her darkest hour when all light had gone out in her evolutions, for there was not a single individual on the planet who gave adoration to the God Presence. Sanat Kumara and the band of 144,000 souls of light who accompanied him volunteered to keep the flame of life on behalf of earth's people. This they vowed to do until the children of God would respond to the

love of God and turn once again to serve their mighty I AM Presence. Sanat Kumara's retreat, Shamballa, was established on an island in the Gobi Sea, now the Gobi Desert. The first to respond to his flame was Gautama Buddha, followed by Lord Maitreya and Jesus.

8. Although the physical focus of the Mother flame was lost when Mu went down, the feminine ray has been enshrined on the etheric plane by the God and Goddess Meru in their temple at Lake Titicaca.
9. Gen. 1:26.
10. Gen. 1:27; 5:2.
11. Pagels, *The Gnostic Gospels,* p. 50.
12. *The Great Announcement,* quoted by Hippolytus in *Refutation of All Heresies,* in *Ante-Nicene Fathers,* 5:79.
13. Pagels, *The Gnostic Gospels*, p. 61.
14. Rev. 12:1.
15. Manly P. Hall, *The Secret Teachings of All Ages,* 16th ed. (Los Angeles: Philosophical Research Society, 1969), p. XLV.
16. Adolph Erman, *A Handbook of Egyptian Religion,* trans. A. S. Griffith (London: Archibald Constable & Co., 1907), pp. 244–45.
17. David Frawley, *Wisdom of the Ancient Seers: Mantras of the Rig Veda* (Salt Lake City, Utah: Passage Press, 1992), p. 27.
18. Rig Veda 1:159, in Frawley, *Wisdom of the Ancient Seers,* p. 53.
19. Frawley, *Wisdom of the Ancient Seers,* p. 54.
20. John 1:1, 3.
21. John Woodroffe, *The Garland of Letters* (Pondicherry, India: Ganesh and Co., 1979), p. 4.
22. Ibid.
23. John 14:23.
24. Ramakrishna, quoted in Swami Prabhavananda and Christopher Isherwood, trans., *How to Know God: The Yoga Aphorisms of Patanjali* (New York: New American Library, 1969), p. 109.
25. Sri Aurobindo, *The Mother* (Pondicherry, India: Sri Aurobindo Ashram Press, 1974), pp. 55, 56.
26. Ibid., pp. 34, 35.
27. We understand the Hail Mary to be a salutation to the flame of God as Mother (Hail Ma-Ray). This presence is personified in Mary and also in many other manifestations of God as Mother. Mother Mary conveyed to Elizabeth Clare Prophet the under-

standing that as we enter a new cycle, we should not affirm a sinful nature or our death, but rather our birthright as sons and daughters of God and our victory. She therefore gave a new version of the Hail Mary: "Hail, Mary, full of grace. The Lord is with thee. Blessed art thou among women, and blessed is the fruit of thy womb, Jesus. Holy Mary, Mother of God, pray for us, sons and daughters of God, now and at the hour of our victory over sin, disease, and death."

28. To ascend you must: balance your threefold flame; align your four lower bodies; attain mastery on all seven rays; achieve mastery over outer conditions; fulfill your divine plan; transmute your electronic belt; raise the Kundalini; and balance at least 51 percent of your karma. For further teaching on the ascension, see Serapis Bey, *Dossier on the Ascension* (1978).
29. James M. Robinson, "Very Goddess and Very Man: Jesus' Better Self," in Karen L. King, ed., *Images of the Feminine in Gnosticism* (Harrisburg, Pa.: Trinity Press International, 2000), p. 117.
30. Odes of Solomon 24:1–2, in H. F. D. Sparks, ed., *The Apocryphal Old Testament* (Oxford: Clarendon Press, 1984), pp. 715, 724.
31. Ibid., 36:1–3, in Robinson, "Very Goddess and Very Man," p. 118.
32. The Gospel of Philip 60.1, in Robinson, *Nag Hammadi Library,* p. 146.
33. Ibid. 55.23–26, 33–36, in Robinson, *Nag Hammadi Library,* p. 143.
34. Acts 2:1–4.
35. Exod. 40:20, 34–35.
36. Gershom G. Scholem, *Major Trends in Jewish Mysticism* (New York: Schocken Books, 1961), p. 230.
37. Louis Ginzberg, ed., *The Legends of the Jews,* trans. Henrietta Szold (Philadelphia: The Jewish Publication Society of America, 1920), vol. 2, p. 260.
38. Ibid.
39. Ibid.
40. Leo Schaya, *The Universal Meaning of the Kabbalah,* trans. Nancy Pearson (Secaucus, N.J.: University Books, 1971), p. 67.
41. Charles Poncé is a widely known lecturer on philosophy, psychology and comparative religion.

42. Charles Poncé, *Kabbalah: An Introduction and Illumination for the World Today* (Wheaton, Ill.: Quest Books, 1978), p. 253.
43. Ibid., p. 254
44. Scholem, *Major Trends in Jewish Mysticism,* p. 111.
45. Moshe Idel, *The Mystical Experience in Abraham Abulafia,* trans. Jonathan Chipman (Albany, New York: State University of New York Press, 1988), p. 84.
46. Ya'qub ibn Yusuf, Forum, *Gnosis Magazine* 5 (Fall 1987):4, 5.
47. Ibid.
48. Ibid.
49. Ibid.
50. Ibid.
51. Raymond E. Brown, Joseph A. Fitzmyer and Roland E. Murphy, eds., *The New Jerome Biblical Commentary* (Englewood Cliffs, N.J.: Prentice Hall, 1990), p. 450 (27:16), p. 513 (33:12).
52. Prov. 8:22 (Jerusalem Bible).
53. Book of Wisdom 9:1, 4, 9 (Jerusalem Bible).
54. Ibid. 1:6 (Jerusalem Bible).
55. Ibid. 7:26, 27 (Jerusalem Bible).
56. I Cor. 1:24.
57. Trimorphic Protennoia 35.1, 2, 30–32, in Robinson, *Nag Hammadi Library,* p. 513.
58. The Sophia of Jesus Christ 104.17–19, in Robinson, *Nag Hammadi Library,* p. 231.
59. Mead, *Pistis Sophia,* p. 82.
60. Prov. 3:13–20; 4:5–9; 8:12–17.

CHAPTER 5
GNOSTIC TEACHINGS ON MALE AND FEMALE

1. Rev. 1:8; 21:6; 22:13.
2. The First Apocalypse of James V 41.15–18, in Robinson, *Nag Hammadi Library,* p. 267.
3. Kurt Rudolph, *Gnosis: The Nature and History of Gnosticism* (San Francisco: Harper & Row, 1987), p. 272.
4. Exegesis on the Soul 127.19–21, in Robinson, *Nag Hammadi Library,* p. 192.
5. The Gospel of Mary 9.6–15, in Jean-Yves Leloup. *The Gospel of Mary Magdalene* (Rochester, Vt.: Inner Traditions, 2002), p. 29; 9.16–18, in Robinson, *Nag Hammadi Library,* p. 525.

6. The Gospel of Thomas, logion 114, in John S. Kloppenborg et al., *Q–Thomas Reader* (Sonoma, Calif.: Polebridge Press, 1990), p. 111.
7. Stephen J. Patterson's introduction to *The Gospel of Thomas,* in Kloppenborg, *Q–Thomas Reader,* p. 111.
8. Ibid., pp. 111–12.
9. The Gospel of Thomas, logion 1, in Meyer, *The Secret Teachings of Jesus,* p. 126.
10. The Gospel of Mary 17.10–18:15 in Marvin Meyer, *The Gospels of Mary: The Secret Tradition of Mary Magdalene, the Companion of Jesus* (New York: HarperSanFrancisco, 2004), p. 22; 18.15–19, in Robinson, *Nag Hammadi Library,* p. 527.
11. Mead, *Pistis Sophia,* p. 135.
12. Ibid.
13. Matt. 16:18.
14. John 20:1–18.
15. Mead, *Pistis Sophia,* p. 20.
16. Ibid., p. 193.
17. The Gospel of Mary 18.12–15, and the Gospel of Philip 63.32–64:2, in Robinson, *Nag Hammadi Library,* p. 527, 148.
18. The Gospel of Mary 8.22–9.2, in Robinson, *Nag Hammadi Library,* p. 525.
19. Zostrianos VIII 131.5–8, in Meyer, "'Male' and 'Female' in the Gospel of Thomas," *New Testament Studies* 31 (1985), p. 567.
20. Frederik Wisse, "Flee Femininity: Antifemininity in Gnostic Texts and the Question of Social Milieu," in King, *Images of the Feminine in Gnosticism,* p. 300.
21. Ibid., p. 301.
22. Ibid.
23. The Book of Thomas the Contender 144.8–10, in Wisse, "Flee Femininity," p. 303.
24. The Teachings of Sylvanus 93.3–13, in Robinson, *Nag Hammadi Library,* pp. 384–85.
25. Wisse, "Flee Femininity," pp. 305–06.
26. Kari Vogt, "'Becoming Male': One Aspect of an Early Christian Anthropology," in Elizabeth Schüssler Fiorenza and Mary Collins, eds., *Women—Invisible in Theology and Church* (Minneapolis: Fortress Press, 1985), p. 76.
27. Origen, *Homilies on Genesis* I, 12–14, in Vogt, "'Becoming Male,'" p. 76.

28. Origen, *Homilies on Joshua,* in Vogt, "'Becoming Male,'" p. 76.
29. Vogt, "'Becoming Male,'" p. 76.
30. Matt. 3:17; Mark 1:11; Luke 3:22; 2 Peter 1:17.
31. Bentley Layton, *The Gnostic Scriptures: A New Translation with Annotations and Introductions* (Garden City, N.Y.: Doubleday and Co., 1987), p. 399, note f.
32. Ibid., p. 399.
33. Bertil Gärtner, *The Theology of the Gospel According to Thomas* (New York: Harper & Brothers, 1961), p. 254.
34. *Pseudo-Clementines,* Hom. II, ch. 15, in *Ante-Nicene Fathers,* 8:231.
35. According to HarperCollins.com, Marvin Meyer is one of the foremost scholars on Gnosticism, the Nag Hammadi library, and texts about Jesus outside the New Testament. He is Griset Professor of Bible and Christian Studies and director of the Albert Schweitzer Institute at Chapman University, Orange, California. Among his more recent books are *The Gospel of Thomas: The Hidden Sayings of Jesus, The Gnostic Bible, Secret Gospels: Essays on Thomas and the Secret Gospel of Mark* and *The Gospels of Mary: The Secret Tradition of Mary Magdalene, the Companion of Jesus..*
36. Meyer, *The Secret Teachings of Jesus,* p. 108.
37. Marvin W. Meyer, trans., *The Gospel of Thomas* (New York: HarperSanFrancisco, 1992), p. 109.
38. Philo of Alexandria, *Quaestiones et Solutiones in Exodum* book 1, 8; Marvin W. Meyer, "'Male' and 'Female' in the Gospel of Thomas," p. 564.
39. Meyer, "'Male' and 'Female' in the Gospel of Thomas," pp. 565–66.
40. An introduction to the Teachings of the Ascended Masters may be found in Mark L. Prophet and Elizabeth Clare Prophet, *Keys to the Kingdom* (2003), available from Summit University Press.
41. Jesus Christ, July 7, 1985, "The Law of Your Twin Flames," in *Pearls of Wisdom,* vol. 28, no. 38, September 22, 1985.
42. Elizabeth Schüssler Fiorenza, "Word, Spirit and Power: Women in Early Christian Communities," in Rosemary Ruether and Eleanor McLaughlin, eds., *Women of Spirit: Female Leadership in the Jewish and Christian Traditions* (New York: Simon and Schuster, 1979), pp. 48–49.
43. The Gospel of Philip 68, in Meyer, *The Gnostic Gospels of*

Jesus, p. 68.

44. Ibid.
45. Ibid.
46. Ibid. 70, in Meyer, *The Gnostic Gospels of Jesus,* p. 70.
47. For more information about dynamic decrees and the use of the Science of the Spoken Word as it is taught by the ascended masters, see Mark L. Prophet and Elizabeth Clare Prophet, *The Science of the Spoken Word* (2004).
48. The Gospel of Thomas, logion 22, in Meyer, *The Secret Teachings of Jesus,* pp. 23–24.
49. John 1:1, 3.
50. In Hinduism the four-armed goddess Kali (Sanskrit, "the black one" or "the power of time") symbolizes the fierce aspect of the Divine Mother. She is a consort of Shiva, the Destroyer, i.e., the Transformer of the energies of Darkness to the original polarization of Light. As Third Person of the Hindu Trinity, Shiva is the incarnation of the Holy Spirit whose action in the world of form is crystallized through his Shakti, or feminine counterpart. Kali is usually depicted with a terrifying countenance, her tongue protruding, wearing a necklace of human skulls or heads and a belt of severed arms. In one hand she holds a sword, in the other she may hold the severed head of a demon, a shield or a noose; her hands may also make the sign of fearlessness and offer blessings and benefits. Kali's dread appearance symbolizes her boundless power. Her destructiveness is seen as ultimately leading to transformation and salvation. She shatters delusions of the ego as well as the form and substance of human creations that are not aligned with the will of her consort, thus blessing and liberating those who seek the knowledge of God.
51. The word *Tao,* which literally means "Way," is the animating principle of life that sustains all creation and is in all creation. According to the teachings of Taoism, it is the transcendental First Cause, the Absolute, the Ultimate Reality.

CHAPTER 6
THE MESSAGE IS SUPPRESSED

1. For additional information about the resurrection flame and how it may be invoked for healing, see Prophet, *Science of the Spoken Word,* pp. 136–39.

2. John 14:6.
3. The Gospel of John records that there were three Marys who kept the vigil with Jesus as he passed through the initiations of the crucifixion and the resurrection: "Now there stood by the cross of Jesus his mother, and his mother's sister, Mary the wife of Cleophas, and Mary Magdalene" (19:25).
4. John 20:17.
5. John 14:2.
6. John 20:26–27.
7. Luke 8:43–48; Mark 5:25–34.
8. Passages in the Gospels which show Jesus teaching but do not record his words: Mark 6:34 (Luke 9:11); Luke 24:27; Matt. 9:10, 13; Mark 2:15, 17; Luke 5:29, 32; Luke 10:39; Matt. 9:35 (Mark 6:6); Matt. 13:54 (Mark 6:2); Matt. 16:21 (Mark 8:31); Mark 1:21 (Luke 4:31); Mark 1:39 (Luke 4:44); Mark 2:2 (Luke 5:17); Mark 2:13; Luke 2:46, 47; 4:15; 5:3; 6:6; John 4:40–42.
9. Passages in the Gospels which recount some of Jesus' words but imply that not all of what he said is recorded: Matt. 4:17 (Mark 1:14, 15); Matt. 4:23ff.; 10:27; 21:23ff. (Luke 20:1ff.); Mark 4:33, 34; 10:1ff.; Luke 13:10–21; 13:22–35; John 7:14ff.; 8:2ff.
10. Acts 1:3.
11. Irenaeus, *Against Heresies* 2.22.5, in *Ante-Nicene Fathers,* 1:391–92.
12. Mead, *Pistis Sophia,* p. 1.
13. Luke 4:16–20.
14. Letter from Clement of Alexandria to Theodore, quoted in Morton Smith, *The Secret Gospel: The Discovery and Interpretation of the Secret Gospel According to Mark* (New York: Harper & Row, 1973), p. 15.
15. Matt. 5:48.
16. Clement, quoted in Smith, *The Secret Gospel,* p. 15.
17. Mark L. Prophet (1918–1973) was trained by the ascended master El Morya to be a messenger for the Great White Brotherhood. In 1958, under El Morya's direction, he founded The Summit Lighthouse as an organization dedicated to the publishing of the Teachings of the Ascended Masters. In 1961 he was joined in this work by his twin flame, Elizabeth. Mark made his ascension on February 26, 1973, and is now known to us as the ascended master Lanello. Some of his embodiments include Abraham's nephew Lot, the Egyptian Pharaoh Ikhnaton, Mark

the Evangelist, Origen of Alexandria, Saint Bonaventure, Louis XIV and Henry Wadsworth Longfellow.

After he ascended, his twin flame, the messenger Elizabeth Clare Prophet, carried on the work of The Summit Lighthouse. As Lanello, he continues to direct the activities of The Summit Lighthouse, the "Ever-Present Guru" who has said, "Ours must be a message of infinite love and we must demonstrate that love to the world."

18. Mark 1:40–41.
19. Pagels, *The Gnostic Gospels,* p. 57.
20. Tertullian, *On Prescription Against Heretics,* in *Ante-Nicene Fathers,* 3:263.
21. Mother Mary, November 2, 1977.
22. The seven rays are the light emanations of the Godhead, the seven spiritual light rays of God. These seven rays emerge out of the white light, through the prism of the Christ consciousness. Each ray focuses a frequency, or color, and specific qualities. The rays and their qualities are (1) blue—faith, will, power, perfection and protection; (2) yellow—wisdom, understanding, enlightenment and illumination; (3) pink—compassion, kindness, charity, love and beauty; (4) white—purity, discipline, order and joy; (5) green—truth, science, healing, music, abundance and vision; (6) purple and gold—ministration, service, peace and brotherhood; (7) violet—freedom, mercy, justice, transmutation and forgiveness.
23. J. N. Sanders, "The Literature and Canon of the New Testament," in Matthew Black, ed., *Peake's Commentary on the Bible* (Walton-on-Thames, Surrey: Thomas Nelson and Sons, 1981), p. 680.
24. Irenaeus, *Against Heresies,* in *Ante-Nicene Fathers,* 1:429.
25. Tertullian, *On Prescription Against Heretics,* in *Ante-Nicene Fathers,* 3:250.
26. Arthur Guirdham, "Reincarnation and the Practice of Medicine," delivered on March 25, 1969, before the College of Psychic Science, London; quoted in Joseph Head and S. L. Cranston, comp. and ed., *Reincarnation: The Phoenix Fire Mystery* (New York: Julian Press / Crown Publishers, 1977), pp. 163–64.
27. Helena Blavatsky, quoted in Manly Palmer Hall, *Orders of the Quest: The Holy Grail* (Los Angeles: Philosophical Research Society, 1976), p. 28.

28. Margaret Starbird describes how the "Inquisition's ruthless campaign against the Albinesian heresy and the prominent families of Provence, many of whom were Templars, squelched the budding of the feminine and its corollary branches of art and science." This growing appreciation for the feminine was rooted in Provence, the same area that "had been the center of a cult of Mary Magdalene for centuries—witness the numerous chapels, fountains, springs, and other geographical landmarks in the region that bear her name," writes Starbird. (Starbird, *The Woman with the Alabaster Jar,* pp. 68–69).

    The feminine found lasting expression in many of the Templars' surviving works, "such as their idiosyncratic round churches, in this case symbolizing the rotundity of the Earth Mother, the big belly of the pregnant goddess," writes Lynn Picknett in *Mary Magdalene: Christianity's Hidden Goddess.*

    "The Templars' passionate devotion to the Magdalene is most evident from their oath, which was sworn to 'God and Our Lady': that this particular 'Notre Dame' was *not* the Virgin, is suggested by the words of their Absolution: 'I pray God that he will pardon you your sins as he pardoned them to St Mary Magdalene and the thief who was put on the cross,'" says Picknett (Picknett, *Mary Magdalene: Christianity's Hidden Goddess* [New York: Carol & Graf Publishers, 2004], pp. 104, 105).

    During this era of the suppression of the feminine, writes Starbird, "beautiful and important epithets that once belonged to the Magdalene were shifted to the Blessed Virgin Mary and churches built to 'Our Lady' ostensibly honored the mother of Jesus as the preeminent bearer of the archetypal feminine—'alone of all her sex.' After the mid-thirteenth century, the 'voice of the bride' was effectively silenced, although it is whispered that the masons of Europe kept the true faith and built its symbols into the very stones of their Gothic cathedrals....

    "The sacred stones of the vaulting arches in Europe's medieval churches themselves cry out to all who enter that they honor the Goddess, the eternal feminine. This includes, above all, the Magdalene," concludes Starbird (Starbird, *The Goddess in the Gospels,* p. 152).

29. Authoritative Teaching 32.30–33.3, in Robinson, *Nag Hammadi Library,* p. 309.

30. Pagels, "Visions, Appearances, and Apostolic Authority," p. 430.
31. Pagels, *The Gnostic Gospels,* pp. xviii, xxiv.
32. Will Durant, *The Age of Faith,* vol. 4 of *The Story of Civilization* (New York: Simon & Schuster, 1944), p. 46.

CHAPTER 7
CLERICAL CELIBACY AND THE DOCTRINE OF ORIGINAL SIN

1. Mark 1:30–31; Luke 4:38–39.
2. Alan Richardson and John Bowden eds., *The Westminster Dictionary of Christian Theology* (Philadelphia: The Westminster Press, 1983), p. 89.
3. Ibid. The bearing of children was very much an obligation under Jewish law and custom. God's first instruction to the man and woman he had created was to "be fruitful, and multiply" (Gen. 1:28). This was also God's instruction to Noah and his sons after the Flood (Gen. 9:1) and to Jacob, the progenitor of the twelve tribes (Gen. 35:11). God's great blessing to Abraham was that his progeny would be innumerable, like the stars of heaven and the sand of the seashore (Gen. 22:17).

   Many of the Jewish laws and customs regarding marriage and sexual relations served to facilitate this goal (e.g., Deut. 24:5), including the allowance of polygamy—exemplified in Abraham, Jacob, David and Solomon, and still practiced in New Testament times. The levirate marriage sought to prevent the misfortune of a man dying childless (Deut. 25:5). See Elaine Pagels, *Adam, Eve, and the Serpent* (New York: Random House, 1988), ch. 1.

   The Bible itself provides evidence that much of the early Christian church followed the Jewish precedent in expecting that religious leaders *should* be married. The first Epistle to Timothy says, "A bishop then must be blameless, the husband of one wife, vigilant, sober, of good behaviour, given to hospitality, apt to teach;... one that ruleth well his own house, having his children in subjection with all gravity; (for if a man know not how to rule his own house, how shall he take care of the church of God?)" (I Tim. 3:2, 4–5) Although this epistle was probably not written by Paul himself, it dates from very early in the history of Christian community and reflects practices at that time.

4. Pagels, *Adam, Eve, and the Serpent,* p. 109.
5. Ibid.
6. Augustine, *City of God* 15.1, in Pagels, *Adam, Eve, and the Serpent,* p. 114.
7. Augustine, *City of God* 2.5, in Philip Schaff, ed., *Nicene and Post-Nicene Fathers of the Christian Church* (Grand Rapids, Mich.: Wm. B. Eerdmans Publishing Company, n.d.), 5:332.
8. Ibid., 15.1, in *Nicene and Post-Nicene Fathers,* 2:285.
9. Catholic Church, *Catechism of the Catholic Church* (New York: Doubleday, 1995) 389, p. 98.
10. Jerome, *The Virgin's Profession,* quoted in H. L. Mencken, *A New Dictionary of Quotations on Historical Principles from Ancient and Modern Sources* (New York: Alfred A. Knopf, Borzoi Book, 1942), p. 738.
11. Kenneth Scott Latourette, *A History of Christianity* (New York: Harper & Row, 1975), vol. I, p. 182.
12. Rev. 12:7–17. For more information about the original fall of the fallen angels, see Elizabeth Clare Prophet, *Fallen Angels and the Origins of Evil.*
13. John 9:4.
14. John 3:15–17.
15. Pope Pius IX, *Ineffabilis Deus,* quoted in Bernhard Lohse, *A Short History of Christian Doctrine* (Philadelphia: Fortress Press, 1966), p. 203.
16. John 2:1–11.
17. I Cor. 7.
18. Gautama Buddha, the "Compassionate One," was born Siddhartha Gautama in northern India, c. 563 B.C. He was the son of King Suddhodana and Queen Mahamaya, rulers of the Sakya kingdom, and thus a member of the Kshatriya (warrior or ruling) caste. At sixteen, after proving his skill in a contest of arms, Prince Siddhartha married his beautiful cousin Yasodhara. He soon grew pensive and preoccupied, but the turning point of his life did not occur until the age of twenty-nine, when he set out on four journeys which presented in turn the four prophesied sights—an old man, a diseased man, a dead man and a holy man.

    On his way back to the palace, he received news of the birth of his son, whom he named Rahula, or "obstacle." That night he went to the bedchamber for a farewell look at his sleeping wife and son. He then rode all night and at dawn assumed the guise of an ascetic, seeking out the most learned teachers of his day to instruct him in the Truth.

After six years of asceticism had not led him to his goal, he vowed to remain under the Bo tree until he attained enlightenment. After meeting the challenges of Mara, the temptress, he spent forty-nine days in meditation, returning with the key elements of his teaching—the Four Noble Truths, the Eightfold Path and the Middle Way.

19. The ascended masters have revealed that Mary Magdalene was the twin flame of Jesus.
20. Mother Mary, April 21, 1987, "The Old Order Must Pass Away," in *Pearls of Wisdom,* vol. 30, no. 21, May 24, 1987.
21. According to Sipe's study, "about 28% of priests are engaged in relationships, many of them enduring, with women. An additional 10% to 13% indulge in intimacies with adult men, and 6% pursue adolescents or children, usually boys." Church officials argue that Sipe's findings are skewed because half the priests in his study were already in therapy. However, even if the real figures are half what Sipe reports, this still indicates a very serious problem. Anastasia Toufexis, "What to Do When Priests Stray," *Time,* September 24, 1990, p. 79.
22. Hank Whittemore, "Ministers Under Stress," *Parade Magazine,* 14 April 1991, p. 5.
23. Robert T. Zintl, "Big Gamble on the Priesthood," *Time,* November 5, 1990, p. 83.
24. II Tim. 2:15.

CHAPTER 8
THE FORGIVENESS OF MARY MAGDALENE

1. Gen. 3:20.
2. Isa. 1:18.
3. Matt. 6:12.
4. Luke 7:36–50.
5. John 8:3.
6. Over the span of approximately 2,150 years, the position of the sun against the fixed stars at the time of the Spring equinox moves 30 degrees through the heavens. This movement of the

equinox through the constellations of the zodiac defines the astrological ages that the earth passes through. Thus, approximately four thousand years ago, the earth entered the age of Aries. Approximately 2000 years ago, the earth entered the age of Pisces. (The symbol of the fish has thus been very appropriate for the dispensation of Christianity.) At this time, we are entering the age of Aquarius.

7. John 8:4.
8. John 8:5–8.
9. John 8:9.
10. Heb. 6:20.
11. John 8:10–11.
12. John 3:17.
13. John 8:12.
14. Mark 16:9; Luke 8:2.
15. Rom. 3:23.
16. John 1:14.
17. Matt. 28:1–7.
18. John 20:2–18.
19. The ascended master Saint Germain was embodied as Joseph, the father of Jesus.
20. The violet flame is the seventh ray aspect of the Holy Spirit, the sacred fire that transmutes the cause, effect, record and memory of sin and the karma that is the record of and the penalty for that sin. The violet flame is also called the flame of transmutation, freedom and forgiveness. It is the gift of the Holy Spirit that comes to us under the sponsorship of Saint Germain, Lord of the Seventh Ray and hierarch of the Age of Aquarius. The violet flame works in microcosmic and macrocosmic worlds and is the key to individual and world transmutation.
21. Isa. 1:18.

CHAPTER 9
A REVOLUTION OF THEOLOGY IN THE MAKING

1. See Michael Baigent, Richard Leigh, and Henry Lincoln, Holy Blood, Holy Grail (New York: Delacorte Press, 1982); Laurence Gardner, *Bloodline of the Holy Grail: The Hidden Image of Jesus Revealed* (Shaftesbury, Dorset; Boston, Mass.: Element, 1998); and Margaret Starbird, *The Woman with the Alabaster*

Jar: Mary Magdalen and the Holy Grail (Santa Fe, N.M.: Bear & Co. Pub., 1993).

2. See Holger Kersten, *Jesus Lived in India: His Unknown Life Before and After the Crucifixion* (Longmead, Shaftesbury, Dorset: Element Books Ltd., 1986); Khwaja Nazir Ahmad, *Jesus in Heaven on Earth: Journey of Jesus to Kashmir, His Preaching to Lost Tribes of Israel, and Death and Burial in Srinagar* (Columbus, Oh.; Ahmadiyya Anjuman Isha'at Islam Lahore Inc., 1998).
3. The ascended master El Morya has revealed that Jesus journeyed to Kashmir after his resurrection and lived there until his passing at age 81, in A.D. 77. See El Morya and Saint Germain, April 22, 1984, "A Document from the Darjeeling Council," in *Pearls of Wisdom,* vol. 27, no. 31A, June 8, 1984; Jesus, April 19, 1992, "The Descent of the Crystal Fire Mist: From My Sacred Heart I Pour Out the Vial," in *Pearls of Wisdom,* vol. 35, no. 18, May 3, 1992; Jesus, June 27, 1993, "The Path of the Builders," in *Pearls of Wisdom,* vol. 36, no. 36, September 1, 1993. See Questions and Answers for further discussion.
4. See Magda, April 1, 1983, "The Mystical Union of Twin Flames," in *Pearls of Wisdom,* vol. 26, no. 29, July 17, 1983; Magda and Jesus, April 9, 1982, "Believability: A Message to the American Woman," in *Pearls of Wisdom,* vol. 25, no. 24, June 13, 1982; Jesus, November 22, 1990, "The Marriage of the Lamb Is Come," in *Pearls of Wisdom,* vol. 33. no. 46, November 25, 1990.
5. I Cor. 15:50, 53.
6. At the point of death, the crystal cord and the threefold flame are withdrawn from the physical body and the soul moves to other octaves to continue her evolution. When the soul reembodies, the threefold flame is reignited in the physical body at the moment of birth.
7. Layton, *Gnostic Scriptures,* p. 359.
8. Fida Hassnain, *A Search for the Historical Jesus* (Bath, U.K.: Gateway Books, 1994), pp. 200, 173–82.
9. John 14:16.
10. John 14:26.

EPILOGUE
THE UNIVERSAL DIVINE FEMININE

1. The electronic belt is formed of the individual's misqualification of God's energy as it collects and intensifies in the subconscious to form a negative spiral shaped like a kettledrum surrounding the chakras below the heart.

MARY MAGDALENE'S MEMORIAL

1. Edith Filliette, *Saint Mary Magdalene: Her Life and Times, as Seen in the Gospels, History, & Tradition* (Newton Lower Falls, MA: Society of Saint Mary Magdalene, 1983), pp.173–74.

QUESTIONS AND ANSWERS

Material in Questions I and II is excerpted from "Following the Grail," *Heart: For the Coming Revolution,* Winter 1985. Material in Question III is excerpted from Prophet, *The Lost Years of Jesus,* pp. 418–429.

1. Acts 1:8.
2. John 19:38.
3. Acts 8:1.
4. Acts 8:1, 4.
5. Starbird, *The Woman with the Alabaster Jar,* p. 26.
6. Rev. 14:1.
7. Luke 23:50–53.
8. For further information on the legends of Jesus at Glastonbury, see C. C. Dobson, *Did Our Lord Visit Britain as They Say in Cornwall and Somerset?* (London: Covenant Publishing Co., 1974); Lionel Smithett Lewis, *St. Joseph of Arimathea at Glastonbury* (Cambridge: James Clarke & Co., 1955); George F. Jowett, *The Drama of the Lost Disciples* (London: Covenant Publishing Co., 1980); and E. Raymond Capt, *The Traditions of Glastonbury* (Thousand Oaks, Calif.: Artisan Sales, 1983).
9. Raymond E. Brown, *The Birth of the Messiah* (Garden City, N.Y.: Doubleday &Co., 1977), pp. 143–53.
10. Reginald C. Fuller, ed., *A New Catholic Commentary on Holy Scripture* (London: Thomas Nelson, 1975), p. 907.
11. Phipps, *Was Jesus Married?* pp. 39–40.

12. Ibid., pp. 40–41.
13. Ibid., p. 41.
14. Ibid., p. 42.
15. Telephone interview with Dr. John Trever, November 9, 1984.
16. Phipps, *Was Jesus Married?* p. 43.
17. Brown, *The Birth of the Messiah*, p. 132.
18. Haskins, *Mary Magdalene,* pp. 94–95.
19. John William Taylor, *The Coming of the Saints: Imaginations and Studies in Early Church History and Tradition* (London: Covenant Publishing Co., 1969), p. 36.
20. Haskins, *Mary Magdalene*, pp. 25–26.
21. Elizabeth Clare Prophet, *Pearls of Wisdom,* vol. 33, no. 46, November 25, 1990, note 5.
22. Picknett, *Mary Magdalene,* pp. 124, 125.
23. Ibid., pp. 96–97.
24. Gardner, *Bloodline of the Holy Grail,* p. 121.
25. Picknett, *Mary Magdalene,* p. 111.
26. Ibid., p. 134.
27. Starbird, *The Woman with the Alabaster Jar,* p. 32.
28. Starbird, *Magdalene's Lost Legacy,* p. 63.
29. Picknett, *Mary Magdalene,* p. 134.
30. Gardner, *Bloodline of the Holy Grail,* p. 122.
31. Starbird, *The Woman with the Alabaster Jar,* p. 61.
32. Ean Begg, *The Cult of the Black Virgin*, p. 6.
33. Ibid., pp. 49, 2–3.
34. Picknett and Prince, *The Templar Revelation,* p. 76.
35. Starbird, *The Woman with the Alabaster Jar,* pp. 148–49.
36. Starbird, *The Goddess in the Gospels,* p. 49.
37. Ibid., p. 145.
38. Luke 24; John 20 & 21; Acts 1:13–15; 2: 1–21; 24:51.
39. Elizabeth Clare Prophet, "The Golden Age of Jesus Christ on Atlantis," April 28, 1991.
40. Elizabeth Clare Prophet, interview, March 8, 1996.
41. Elizabeth Clare Prophet, "The Gospel of Thomas," October 13, 1991.
42. Nisibis, near Edessa, is now Nusaybin on the Turkish side of the border of Syria.
43. Ahmad, *Jesus in Heaven on Earth*, pp. 384, 386.
44. Ibid., p. 388.
45. Ibid., p. 426.

Picture Credits

Cover, p. 39 and p. 95 *Mother of the World* by Nicholas Roerich, © Nicholas Roerich Museum, New York. Used by permission.

p. 45 *Madonna and Child between St. Catherine and Mary Magdalen,* Giovanni Bellini. Academia, Venice, Italy. Cameraphoto Arte, Venice / Art Resource, NY.

p. 72 Cliffs at Jabal al-Tarif, Nag Hammadi, Egypt. Institute for Antiquity and Christianity, Claremont, California.

p. 106 Ardhanarisvara. Werner Forman / Corbis.

p. 141 Portrait of Origen, engraving by Michael Burghers. Art Resource, NY.

p. 157 Portion of the Gospel of Thomas from the Nag Hammadi Codex II. Institute for Antiquity and Christianity, Claremont, California.

p. 177 St. Peter's, Rome. Lingbeek / iStockphoto.

p. 193 *Mary Magdalen,* by Carlo Dolci. Uffizi, Florence, Italy. Scala / Art Resource, NY.

p. 199 *The Penitence of the Magdalen,* by Giovanni da Milano. S. Croce, Florence, Italy. Scala / Art Resource, NY.

p. 208 *Noli Me Tangere,* mural by Fra Angelico. Museo di S. Marco, Florence, Italy. Erich Lessing / Art Resource, NY.

p. 238 *Mary Magdalene Traveling to France,* anonymous, 14th century. Lower Church, S. Francesco, Assissi, Italy. Scala / Art Resource.

p. 272 *La Morenata,* the Black Madonna of Montserrat. Charles & Josette Lenars / Corbis.

p. 277 *Our Lady of Czestochowa.* Jasna Gora Monastery, Czestochowa, Poland. Nicolas Sapieha / Art Resource.

About The Summit Lighthouse

The Summit Lighthouse is an internationally recognized spiritual center for the advancement of inner awakening. Our international organization is a global family that is inspired, guided, and sponsored by those known as the ascended masters.

The ascended masters are the most beloved and trusted transcendent beings guiding our planet's material and spiritual evolution. Most of the world's religions are currently based on the revelations of one or more of these masters before their ascension. We openly embrace spiritual seekers from all paths of light including the mystical traditions of the world's religions.

The ascended masters and their messengers have given us over fifteen thousand hours of invaluable inner wisdom and insightful instruction, and they have provided the means for our direct initiation into higher consciousness.

For the ascended masters . . . no subject is off limits! Their teachings contain amazing truths and awesome answers on spirituality, alchemy, astrology, sacred geometry, spiritual science, karma, reincarnation, ascension, archangels (and fallen angels), and even those issues that are considered taboo or "out of this world."

Primary Goals of the Teachings of the Ascended Masters

The ascended masters challenge us daily to be bold, to dare to be who we truly are, and to face adversity with courage, patience, perseverance, honesty, integrity, inner love, discipline, and discernment—all for a greater sense of inner peace, fearlessness, stillness and silence, harmony, self-mastery, compassion, and wisdom.

These teachings help our souls get back to the origin of their individualized inner source of True Self Love—the Higher Self, or I AM Presence. Our point of contact with our Higher Self is the "Spark of Life" or "Sacred Fire of the Heart," the place where our consciousness expresses its true divine nature of unconditional love and happiness, universal oneness, and an authentic desire to serve others.

How Our Teachings Came into Being

Our teachings were all released through highly trained and trusted messengers, Mark L. Prophet and Elizabeth Clare Prophet. Mark was contacted by the ascended master El Morya at the age of eighteen and received training from him for many years before he was instructed to establish The Summit Lighthouse in 1958 in Washington, D.C.

With his ascension in 1973, Mark passed the torch for the mission to his gifted wife, Elizabeth Clare Prophet, who continued her service until her retirement in 1999.

The dictations of the ascended masters were regularly given in public. The ascended masters also inspired thousands of lectures delivered by the messengers. The content of the dictations are, by most human standards, beyond the mind's ability to construct in real time. They carry very powerful frequencies of light, awakening us to the highest truths we've ever experienced.

We leave it up to you to decide the value for yourself.

Moving toward Your Victory

No matter what path of light you are on, spiritual freedom is attained using tools that have been passed down in wisdom teachings through the millennia: meditation, selfless service, devotional music, prayer, mantra, and the science of the spoken Word. The masters bring an accelerated understanding of these principles, especially suited for the challenges of the modern world, including dynamic decree work and the use of the violet flame.

Next Steps

We are genuinely excited to meet you on the Path and hope you are too. We extend a warm welcome from everyone at The Summit Lighthouse, and we invite you to explore the teachings of the ascended masters at **www.SummitLighthouse.org.** Check out our free online lessons and hundreds of articles on a wide range of spiritual subjects. Browse through our online bookstore. And if you would rather talk to someone in person, please feel free to contact us today!

The Summit Lighthouse®
63 Summit Way
Gardiner, Montana 59030 USA
1-800-245-5445 / 406-848-9500
Se habla español.
info@SummitUniversityPress.com
SummitLighthouse.org

ELIZABETH CLARE PROPHET is a world-renowned author. Among her best sellers are *Fallen Angels and the Origins of Evil, Saint Germain's Prophecy for the New Millennium,* her 10-book series *Pocket Guides to Practical Spirituality* including *How to Work with Angels, Soul Mates and Twin Flames* and *Alchemy of the Heart,* and *The Lost Years of Jesus: Documentary Evidence of Jesus' 17-Year Journey to the East.* She has pioneered techniques in practical spirituality, including the use of the creative power of sound for personal growth and world transformation. Her books have been translated into more than twenty languages.

ANNICE BOOTH has been a faculty member of Summit University for over twenty years. She has taught classes on practical spirituality, including secrets of prosperity, spiritual alchemy, the ascension, your divine plan and the spiritual dimensions of love and relationships. Mrs. Booth has traveled throughout the world giving workshops on these subjects. She is the author of three books, *The Path to Your Ascension: Rediscovering Life's Ultimate Purpose, Secrets of Prosperity: Abundance in the 21st Century* and *Memories of Mark: My Life with Mark Prophet.* She is also the compiler and editor of *The Masters and Their Retreats,* by Mark L. Prophet and Elizabeth Clare Prophet.

Printed in the USA
CPSIA information can be obtained
at www.ICGtesting.com
CBHW071553081224
18582CB00011B/44